WOMEN'S FAITH D...

Presenting a rich account of women's faith lives and mapping women's meanings in their own right, this book offers an alternative to dominant accounts of faith development which fail to account for women's experience. Drawing on Fowler's faith development theory, feminist models of women's faith and social science methodology, the text explores the patterns and processes of women's faith development and spirituality in a group of thirty women belonging to, or on the edges of, Christian tradition.

Integrating practical theological concern with Christian education and pastoral practice, this book will be of interest to all concerned with women's faith development, spirituality, education and formation, and to those working in the fields of practical theology, pastoral care, adult theological education, spiritual direction and counselling.

Explorations in Practical, Pastoral and Empirical Theology

Series Editors: Leslie J. Francis, University of Wales, Bangor, UK
and Jeff Astley, University of Durham and Director of the North of England
Institute for Christian Education, UK

Theological reflection on the church's practice is now recognised as a significant element in theological studies in the academy and seminary. Ashgate's new series in practical, pastoral and empirical theology seeks to foster this resurgence of interest and encourage new developments in practical and applied aspects of theology worldwide. This timely series draws together a wide range of disciplinary approaches and empirical studies to embrace contemporary developments including: the expansion of research in empirical theology, psychological theology, ministry studies, public theology, Christian education and faith development; key issues of contemporary society such as health, ethics and the environment; and more traditional areas of concern such as pastoral care and counselling.

Other titles published in this series:

Ordinary Theology
Looking, Listening and Learning in Theology
Jeff Astley
ISBN 0 7546 0583 3 (Hbk)
ISBN 0 7546 0584 1 (Pbk)

The 'Empty' Church Revisited
Robin Gill
ISBN 0 7546 3462 0 (Hbk)
ISBN 0 7546 3463 9 (Pbk)

Sin and Forgiveness
New Responses in a Changing World
Kay Carmichael
ISBN 0 7546 3405 1 (Hbk)
ISBN 0 7546 3406 X (Pbk)

A Christian Theology of Place
John Inge
ISBN 0 7546 3498 1 (Hbk)
ISBN 0 7546 3499 X (Pbk)

God, Human Nature and Education for Peace
New Approaches to Moral and Religious Maturity
Karl Ernst Nipkow
ISBN 0 7546 0863 8 (Hbk)
ISBN 0 7546 0872 7 (Pbk)

Women's Faith Development

Patterns and Processes

NICOLA SLEE
The Queen's Foundation for Ecumenical
Theological Education, Birmingham, UK

ASHGATE

Published by
Ashgate Publishing Limited
Gower House, Croft Road
Aldershot, Hants
GU11 3HR
England

Ashgate Publishing Company
Suite 420
101 Cherry Street
Burlington, VT 05401–4405
USA

Ashgate website: http://www.ashgate.com

British Library Cataloguing in Publication Data
Slee, Nicola M.
  Women's faith development: patterns and processes. –
  (Explorations in practical, pastoral and empirical theology)
  1. Faith development 2. Women–Religious life 3. Experience
  (Religion) 4. Feminist theology
  I. Title.
  270'.082

Library of Congress Cataloging-in-Publication Data
Slee, Nicola.
  Women's faith development: patterns and processes / Nicola Slee.
     p. cm. – (Explorations in practical, pastoral, and empirical theology)
  Includes bibliographical references and index (alk. paper).
  1. Women–Religious life. 2. Faith development. 3. Feminist theology. 4. Theology,
  practical. I. Title. II. Series.
  BV4527.S52 2003
  261.8'344–dc21   2003052241

Reprinted 2005, 2008

ISBN 0 7546 0885 9 (Hbk)   ISBN 978 0 7546 0885 1 (Hbk)
ISBN 0 7546 0886 7 (Pbk)   ISBN 978 0 7546 0886 8 (Pbk)

Typeset in Times by Owain Hammonds, Ceredigion.

Printed and bound in Great Britain by MPG Books, Bodmin.

For the women who came before,
and in memory of my grandmothers

Leafy Slee, 1903–1992 and Mollie Moodie, 1906–1984

To the women who will come after,
and with love to my god-daughters

Nathalie Richards, Hannah Skinner and Morven Cameron

Contents

Preface and Acknowledgements

This book began life as a doctoral thesis, presented to the University of Birmingham in 1999, and numerous people have supported and encouraged me, both through the process of bringing the doctorate to successful completion, and then through the subsequent stages of shaping and revising it into its present form. In particular, I am grateful for the help and humanity of my supervisor and friend, Professor John Hull; for a detailed reading and critique of an early draft of the thesis by Pam Lunn; and for the thoughtful and challenging responses of many different groups to whom I have presented my findings and reflections at various stages over the last ten years. I value greatly the encouragement of my colleagues on the Southwark Ordination Course (1990–93), the Aston Training Scheme (1993–97) and the Queen's Foundation (1997–present). In particular, the culture of freedom and risk-taking on the Aston Scheme enabled me to come to a place where I could abandon an earlier, abortive Ph.D. and choose the work I really wanted to do. My family has cheered me on from a distance, and to them I owe an upbringing in which faith was as much a part of life as green fields and muddy lanes, and a sense of connection to land, to sea, to God and to kin which has endured many struggles and which I prize perhaps more than they know. Many friends have seen me through the deadlocks, confusions and breakthroughs of this project; only those who have accompanied me most closely know how real the struggle with paralysis, which is a central theme of this book, has been for me, and what personal significance the publication of this book represents. I am especially grateful to Jo Jones, Kate Lees, Gavin D'Costa and Peter Kettle, who have stood by me over the long haul and, in their different ways, taught me the meaning of faithful friendship. Maggie Rowe, Deirdre Burton, Sr Valeria Moore (CSMV), Abbess Mary John Marshall (OSB) and Ramona Kauth have supported me in particular ways, with great skill and insight, without whom I would not have come this far. More recently, Rosie Miles has come to share very closely in the process of bringing this work to completion, and I am more grateful than I can say for her companionship and belief in me, as well as the critical intelligence she has brought to bear on the manuscript.

Three communities offered me generous hospitality at various stages of this project. Mother Abbess and the Benedictine community of St Mary's Abbey, West Malling – which has long been a place of pilgrimage and sustenance for me – generously provided me with a house, and with their ongoing friendship and prayer, during a three-month sabbatical in 1997, which allowed me to immerse myself in the data from the interviews and write up the bulk of my findings. Subsequently, the Sisters of Sion in Birmingham welcomed me into their home, for what they thought was going to be three months but turned out to be eighteen, and offered me companionship and space during a time of protracted illness when progress on the thesis was very slow. At the same time, the Revd Peter Fisher, then Principal of the Queen's Foundation, with staff at Queens, welcomed me into their midst as a Visiting Scholar, and gave me a place to recover and, finally, complete the thesis. During this time, I also received generous financial assistance from the Hockerill Educational Foundation and from the Keswick Hall Trust, for which I am grateful. After my original year's stint as a Visiting Scholar at Queens, the governors and staff gladly supported my move into freelance work, and I continue to appreciate the hospitality and collegiality I receive from students, staff and friends of Queens.

And of course, I am enormously grateful to all the women – more than thirty – who shared with me their faith stories and, in so doing, allowed me into the sacred spaces of their lives, in interviews which not only provided me with the material for this study, but moved me profoundly by their honesty, courage, integrity and fidelity. I cannot thank them by name, since to do so would be to break the contract of confidentiality I made with them, but that does not make my thanks any less sincere. I have been enriched immeasurably by the whole process of listening to, working with and reflecting on the stories of these women which I now carry inside me, and which have become part of who I am. These women, themselves, are representative of so many other women who have, throughout my life, taught me, by their lives and spirit, what it means to be a woman of faith: my grandmothers, mother, sisters and aunts; many teachers, ministers, pastors, religious and lay women; numerous colleagues, friends, mentors and women students. They have all inspired this project, and I am glad to share its fruits with them. Conscious of standing in a long line of women stretching back into the shadows of history which will pass through my short life into a future I can only begin to dream, I dedicate this work to the memory of my grandmothers and the generations of women who came before me, and to my god-daughters and the generations who will come after me.

Nicola Slee
The Queen's Foundation for Ecumenical Theological Education
Birmingham
March 2003

Chapter 1

The Nature and Aims of the Study

Feminist practical theology is beginning to emerge as women cease to remain complicit in networks of institutional power that work against our wellbeing.

Heather Walton[1]

... This requires a refusal of the pretense of pure objectivity, an invitation of face-to-face encounter, confrontation, and messiness, and a willingness to participate proactively in a revisionary project that changes the lives of the marginalized and of all the participants.

Bonnie J Miller-McLemore[2]

What we want to change we curse and then
pick up a tool ... If you
can't bless it, get ready to make it new.

Marge Piercy[3]

Introduction

This study is an examination of the patterns and processes of women's spirituality and faith development[4] in a group of thirty women belonging to, or on the edges of, Christian tradition. It is offered as a piece of interdisciplinary and practical theological reflection written from a perspective of Christian feminist commitment, arising out of my own experience and using the tools of social science research methodology, to investigate an area of central concern to the life of the churches and to the women's movement within and on the edges of the churches. In this chapter, I set out to acknowledge as explicitly as I can, the factors which have shaped the study. I begin by describing the personal and professional context of my own experience out of which the research took shape. Next, I summarise the basic aims of the study, before going on to delineate the broader academic context which provided the theoretical background to the study. Finally, I provide an overview of the book.

---

[1] Walton (2001), p. 7.

[2] Miller-McLemore (1999), p. 92.

[3] From 'The art of blessing the day' in Piercy (1998), p. 2.

[4] I recognise that there is some ambivalence in using the language of 'faith development' and 'spirituality' in conjunction. The two phrases are not synonymous. Whilst 'faith development' as a term is associated quite specifically with the work of Fowler and has a clear set of meanings in the literature, the term 'spirituality' is much looser and is widely used in a number of different settings, not only religious ones. Cf. Sheldrake (1995), Chapter 2, for an excellent discussion of the range of meanings accruing to 'spirituality' in a Christian context.

The Personal and Professional Context of the Study

At the outset, it is important for me to acknowledge the rooting of the study in my own personal and professional commitments. This is a way of insisting upon the hermeneutical bias of all research and, in particular, a way of naming the specific precommitments of this study so that readers can understand and interpret accordingly the factors which have shaped it. It is a way of saying how and why this study matters to me, how it emerges out of my own lived experience and grapples with issues pertinent to my life and my work, and how it has come to take the particular shape and focus that it has. A writer necessarily writes out of her own life context and writes at least partly to make sense of and shape that life experience. The life makes sense of the work, but, in a reciprocal way, the work makes sense of the life. This is as true in social scientific empirical research, I suggest, as it is in fiction, biography, poetry or 'pure' theology (whatever that is!), although not all traditions of social science acknowledge the subjective rooting of scientific enquiry as openly as others. My own commitment to a qualitative rather than a quantitative research approach arises at least in part because of the transparency of such an approach to its own grounding in subjectivity – both the subjectivity of the researcher and the subjectivity of those participating in the research. But this is to anticipate a more expanded discussion of qualitative research further in this chapter and, more substantially, in Chapter 3. At this point, my intention is to name as transparently as I can the precommitments which have motivated and inspired this study, as well as limited its sights and insights.

The study has its roots in my personal faith journey as a lay Christian woman and my work as a professional religious educator involved in adult faith formation within the churches. In my nurturing and development as a Christian, women have, from the beginning, played a crucial role. I do not want this to be read as a negation of the nurturance and inspiration I have received from many men, from my grandfather and father to many teachers, ministers, friends and colleagues subsequently. However, as a woman I have needed to know in a very particular way that women before me have walked the way of faith and paved a way, leaving some signs – landmarks, cairns or marks on a map – for other women, including myself, to follow. Though few of my formal theological teachers or pastors have been women, women have been significant as those who have mediated to me the reality and understanding of what it means to be a follower of the way of Jesus. Women in my family – my mother, two sisters, my grandmothers, my Devon aunts, my cousins – and female friends, colleagues and members of the churches I have belonged to or had contact with have lived out faithful discipleship in ways which have inspired, empowered and enlarged my own growing Christian identity. Yet, despite such female faithfulness at the core of living Christian tradition, women's faith lives have generally not been accorded significance, their stories have not been recorded, their struggles and conflicts have not been noted, their gifts and ministries have not been accorded public recognition in the literature, traditions and practices of the churches. With the advent and flourishing of feminist theology since the 1960s, this is gradually changing, and there is a growing literature in women's spirituality (for example, Spretnak, 1982; King, 1989; Zappone, 1991), faith history (Fiorenza, 1983; MacHaffie, 1986; Coon et al., 1990), ministry (Herzel, 1981; Ruether, 1985; Russell, 1993) and pastoral care (Graham and Halsey, 1993; Glaz and Stevenson-Moessner, 1991; Bons-Storm, 1996;

Miller-McLemore and Gill-Austern, 1999), as well as formal feminist theology (Ruether, 1983; Fiorenza, 1983; Loades, 1990). I see my study as part of this wider feminist project of reclaiming and describing in its own terms women's religious experience, in ways which can both complement, challenge, widen and enlarge the androcentric traditions of faith and spirituality we have inherited.

In my professional work as a religious educator, I have worked for some twenty years teaching adults in a variety of church-related institutions. I have worked with both men and women colleagues and taught both male and female students, and learnt much from both, finding my own faith and educational practice constantly challenged, enriched and extended. Yet my developing sensitivity to the reality of women's marginalisation within Christian tradition has alerted me to the particular spiritual and educational struggles and needs of female students and colleagues. I have become increasingly aware of the myriad ways in which the realities of institutional life within both the church and the academy function to silence and disempower women, as well as other groups such as black, working-class and gay people. Here, it is important to acknowledge the myriad and often subtle forms of discrimination that operate within church and academy, themselves both reflecting wider patterns of social exclusion, of which gender is only one of the more obvious. It is essential to pay attention to the interlocking forms of discrimination in which race, class, age, sexuality, geographical location and physical and mental abilities play a crucial part alongside gender. At the same time as acknowledging the multiple forms of what Miller-McLemore describes as 'exploitative classificatory systems' (1999, p. 79), gender itself, of course, is undergoing constantly shifting reconfigurations, both in terms of its expression in diverse settings and communities, and in terms of its academic analysis and explication.

Nevertheless, without buying into simplistic notions of gender oppression which themselves are liable to perpetuate binary ways of thinking and operating, I do not believe we have achieved a post-feminist era in which we may safely abandon the agenda of women's liberation. Certainly within the churches, the project of female liberation has barely begun, and has a very long way to go before women and men can be sanguine about its fruits. In the relatively small world of British theological education, which nevertheless might be expected to be more rather than less attuned to the voices and interests of marginalised groups and individuals than the wider church it serves (if only because it is likely to be more abreast of contemporary thinking than the wider church), there is movement towards gender equality but significant obstacles still to be overcome. Patterns of training, ways of learning and modes of practice have not, by and large, reflected or served the needs of women, thereby functioning to perpetuate women's marginalisation and oppression. Many of the existing theological, psychological and educational models of spiritual maturity which have shaped the church's praxis are more or less androcentric in nature, predicated upon the experience of boys and men and, to greater or lesser extent, impervious to the particular struggles and gifts of women.[5]

---

[5] Although there is little sustained reflection on women's religious education in the United Kingdom, there is a significant, if slight, literature mostly emanating from North America (for example, Cornwall Collective, 1980; Giltner, 1985; Mud Flower Collective, 1985; Harris, 1988; Chopp, 1995), which has informed my understanding and practice, and helped to shape this study.

Out of these different but related contexts of church and educational settings, this study has been generated. It is rooted in my growing concern for and commitment to, the religious development and education of women and girls within the churches – a concern which should be at the heart of practical theology, but which, at least in the British context, has barely begun to be articulated. The *developmental, pastoral* and *educational* focus of the work is what sets it apart from myriad other studies of women's spirituality, both popular and academic. It is concerned with women's faith and spirituality as something that is dynamic, contextually specific and in the process of change. It seeks to explore the dynamics and possible patternings of that process of change, as well as to identify particular developmental crises and opportunities in the unfolding of women's faith lives. When I began this study, I could find no single published work which corresponded to my own concerns (with the possible exception of Joann Wolski Conn's pioneering anthology of texts on *Women's Spirituality*, which first appeared in 1986). Since then, several volumes have appeared from the United States which address these issues centrally, most particularly Carol Lakey Hess's *Caretakers of Our Common House: Women's Development in Communities of Faith* (Abingdon, 1997) and Joanne Stevenson-Moessner's edited collection of essays, *In Her Own Time: Women and Developmental Issues in Pastoral Care* (Fortress, 2000). I am delighted to add to this select but vital literature on the religious development and education of women and girls. In the British context, no study has previously been conducted, to my knowledge, of the specific religious developmental needs of women, nor have I been able to locate any published work, beyond the occasional article, in the wider European context. For all its manifold failings (of which I am only too aware), my study may at least have the merit of calling the attention of both practioners and reflectors within the churches to a much neglected area.

The Aims of the Study

The overarching purpose of my study is to examine the patterns and processes of women's spirituality and faith development in a group of women belonging to, or on the edges of, Christian tradition. A subsidiary aim is to discern whether current models and theories of faith development are able adequately to account for women's experience. In relation to this second aim, I dialogue in particular with the faith development theory of James Fowler and suggest ways in which this theory both illuminates women's faith development and itself needs to be reframed in the light of my own findings. I recognise at the outset that, since the study is not a comparative one, any findings can only be hypothesised to be distinctive of women, and would require further testing on mixed, or men-only, samples, before any hard and fast claims could be made about differences between men and women. Nevertheless, my hope is to have produced a qualitatively rich account of women's faith lives which is self-authenticating in its own terms, which allows theoretical constructs to be developed from the 'ground' upwards, and which suggests avenues for further exploration and study. The intention is to listen to women's stories as valid in their own right, and to 'map' women's meanings in as much detail as possible, as a way of providing an alternative and a corrective to dominant accounts of faith development which have been shaped within an androcentric culture.

Within the broad terms of the study, I gradually formulated a number of more discrete aims and objectives, as the research proceeded, allowing for a sharper focus, as follows. First, how do women of faith, in different contexts and at different stages of development, describe and understand their faith? What images, metaphors, models and stories do they employ? What themes, issues, tensions or questions emerge as salient? What models of mature faith emerge? Second, is it possible to identify common and recurring developmental patterns? Are there common developmental phases or stages, crises or transitional points? Can one identify developmental 'triggers' or spurs to faith? Third, what are the significant differences in women's accounts of faith development? What are the surprising, unexpected or neglected aspects of the woman's accounts which might be hypothesised to be distinctive? Where are the conflicts, tensions and differences *between* the women's accounts, as well as *within* each woman's account?

In practice, my findings allowed some of these questions to be addressed more fully than others, although the data yielded at least indicative responses to each. In addition, the data suggested other areas of potential exploration which there has not been scope to investigate within the limits of the present study. However, these were the questions that were in my mind at the outset of the study and that shaped the research design.

The Nature of the Study

This study is contextualised within, and offered as an example of, *feminist practical* or *pastoral theology*, a newly emerging field within the broader literature of feminist theology (for example, Glaz and Stevenson-Moessner, 1991; Demarinis, 1993; Graham and Halsey, 1993; Bons-Storm, 1996; Neuger, 1996; Stevenson-Moessner, 1996, 2000; Graham, 1997; Ackermann and Bons-Storm, 1998; Miller-McLemore and Gill-Austern, 1999), concerned with a feminist theological analysis, critique and transformation of the life and practice of the Christian community, and having its roots within practical and pastoral theology more widely as well as feminist discourse and theory, including feminist theology. In order to explicate my understanding of a feminist practical theology, let me first delineate my understanding of practical theology more generally, including an understanding of how it relates to social science theory and qualitative empirical research, before going on to outline the feminist theological commitment of such a theology.

Practical or pastoral theology[6] can be understood as the theological discipline concerned with the life or practice of the Christian community.[7] Although in the

---

[6] There exists in the field a variety of terminology. 'Practical theology', 'pastoral studies' or 'pastoral theology' and 'ministerial studies' are all used, sometimes interchangeably, sometimes with rather distinctive meanings. Cf. Ballard and Pritchard (1996), pp. 23–5 and Woodward and Pattison (2000), pp. 1–19 for discussions of the terminology. In common with British usage, I shall use both terms more or less interchangeably, with something of a preference for 'practical theology' as the term with the wider, socio-political reference, except when I am explicitly concerned with a more narrowly pastoral focus.

[7] Whilst Woodward and Pattison (2000) eschew definitions, they suggest some commonalities which at least hint towards an agreed focus: both pastoral and practical

past practical theology has been concerned narrowly with matters of ministerial formation, it is now generally understood in a much wider sense as the articulation of the theological meaning of the practice of the whole church. Thus, Laurie Green describes practical theology as 'an active and critical ministry' of the church, which 'investigates and reflects upon God's presence and activity in our lives, and asks what that means for us' (1990, p. 12). Carol Lakey Hess defines the aim of practical theology as 'discerning God's call (Holy Spirit to human spirit) for just and righteous life together in this world and in particular concrete communities of faith' (1997, p. 17). Paul Ballard and John Pritchard offer the following description:

> [Practical theology] focuses on the life of the whole people of God in the variety of its witness and service, as it lives in, with and for the world. It asks questions concerning Christian understanding, insight and obedience in the concrete reality of our existence. It is, therefore, a theological activity, descriptive, normative, critical and apologetic, serving both the Church and the world in its reflective tasks. (1996, p. 27)

Practical theology can be understood both as a separate theological discipline in its own right, with its own subject area (the practice of the Christian community within the world) and methodology (the hermeneutical circle or pastoral cycle method), and as a way of delineating the orientation of *all* theology towards practice and 'rooting all theology in its existential responsibility' (Ballard and Pritchard, 1996, p. 27).

Practical theology is thus particularly concerned with the relation between Christian belief and practice. There is a variety of models for understanding and explicating this relationship. The model which has informed the present study most profoundly is the praxis model, particularly as this has been expressed in the so-called 'pastoral cycle' method of doing theology. The praxis model emerged out of the political theologies of liberation (for example, Gutierrez, 1988; Cone, 1974; Bonino, 1975; Segundo, 1977; Boff, 1987), feminist (Russell, 1974; Ruether, 1983; Fiorenza, 1983) and womanist theologies (Weems, 1988; Grant, 1989; Williams, 1993), as well as a broader movement of local and contextual theologies (Winter, 1980; Donovan, 1982; Schreiter, 1985; Amirtham and Pobee, 1986). It has been very widely adopted and employed by pastoral theologians, both in Britain and the United States (Holland and Henriot, 1983; Green, 1990; Ballard and Pritchard, 1996; Lartey, 1997).

The praxis model explicitly roots all theological enquiry in concrete, historical and social experience as the 'first act' of theology, upon which the 'second act' of reflection is dependent. It holds a strong commitment to story as the primary data of theology, the first-hand stories of those in a particular situation whose experience constitutes the lived reality of faith. Yet 'experience' is never understood in a naive sense as 'given', as socially or politically innocent, uninformed by values or commitments. Thus a hermeneutics of suspicion has to be brought to bear upon

---

theology are concerned with practice, with the relation of practice to Christian theological tradition, are focused in the Christian community and closely associated with the ministry of the church, as well as relating to 'contemporary practices, issues, and experiences that bear upon or form a concern for the Christian community' (p. 6).

experience in the first place, to render visible the politics of bias inherent in any given social situation, including the reality of the church's institutional life, which is always situated in historical time and political place. The critical analysis of experience upon which the praxis model of theology is grounded is then brought into interaction with the wisdom, insights and practice of Christian tradition, via a reading of the scriptures, tradition, liturgy and spirituality of the church. Out of the dialogue and interaction between experience and Christian tradition, a new praxis is born, a critically informed social action which must itself then be submitted to fresh and ongoing analysis.

This cyclical method for doing theology has been expounded in a number of forms, but is generally understood in terms of a four-fold movement from the present concrete situation (Experience, or, as Holland and Henriot [1983] describe it, Insertion) to a critical analysis of that situation, using in particular the tools of social science enquiry (Exploration or Social Analysis), into the dialogue between analysed experience and the wisdom of Christian tradition enshrined in its scriptures, doctrinal formulations and heritage of spirituality (Theological Reflection), and finally, to some form of committed action or Response. Together these four elements constitute the basic rhythm of theology and create the 'spiral' of theological activity. The four elements should not be thought of as rigidly compartmentalised or discrete spheres of activity. In practice, it is not always easy to differentiate sharply between them, because they flow out of and into each other in complex and intricate ways, with a kind of organic fluidity which is intrinsic to any genuinely creative activity.

Although I have not followed the four moments of the pastoral cycle slavishly, I have attempted to engage each of them at some level. Fundamentally, the study is rooted in my own and other women's *experience* of faith and spirituality, and a fundamental aim of the study is to listen to and to 'hear into speech' (Morton, 1985) women's stories, to map out and render visible women's faith experience. The first 'moment' of this study is the attempt to 'insert' myself into the lived experience of women's faith within and on the edges of the churches. The *exploration* of women's faith is conducted largely via the use of social science research methodology, which provided the tools for the gathering as well as analysis of women's faith stories. The *reflection* element is woven throughout the study, as I attempt to bring to bear insights from faith development theory, women's psychological development and feminist practical theology to the data gathered from the interviews. The moment of *response* is attended to at the end of the study in the consideration of the implications of the findings for pastoral and educational praxis within the churches.

It is clear, even from a most cursory outline of the pastoral cycle, that the praxis model of theology is necessarily *interdisciplinary* in orientation. Rather than seeing theology over and against the other 'human' disciplines, in opposition to and judgement upon them, the praxis model affirms that God's truth is one, and to be discerned in every area of human enquiry and knowledge, and that theology needs the wisdom, insights, tools and methods of the arts and humanities and the natural and social sciences. Whilst no one individual can possibly master the full range of human knowledge which theology needs to call upon in its pursuit of incarnated truth, the body of the church as a corporate fellowship gathers together a great wealth and breadth of human insight, skill and experience, all of which needs to be utilised in the work of theology. Thus, it is axiomatic in the praxis model that theology is a *corporate* act of the whole church across time as well as place, and not something conducted by a professional elite on behalf of others. As Miller-McLemore suggests, 'serious practical theology takes time, requires a rich variety of complex resources, and works best, despite the vast complications, with multiple authors' (1999, p. 93).[8] Both of these features – the interdisciplinary and corporate aspects of practical theology – have informed the present study. It is explicitly interdisciplinary, drawing upon theology, psychology, social science methodology and the practice of education and pastoral care, as well as poetry and fiction, in its design and the range of literature studied. It is also a corporate act of reflection which, at every stage of the research, has been rooted in consultation and shared reflection with others. From reading the works of others to discussions with scholars and practioners, through the central act of the conversations I conducted with the thirty women who formed my research group, and through a series of seminars I conducted in which I shared my findings and initial analysis with several groups of women, this study is conversational at its core.

Whilst the praxis model of theology is broadly interdisciplinary, it has tended to lay special emphasis upon the importance of the *social sciences* as a primary tool of theology. In its efforts to investigate and critique human experience with rigour, precision and critical openness, the theoretical concepts and methods of enquiry provided by the social sciences are deemed to be particularly important. This bias towards the social sciences has been rightly critiqued by some, and an attempt made to reinstate the arts and popular culture as equally significant hermeneutical tools within pastoral theology which need also to play their part in the interpretation of lived experience (for example, Couture, 1999; Bennett Moore, 2001).[9] Whilst sharing practical theology's traditional commitment to the social sciences, I have attempted also to remain open to wider sources, in particular drawing upon both the content and language of poetry as a means of enhancing and enlarging social scientific methods of analysis and interpretation, as well as attempting to employ such methods themselves in an essentially aesthetic way which takes account of the irreducible particularity, subjectivity and qualitative richness of human experience.

My study draws upon the social sciences in two main ways: first, in its employment of *developmental psychology* in elucidating the key concepts of faith development and women's development; and second, in its use of the methods of *qualitative research* to conduct the study of women's faith lives. Within the broad field of *developmental psychology*, there are two main strands to the theoretical background which informs the study. First, I have drawn on faith development research and theory, particularly the work of James Fowler (1980, 1981, 1991 et al.),

---

[8] See Woodward and Pattison (2000), pp. 13–16 for a helpful discussion of the essential characteristics of practical/pastoral theology.

[9] Cf. Zoe Bennett Moore: 'Pastoral theology as an interpretative discipline rightly uses the tools of social analysis and pays attention to the prevalent material power issues and sociocultural narratives … It is, however, important that the whole range of human experience is reflected on with a corresponding range of methods … The world must be interpreted through its literary productions, through its symbols and language, as well as through its social structures and institutions and its distribution of power and wealth' (2001, p. 13).

as well as broader theories of human development within which Fowler's work is, itself, situated (for example, Piaget, 1929, 1962; Kohlberg, 1981, 1984; Erikson, 1980; Selman, 1980; Loevinger, 1976). The faith development paradigm has contributed greatly to a rich and multidimensional understanding of faith. Fowler invites us to see faith as a human universal which, whatever a person's beliefs, is exercised as part of the meaning-making journey. He invites us to recognise that faith is dynamic and changing over time, involving cognitive, affective and behavioural aspects. He proposes that, despite its many manifestations in many different contexts, faith possesses certain formal characteristics at the deep level of structure. These are described in terms of a hierarchy of qualitatively distinct developmental stages. Nevertheless, in spite of the significance of Fowler's contribution to the psychological study of faith, feminist analysis reveals serious limitations in his work at a number of different levels. The sources drawn upon, the images and metaphors of faith employed, the models of mature faith adumbrated, the theoretical understanding and operationalization of faith, and the account of stage development proposed can all be critiqued for their inbuilt androcentric bias. Something more is needed for an adequate understanding of women's faith lives.

In order to correct this imbalance, a second strand of theory is drawn upon in my study. I have utilised the work of feminist psychologists and theologians and studies of women's moral and identity development, as well as feminist pastoral theology texts, to critique the work of Fowler, and to develop alternative models of women's faith development. The work of theologians such as Carter Heyward (1982, 1984), Mary Grey (1989, 1993) and Katherine Zappone (1991) complements the insights of developmental psychologists such as Jean Baker Miller (1976), Carol Gilligan (1982, et al.), Nancy Chodorow (1978) and the work of the Stone Center (Jordan, 1991, 1997) in suggesting that women's spirituality is essentially relational in character, rooted in a strong sense of connection to others and an ethic of care and responsibility. There is a certain measure of consensus (as well as some critique and a growing differentiation of the notion) that the pattern of women's faith development proceeds within the context of such connectedness. This is in contrast to the classic pattern of male development as enshrined in the major psychological accounts of Freud (1973), Erikson (1980) and Kohlberg (1981, 1984), which describe a process of individuation via separation from the other. A number of empirical studies of women's faith development (for example, Cooney, 1985; Leary, 1988; Devor, 1989) as well as broader models of women's faith development (Christ, 1986; Osiek, 1986; Harris, 1989) and pastoral theological discussions (Hess, 1997; Neuger, 1999; Stevenson-Moessner, 2000) lend broad support to this relational thesis and are discussed in Chapter 2. Whilst I argue that the relationality thesis must not be iterated nor received simplistically or overgeneralised, it is nevertheless inconceivable that it could be ignored in any discussion of women's faith development.

Whilst the literature of developmental psychology and feminist theology provided the theoretical framework for the elucidation of the concepts of women's spirituality and faith development, the field of *qualitative research* provides the framework for the conduct of the research itself. At its simplest, the distinction between quantitative and qualitative approaches can be described in terms of a distinction between approaches which are concerned with number, measurement and quantification, on the one hand, and those which are concerned with meanings and the relationships between meanings, on the other. Whilst there is great variety under the broad umbrella of qualitative research (cf. Jacob, 1987; Tesch, 1990), it is possible to identify a range of characteristics which most qualitative research shares. Miles and Huberman (1994, pp. 6–7) suggest the following key features:

- Qualitative research is conducted through an intense and/or prolonged contact with a 'field' or life situation. These situations are typically 'banal' or normal ones, reflective of the everyday life of individuals, groups, societies and organisations.
- The researcher's role is to gain a 'holistic' (systemic, encompassing, integrated) overview of the context under study: its logic, its arrangements, its explicit and implicit rules.
- The researcher attempts to capture data on the perceptions of local actors 'from the inside', through a process of deep attentiveness, of empathetic understanding (*Verstehen*), and of suspending or 'bracketing' preconceptions about the topics under discussion.
- Reading through these materials, the researcher may isolate certain themes and expressions that can be reviewed with informants, but that should be maintained in their original forms throughout the study.
- A main task is to explicate the ways people in particular settings come to understand, account for, take action, and otherwise manage their day-to-day situations.
- Many interpretations of this material are possible, but some are more compelling for theoretical reasons or on grounds of internal consistency.
- Relatively little standardised instrumentation is used at the outset. The researcher is essentially the main 'measurement device' in the study.
- Most analysis is done with words. The words can be assembled, subclustered, broken into semiotic segments. They can be organised to permit the researcher to contrast, compare, analyse and bestow patterns upon them.

It is evident from this overview of the characteristic features of qualitative research that there is a strong convergence between this approach and the praxis model of theology as exemplified by the pastoral cycle. The two models, or methods of enquiry, share a strong commitment to naturalistic knowledge, the immersion of enquiry in concrete, historical situations, the development of theoretical constructs from the ground upwards, the dynamic interaction between prior knowledge and lived experience, and the pragmatic application of acquired knowledge to the historical situation. This convergence between the pastoral cycle approach to theology and qualitative research methodology was a strong reason for choosing the latter.

The choice of a qualitative approach was also made on other grounds: partly on the grounds of the state of the research field, where little systematic or detailed study has been made of the faith lives of women, and partly on the grounds of my own personal inclinations and abilities which were more applicable to a qualitative approach. In terms of the former, a qualitative study was deemed more likely to elicit issues, meanings, themes and possible trends or patterns which could contribute to an opening-up of the research field, in contrast to a quantitative approach which presupposes a degree of closure of the issues in order to test a narrowly defined set of hypotheses. In terms of the latter, my experience of women's groups and involvement in feminist projects, and my academic background in the humanities predisposed me to a qualitative approach. Whilst a qualitative approach is limited in the extent to which it can establish firm and general conclusions, it is particularly suited to the generation of concepts, questions and issues which can then be subjected to more rigorous testing at a later date, as well as to the elicitation of rich data. Moreover, whilst I do not subscribe to the view that only qualitative approaches are compatible with a feminist commitment, the holism, naturalism and empathetic approach of qualitative research are certainly consistent with feminist values.[10]

Specifically, it was decided that the use of interviews would permit the creation of an open yet supportive context within which to explore freely the patterns and processes of women's faith lives. Many feminists have championed and made significant contributions to the interview as a form of research rich in potential for exploring issues in women's lives and capable of making a significant contribution to women's own development and empowerment (for example, Oakley, 1981; Finch, 1984; Graham, 1984; Ribbens, 1989; Anderson and Jack, 1991; Minster, 1991; Cotterill, 1992; Opie, 1992). Although recent debate has highlighted the complexity of the interview situation as a social, political and personal exchange, and some doubts have been cast on the more cavalier claims about mutuality in the research enterprise, there is no doubt that the interview continues to offer a meaningful method for feminist research. The conversations between myself and the thirty women I interviewed form the linguistic and narrative heart of this book; they are its primary data, its lifespring and its inspiration. They keep the text earthed in real women's situations, dilemmas, growing pains and achievements. They keep the study conversational at its core.

The *feminist Christian commitment* of the present study is the basic hermeneutic which underpins the whole work at every level, providing the original impetus for the study and the overarching rationale for its nature, aims and shape. At the start of the twenty-first century, *feminism* takes a confusing array of different forms, both theoretical and practical, and can be understood in many diverse ways. It is no longer possible, if it ever was, to speak of one feminist perspective; one educational text (Weiner, 1994) distinguishes between at least ten different types of feminism (liberal, radical, Marxist, black or womanist, separatist, lesbian, psychoanalytic, postmodern, poststructural and various forms of religious feminisms). Without attempting to distinguish or adjudicate between these diverse feminisms, I will simply state that, for me, feminism is a political and personal commitment arising out of an understanding of the structural inequality that pertains, and has pertained throughout all known human history, between the sexes, such that men, as a group, have exercised power and control over women as a group, with the result that women's knowledge, experience and history have been systematically repressed. This structural injustice, which feminist theologians name 'sin', results in a profoundly skewed relation between the sexes and a correspondingly flawed

---

[10] See pp. 43–5.

understanding of gender, such that what it means to be 'male' and 'female' requires radical deconstruction and re-evaluation. As stated above, it is not possible to isolate the particular structural injustice of sexism from other forms of structural injustice – racism, ageism, classism, and so on. In practice, as well as in theory, it is essential to recognize what Fiorenza names the 'kryriachal' nature of oppression, the 'multiplicative structures of oppression' (1995, p. 13). Feminism, and its sister womanism, must be committed to a complex systemic analysis of these interlocking forms of oppression, as well as to their overcoming. Such an understanding of feminism goes beyond the liberal project of mere extension to women of the rights enjoyed by men, to the demand for a more fundamental and wholesale restructuring of the system within which relations between men and women, black and white, rich and poor, lesbian/gay/bisexual and heterosexual, able-bodied and disabled, and all other forms of binary opposition, pertain. As Daphne Hampson puts it, 'Feminism represents a revolution. It is not in essence a demand that women should be allowed to join the male world on equal terms. It is a different view of the world' (1990, p. 1). And bell hooks proclaims: 'Feminism is a struggle to end sexist oppression. Its aim is not to benefit solely any specific group of women, any particular race or class of women. It does not privilege women over men. It has the power to transform in a meaningful way all our lives' (1984, p. 26). This is what I understand as the feminist project, and, whilst feminists may agree on little when it comes to the analysis of the causes of, and solutions to, this structural injustice, they are at least agreed on the problematic nature of our inherited notions of gender and the need for reconstruction of those understandings.

To bring such a feminist commitment to bear upon Christian faith is to subject to radical critique every aspect of that faith tradition in the light of women's experiences, deconstructing and reappraising Christian scriptures, tradition, spirituality and theology. It is also to permit Christian faith to shape and critique one's feminist commitment, in a creative and dynamic dialogue between feminism and religious faith. My Christian feminist commitment has informed this study at every level: it has fuelled my passion to 'hear into speech' the neglected stories of women's faith lives; it has generated the commitment explicitly to foreground and give epistemological priority to women's faith lives; it has provided the hermeneutics of suspicion with which to critique and challenge the androcentric fallacy prevalent in much existing psychology, theology and pastoral and educational theory and practice.[11]

Interestingly, feminist practical and pastoral theology have been slow to emerge within the broader field of feminist theology. Miller-McLemore speaks of a 'one-generational lag' between feminist and womanist publications in other subdisciplines of theology – such as biblical studies, ethics and systematic theology – and those in pastoral theology: 'In contrast to progress made in other areas of systematic, biblical, and historical theology, explicit consideration of feminist and womanist theory in pastoral theology has taken longer to reach the table' (1999, p. 86). Ackermann and Bons-Storm suggest that 'practical theology is probably the theological discipline least influenced by feminist voices' (1998, p. 1). Speculating

---

[11] Elsewhere (Slee, 1996) I have elaborated a more sustained account of my understanding of Christian feminist identity.

on the reasons for this, Miller-McLemore suggests a number. First, 'proximity to the more conserving structures of congregations, designed to preserve traditions, makes the introduction of the politically and spiritually disruptive ideas and practices of feminism and womanism prohibitive and complicated' (p. 87). Second, 'the precariousness of the field itself and the potentially increased liabilities of adding feminism and womanism preclude discussion ... Adding feminist theory to pastoral theology renders its position even more precarious as a discipline peculiarly poised between practice, person, confessional religious congregations, and the academy' (p. 87). Thirdly, and paradoxically, many of the methods and practices of pastoral theology are already, to a degree, reflective of key feminist principles and concerns, so it may have been perceived that there is less of a need for explicit feminist reformation of the discipline. Heather Walton (2001) speaks of a 'complicit' relation between women and practical theology, emerging out of the fact that women have at the same time identified themselves more closely with the concerns of practical theology than other areas of theology, looked to it for sustenance and life, been able to 'carve out a little niche in [its] soft and feely places', whilst finding it difficult to 'mount a radical critique' of the discipline that has welcomed them and offered a route to ordination and/or jobs (pp. 6–7). The 'feminisation' of practical theology (the close association of the discipline with traditionally female spheres such as caring, teaching, serving and healing) has, in many ways, worked against its radicalisation. However, feminist practical theology is beginning to emerge now as a recognisable subdiscipline of feminist theology, on the one hand, and practical theology on the other. I am glad to offer this study of women's faith lives, and the factors which both promote and inhibit women's faith development, to this newly emerging field, in the hope that it may add to the voices within practical theology which are challenging conventional wisdom and previously unrivalled 'normative' accounts of what it means to be human, to live the Christian life and to practise faith.

An Overview of the Study

The present chapter has contextualised the study in my own personal and professional experience, as well as in the broader, interdisciplinary context of feminist practical theology, developmental psychology and social science methodology. It has attempted to explicate the key features of the study as well as to spell out its main aims. Chapter 2 develops in more detail the understanding of women's spirituality and faith development by drawing upon the literature of faith development theory and critiquing it from the perspective of women's experience, and identifying alternative models of women's faith development. Chapter 3 discusses the development of a feminist research methodology, elaborating the principles which informed the research design and describing the specific research methods used. Chapters 4 to 7, which form the heart of the study, present the key findings. These are organised around two key concepts: first, in Chapter 4, the *processes* of women's faith development describe the strategies the women in my interviews used in making sense of and patterning their experience and finding ultimate meaning in it. Six strategies are identified and described, which I name conversational, metaphoric, narrative, personalised, conceptual and apophatic faithing.

The bulk of the findings, however, is presented in terms of what I have named the *patterns* of women's faith development. Three major *generative themes* are identified within the women's faith stories which seemed to represent basic and recurring patterns in the women's faith lives; these themes are summarised as alienation, awakenings and relationality. Following Harris (1988), I employ the notion of themes to suggest broad areas of human experience which can extend in a number of different directions, and yet which nevertheless cohere. A theme may cohere, not necessarily in terms of tight logical order or sequence, but by means of loose association or metaphoric resemblance. To speak of such themes as 'generative' is to suggest that these areas of women's experience are, themselves, fecund with meaning, generative of insight and illumination, and capable of giving rise to new understandings of women's lives. Whilst they do not constitute a fully worked out, comprehensive model of women's faith development, and are not necessarily developmentally sequential, the three themes together do provide the beginnings of such a model, which is clearly in need of fuller investigation, testing and development. Chapters 5, 6 and 7 describe in detail the ways in which the three themes of alienation, awakenings and relationality were evident in the women's faith accounts, describing the different ways in which they featured and discussing the wider implications. Finally, Chapter 8 draws together the study by considering the implications of the findings, first for faith developmental theory, and second, for the pastoral care and education of women, particularly, but not exclusively, within the churches.

Chapter 2

Women's Faith Development: A Framework

The silence of women in the narrative of adult development distorts the conception of its stages and sequence. Thus, I want to restore in part the missing text of women's development.

Carol Gilligan[1]

When we start on this journey, we discover a couple of things right away. First, the way is largely uncharted, and second, we are all we've got. If women don't tell our stories and utter our truths in order to chart ways into sacred feminine experience, who will?

Sue Monk Kidd[2]

When we women offer our experience as our truth, all the maps change. There are new mountains.

Ursula Le Guin[3]

Introduction

Where do we look to find sources which can illuminate our efforts to understand the faith development of women and girls? There are hardly any texts that treat directly of the area, with one or two noble exceptions already mentioned (Conn, 1986; Hess, 1997; Stevenson-Moessner, 2000), upon which I shall draw freely. Nevertheless, there is no shortage of discourse and theory about human development and, to a lesser degree, faith development, which might be deemed to be pertinent. Indeed, the range of developmental theories which might be consulted is immense, and evergrowing; no one study can possibly absorb and utilise all the relevant literature. Psychodynamic theories rooted in the work of Freud and the post-Freudians compete with Jungian understandings of human development, whilst cognitive-structural theories such as those by Piaget and Kohlberg offer a different account again. Some theories, such as those by Erikson, Selman and Loevinger, seek to integrate both psychodynamic and cognitive-structural approaches. None of these theories can be read naively or applied uncritically to female development however, for, as many critics have highlighted, they are almost all, to a lesser or greater degree, gender-blind, inattentive to women's experience and lives. Many of the

---

[1] Gilligan (1982), p. 156.
[2] Monk Kidd (1996), p. 3.
[3] Le Guin (1989), p. 160.

major psychological accounts of development are based on male-only or male-majority studies, or operate with cultural stereotypes of women, or project misogynist images of women which illuminate the theorist's prejudices and limitations rather more than they do the growing pains and needs of women. As Robert Kegan warns:

> Any time a theory is normative, and suggests that something is more grown, more mature, more developed than something else, we had all better check to see if the distinction rests on arbitrary grounds that consciously or unconsciously unfairly advantage some people (such as those who create the theory and people like them) whose own preferences are being depicted as superior. We had all better check whether what may appear to be an 'objective' theory is not in reality a tool or captive of a 'ruling' group (such as white people, men, Westerners) who use the theory to preserve their advantaged position. (1994, p. 229)

Our use of existing sources, then, must be judicious, nuanced and critical. No one model of human or faith development is likely to be adequate to the task or offer, by itself, a sufficient vocabulary and syntax for speaking about women's faith. In this chapter, we shall consider a number of models of faith development, but it needs to be held in mind throughout that none of these are universally valid or without need of refinement and restatement – even though, ironically, some of them are rooted in assumptions about their universal applicability (a particular problem of the cognitive-structural models which take it as axiomatic that stages of development are invariant and universal, in so far as they are valid). Some of the models we shall examine, such as those by Fowler and his predecessors, are well established and have spawned a large body of secondary research and critical discussion. Others, such as some of those offered by feminist theologians and educators, are rudimentary in form, suggestive rather than fully worked out, and untested in empirical research. Their nature and status need to be borne in mind as the reader attempts to evaluate the significance of different developmental models. I include them in the discussion because I believe they all have some insight to shed on the developmental journeys of women and girls, even if their claims need to be relativised and critiqued in the light of alternative accounts.

The major psychological theory of faith development available at the present time in the English-speaking world is that of James Fowler and, whilst I am not uncritical of Fowler, I have drawn on faith development research and theory widely, and found inspiration from it, not least in some of its axiomatic presuppositions about the nature of faith and the processes of its development. Nevertheless, Fowler's account of faith development will not do on its own; it shares in the limitations of cognitive structural theories more generally, and needs to be set within a broader framework of a variety of developmental models. More specifically, empirical evidence suggests that it neglects certain aspects of women's faith, and more recent accounts of women's faith are necessary to correct and broaden Fowler's theory.

In this chapter, I attempt to provide a broad map of some diverse types of developmental theory, before going on to look at the research on faith development more narrowly, and specifically to consider both empirical and theoretical studies of women's faith.

Development in Diverse Perspective

It is not possible to give a complete account of the full range of human developmental theories here: a vast and constantly growing field of psychological enquiry which is itself dependent on biological understandings of human maturation and on changing philosophical understandings of what it means to be human. Nevertheless, it is necessary to set the discussion of faith development within some kind of coherent framework of developmental discourse, in order to highlight the diversity of perspectives which can be employed to illuminate persons' growth in faith and to illuminate the particular context out of which faith development research and theory has emerged. I shall briefly consider below lifespan theories, structural stage theories, relational psychodynamic theories and so-called 'dialectical' or socio-psychological theories, illustrating each theoretical approach by reference to one or two major exemplars and giving particular attention to the applications of such an approach to women's development. If I pay more attention to the underlying assumptions about development operative in structural stage theories, that is because they have had most impact on faith development research and theory. However, each of these theoretical models has something insightful to offer in the understanding of women's faith development. Nor are they not necessarily mutually exclusive, although there are, of course, tensions between them in terms of how they seek to account for development. The relative weightings they give to such factors as the subconscious and the affective, cognitive ability, familial and social context, and so on, vary greatly; by setting them alongside one another it is possible to highlight the particular strengths and shortcomings of each theoretical approach. And we must bear in mind that each of them has been articulated in more or less androcentric ways, so that no theoretical approach remains immune to feminist critique – although some, by definition, particularly those accounts which pay more attention to the socio-political structuring of development, are more capable of offering a satisfactory account of women's development than others.

Lifespan Theories

Lifespan theories are probably best known to most readers through the work of Erik Erikson (1980), who introduced and elaborated concepts such as the life cycle, identity crises and phases of development, which are now part of common parlance. (Other lifespan theorists include Havighurst [1980], who outlines the developmental tasks of adulthood, and Levinson [1978], who charted the seasons of men's lives in an American study of that name.) Erikson posited the notion of development based on a series of life crises or opportunities for decision, the resolution of which would set the course of development for the next phase. Such crises occur at the intersection of biology, culture and psychology, where the emerging biological organism and individual ego come up against the demands of culture at a particular point in time. If a crisis is resolved positively, the struggle gives birth to a strength or virtue; if it is not, the individual is at risk of vulnerability in successive developmental crises. Moving beyond earlier theories, which had stopped with adolescence, Erikson named eight developmental crises or 'seasons' taking the individual from birth to death: infancy, centring around the establishment of basic trust versus mistrust; early childhood, characterised by autonomy versus shame and doubt; play age, where the choice is between initiative versus role confusion; school age, where the child must choose between industry or inferiority; adolescence, where the tension is between ego identity and confusion; young adulthood, marked by the struggle between intimacy and isolation; middle adulthood, characterised by generativity or self-absorption and stagnation; and finally old age, during which the individual must face the crisis of ego integrity versus despair. Each of these phases is marked by significant bodily changes, accompanied by emotional and cognitive growth, giving rise to new relational modes and social roles.

Unlike Freud, Erikson perceived development as more than biologically and sexually determined; his theory explicitly seeks to take into account the shaping power of culture in relation with biological and psychological factors, thus widening significantly the scope of developmental theory. After Erikson it is impossible to view individual development in isolation from cultural setting and without taking into account such factors as the individual's family, class, education, work, neighbourhood and so on. Nevertheless, whilst Erikson recognised the impact of culture on development, his theory tends to normalise white American cultural patterns of development, and male ones at that. Although Erikson paid some attention to gender and had a more positive attitude to women's identity formation than Freud, his account of women's identity shows a markedly biological focus, centred on the metaphor of the womb which, for Erikson, symbolised women's inwardness, interiority, protectiveness and inclusiveness. Feminists have critiqued Erikson's model for its implicit bias towards separation and autonomy as primary developmental goals, with intimacy only appearing in the later stages; a model which, it is suggested, may describe typically male patterns of development in the western world, but does not do justice to women's experience of connectedness and relationality (for example, Gilligan, 1982), nor to very different cultural models of development where individual identity is considered less important than kinship loyalty and commitment to the group.

Nevertheless, lifespan theories contain important insights into the nature and process of development, and some of their key ideas may helpfully be applied to women's development. Thus, for example, in the early 1980s, Anita Spencer (1982) reworked Levinson's developmental 'seasons' for women, highlighting the way in which particular cultural constraints shaped the lifecycle dilemmas for women distinctively. Whilst essentially accepting Erikson's and Levinson's accounts of the developmental crises rather than challenging them, as later feminists have done, Spencer suggests that these developmental choices are configured very differently for men and for women, and are often far more ambivalent for women, admitting of less complete resolution. Thus, the young adult challenge of forming a dream and giving it a place in the life structure may be experienced by young women as a tension between the choice of a sexual partnership and parenting, on the one hand, and the choice of an occupation or career on the other, whereas for young men there is social support for both of these choices to be engaged simultaneously and they are rarely perceived as mutually exclusive. Or again, the late adult challenge of coming to terms with finitude and accepting the passing of one's generative stage of life may be experienced by women as more intimately connected to biological changes which have negative social value; the loss of a woman's fertility and youthful beauty may be more threatening for her than the equivalent process in a man, because of the way in which culture has defined and valued women for their sexual role and productivity. Whether or not we accept such generalisations, a lifespan approach is useful in so far as it calls attention to the particular social and cultural shaping of developmental crises and provides a framework for assessing both the strengths and the losses of an individual's navigation of these dilemmas.

Structural Stage Theories

In contrast to lifespan theories, structural stage theories are concerned to identify and describe the basic, underlying structures that shape development, which are presumed to be universal and invariant, and therefore independent of and prior to culture. There are two basic types of such theories: psychodynamic stage theories, such as those of Freud and Jung, which identify the basic structures of development in the psychosexual dynamics of human interaction, and cognitive stage theories, such as those of Piaget and Kohlberg, which locate the basic underlying structures of development in the logical processes of cognition. Whilst the two types of stage theory differ widely in their accounts of development, and particularly in terms of the competing priority they give to affect and cognition respectively, their understanding of the basic structures of development is broadly similar, especially the way in which they construct the notion of developmental stages. Here I shall focus on cognitive stage theories, since I shall discuss psychodynamic approaches below in terms of their emphasis on human relationship and connection.

The father of cognitive stage theories is, of course, Jean Piaget (1929, 1962), and his theory of cognitive development in infants and children remains fundamental for all subsequent stage theories. Later theorists have widened the scope of his concern with childhood scientific and logical thinking in various ways: Kohlberg (1981, 1984) by extending the focus to the development of moral thinking, Fowler (1981) by broadening the concern to faith development, Perry (1968) by investigating adult college students' thinking, and Loevinger (1976) by adapting a Piagetian approach to the study of girls' and women's thinking. Whilst the detailed account of development as described by each of these theorists varies widely, the underlying assumptions about the nature and process of development are broadly similar.

For structural stage theories, development is understood to demonstrate certain formal characteristics which are held to be axiomatic and non-negotiable. First, developmental change is *orderly* and *sequential*. Underlying all the surface features of a person's life, there is a pattern of development which has a coherence, logic and order to it, and moves in the direction of increasing autonomy, differentiation, flexibility, equilibrium and integration of experience. These theories make a basic distinction between surface content and deep structure to account for both contextual diversity in persons' thinking and an underlying commonality of pattern. Fowler, for example, claims that 'underlying the wide variety of *contents* which come to be expressive of the faith of persons, there are formally describable *patterns* or *structures* of thought, of valuing, and of constitutive-knowing' (1980, p. 65, original emphasis). According to Oser, 'the cognitive structure of religious reasoning ... is a basic pattern which is ... trans-situational, which means that it is employed in similar fashion in various situations' (Oser and Gmünder, 1991, p. 59).

Secondly, developmental change *takes place in stages*, described by Fowler as 'the deeper structural operations of knowing and valuing which underlie, ground, and organize the thematic content of a person's faith' (1986, p. 27). The notion of 'stage' is one of fundamental qualitative, structural change, rather than mere incremental or quantitative change. Development takes place through qualitative shifts in which the whole structure of thinking and operating reformulates itself into new and more adequate constellations. Because of the qualitative nature of developmental stages, it follows that their order is fixed and invariant, The stages are cumulative, each dependent upon the foundation of the previous stage and taken up into the next stage where it is transformed into a new and more adequate structural whole. This does not mean that a person's actual thinking and behaviour will always be consistent within a given stage. In fact, persons often operate at a variety of stage levels according to circumstance and the level of maturation achieved in a particular area – for example, one's moral thinking could be at a different stage from one's general cognitive level, or stressful circumstances could predispose one to regress to a lower stage than one's normal functioning level. Nevertheless, the hierarchical and cumulative nature of the stage sequence does impose certain theoretical restrictions on how development can be envisaged. It is logically impossible, in terms of the theory, to bypass a stage altogether, or for a person at an early stage of development to have the capacity to operate at a much higher stage, unless they first pass through the intervening stages.

Finally, developmental change is understood to be *consistent and unchanging across diverse cultural contexts*. Despite variations in individuals' circumstances and experience, there is a common genetic and epistemological structure to development which is invariant and universal.

According to structural stage theories, movement from one stage to the next is not an automatic function of biological maturation, chronological age, psychological development, or mental age, though all of these factors play a part. Rather, 'transition itself occurs when the equilibrium of a given stage is upset by encounters with crises, novelties, and experiences of disclosure and challenge which threaten the limits of the person's present patterns of constitutive-knowing' (Fowler, 1986, p. 27). Because each stage has its own functional equilibrium, it is quite possible to stay within a given stage for long periods of time. Some kind of dissonance must occur to upset the equilibrium and force a given stage to deconstruct. This dissonance can be caused by internal changes resulting from biological maturation or external factors such as leaving home, graduation, getting married, the birth of a child, as well as death, illness, divorce and various forms of personal catastrophe.

Whatever the cause of change from one stage to another, the basic dynamic of change itself is likely to be uniform. First, the existing stage is deconstructed, either by events or by internal changes, through a process of disengagement, disidentification, disenchantment and disorientation. This is a time of maximum discomfort and confusion for the individual, for the safety and equilibrium of a normative way of operating is, over time, broken down and discarded. This can happen suddenly and dramatically, or very gradually, almost imperceptibly. However it happens, it is a time of major dislocation when old ways and structures will no longer do, however well they have served in the past. Following the abandonment of previously held beliefs and patterns of being, the individual experiences a transitional time of dissonance and suspension in what Bridges (1980) terms 'the neutral zone'. This is a time of emptiness and waiting, when the old constructs have broken down, but before new ones have taken their place. The new stage does not appear overnight, but has to constellate out of the breakdown of the old, and, again, this can take a considerable time. The transitional phase in between stages may be experienced as profoundly bewildering, yet out of this time in the neutral zone, the new beginnings of the next stage emerge.

As is well known, Piaget distinguished between three main stages of cognitive development: sensory-motor intelligence, during which the infant coordinates perceptive and motor functions and intelligence is entirely bodily; intuitive or pre-operational thinking, in which language facilitates transductive thinking but there is no systematic, logical thought; concrete operations, when the child becomes capable for the first time of inductive and deductive logic, though this is limited to concrete situations and actions; and, finally, formal operational thought, when the capacity to think hypothetically and abstractly is acquired. Kohlberg (1981, 1984) applied these stages to moral thinking, but extended his research beyond adolesence, and identified six structural stages, arranged in three levels: level one, the preconventional, in which the child's thought is dominated by physical, pragmatic considerations, consisting of a punishment and obedience orientation (stage one) and an instrumental relativist orientation (stage two); level two, the conventional level, in which conformity to social order is primary, consisting of an interpersonal concordance – a 'good boy-nice girl' orientation (stage three) and a law-and-order orientation (stage four); and the postconventional, autonomous or principled level, consisting of a social-contract legalistic orientation (stage five) and a universal ethical-principle orientation (stage six).

Cognitive stage theories have been very widely critiqued from all quarters: for placing too high an emphasis on the shaping power of cognition in development and ignoring the role of affect, imagination and the subconscious; for underestimating the capacities of children for logical thinking; for their rigid and inflexible stage constructs which seem to impose a linearity to development which does not accord with experience; for a kind of imperial colonialism which prizes a certain kind of scientific, logical rationalism as the highest form of thought; for describing rather than genuinely accounting for the process of development; for generalising male patterns of thought to the whole population and not taking into consideration gendered patterns of thinking and behaviour.[4] For all these criticisms, most of which have been applied in one form or another to faith development theory, and with which I have some sympathy, we do well not to jettison stage theories entirely. They can be useful in the study of adult faith in calling attention to deep structures of thought which shape the particularities of faith content; they alert attention to the dynamic of development inherent in the human organism, suggesting that faith too, by its very nature must be changing and growing and in a state of perpetually shifting equilibrium rather than static and changeless; they provide a vocabulary for

---

[4] For critical discussions of Piaget's theory, see Brainerd et al. (1978); Donaldson (1978); Brown and Desforges (1979).

discriminating between more or less adequate structures and patterns of faith and, whilst we may argue about the criteria they apply to the judgements of faith, they compel us to address the question of what makes for better or worse faith stances in our world and in our time.

Relational Psychodynamic Theories

In strong contrast to a cognitive approach, there exists a loose network of theories which we might describe as relational psychodynamic approaches in so far as they place a central emphasis on human relational ties as the primary context for development, and draw on the psychodynamic tradition in their description of relationality (although some would align themselves more closely than others with the assumptions of Freud and that tradition). In this category would be included objects relations theory (Freud, 1963; Winnicott, 1971; Bowlby, 1988), self-psychology (Kohut, 1977), the Sullivan or interpersonal school (for example, Stern, 1985) and a broad movement of feminist-inspired research that has highlighted relationality and connectedness in women's development (Miller, 1976; Chodorow, 1978; Gilligan, 1982; Jordan, 1991). As well as highlighting the centrality of relationality in the development of identity, these theories pay particular attention to the early experience of the infant's connection to its primary caregiver, seeing this bond as constitutive of all that follows in later development.

The object relations theorists emphasise the drive or yearning for connection with an other in the infant (described in terms of 'object seeking'), in contrast with Freud's emphasis on biological and sexual drive as the fundamental motor of development. They propose that a variety of significant others are internalised within the inner psyche of the child, taking up internal residence as 'internal objects'. Thus 'a host of satisfying, tantalizing, and tormenting figures or aspects of the self [can] direct behaviour and color perceptions of the external world. These internal objects [become] the source for inner messages of self-worth, self-condemnation, inner conflict, and projection of old relational patterns onto real, external others' (Cooper-White, 2000, p. 94). Self-psychology and the interpersonal school, whilst using different terminology, similarly emphasise the child's early relation to her carers and the quality of the holding environment as the fundamental factors in the development of a stable and positive identity.

Whilst object relations theory and other similar approaches emphasise the centrality of early relationship in human development generally, there is a wide range of research and theory which has focused on the particular significance of relationality in girls' and women's development, suggesting that women's identity is peculiarly rooted in connection with others, both in later life as well as in the early years. Jean Baker Miller's *Toward a New Psychology of Women* (1976) broke new ground by demonstrating how psychological study of women had been distorted by an 'inequality of framework' which largely marginalised women from research and, when it included them, judged their experience by the standard of an alien, male perspective. Miller showed how qualities which women have developed as a result of their structural subservience to men and their social roles as caretakers and nurturers – qualities such as vulnerability, tenderness, cooperativeness and unselfishness – have been consistently devalued and perceived as weaknesses in psychology. Similarly, she called attention to the way in which most theories of psychological development elevate separation and self-determination as the goals of human development, ignoring and devaluing women's experience of affiliation and judging women to be psychologically immature. Miller argued, that, on the contrary, 'women's development *is* proceeding, but on another basis ... Women stay with, build on, and develop in a context of attachment and affiliation with others. Indeed, women's sense of self becomes very much organized around being able to make and then to maintain affiliations and relationships' (p. 87). Whilst she acknowledged that women's rootedness in relationship could be expressed in immature and dependent ways, Miller proposed that women's relational identity possesses psychological strengths which had not been recognised.

Where Miller drew attention to women's affiliative self-identity, Chodorow, in *The Reproduction of Mothering* (1978), sought to explain how this might be accounted for in terms of the early parenting experiences of male and female children. In a culture where parenting is performed largely if not exclusively by women, Chodorow argued that male and female infants experience themselves differently in relation to the mother. Whereas the infant girl knows herself to be essentially a part of the female world represented by her mother and feels no need to separate herself from her, the male child, by contrast, recognising himself to be fundamentally different from the mother, is only able to achieve a sense of identity by differentiating himself from her and identifying himself with the father (or other male role-model). Thus the girl's identity is formed in a context of connectedness and relationality, and mothering – the ability to care for others in close relationships – is reproduced in her. The boy's identity, on the other hand, is formed in a context of separation and a profound experience of otherness. For boys, separation and individuation become allied, whereas for girls, it is attachment which accompanies the individuation process. This leads to differing perceptions of self-identity and relationships in adult life.

Carol Gilligan's (1982, 1983, 1986, 1987) work on moral and identity formation in women and girls is well-known, and has done much to establish a 'different voice' in developmental theory over and against mainstream androcentric accounts. Gilligan conducted a series of interviews with women exploring their moral thinking about real-life issues they had had to face (in contrast to Kohlberg's methodology which employed hypothetical issues). As a result of her research, Gilligan proposed that women's moral thinking and development exhibit distinctive features which are not accounted for by Kohlberg's theory and which are, indeed, systematically downgraded by him. In particular, she concluded that women's moral thinking is characteristically relational and contextual in a way which is not true of men. In contrast to the appeal to abstract moral principles which Kohlberg noted in his more advanced male subjects, Gilligan found that the women in her study appealed to the needs and demands of relationship and to an ethic of responsibility and care, in their attempts to resolve moral dilemmas. Accordingly, she called for the reworking of his theory of stage development in order to account adequately for the 'other voice' of women's experience.

Gilligan's work itself has aroused strong and divided reaction and has spawned an extensive secondary literature which cannot be reviewed here (compare, for example, Boyd, 1982; Brabeck, 1983; Broughton, 1983; Pratt et al., 1984; L.J. Walker, 1984; Kerber et al., 1986; Sher, 1987; Gould, 1988), but there would seem to be grounds for suggesting that her conclusions may need to be modified significantly to take account of a wider range of variables (see Reich, 1997) and to qualify the impression of an absolute distinction between a (male-specific) ethic of justice and a (female-specific) ethic of care. Indeed, Gilligan herself has been careful to dissociate herself from an essentialist gender stance, and in later work has advanced a more nuanced elaboration of her thesis which recognises that both men and women are capable of operating according to both ethics of care and of justice, though women demonstrate a preference for the former, and men for the latter. Whilst debate continues about the extent of the difference between male and female patterns of identity construction, Gilligan's detailed case studies provide rich qualitative evidence of the appeal to relationality and committed connection in women's moral thinking, and demonstrate that higher-level moral reasoning can be conducted in terms other than that of the appeal to abstract principles, as privileged by Kohlberg.

The work of the Stone Center in New York (Jordan, 1991) confirms, in broad terms, the suggestion that women's identity is strongly embedded in connection to others. Surrey (1991) develops the notion of the 'self-in-relation' as the core structure of women's identity. This term is intended to capture 'the recognition that, for women, the primary experience of self is relational, that is, the self is organized and developed in the context of important relationships', as well as relationship 'being seen as the basic goal of development' (Surrey, 1991, pp. 52, 53). Surrey suggests three basic elements which form the self-in-relation. First, 'an interest in, and attention to, the other person(s) which form the base for the emotional connection and the ability to empathize with the other(s)'; second, 'the expectation of a mutual empathic process where the sharing of experience leads to a heightened development of self and other'; and third, 'the expectation of interaction and relationship as a process of mutual sensitivity and mutual responsibility that provides the stimulus for the growth of empowerment and self-knowledge' (pp. 58–9). In other words, there is an experience of 'emotional and cognitive *intersubjectivity*' in relationship, which is formed by 'the ongoing intrinsic inner awareness and responsiveness to the continuous existence of the other or others and the expectation of mutuality in this regard' (p. 61). It is out of this experience of intersubjectivity that women's sense of self is formed.

Relational approaches to the construction of identity provide a strikingly different lens through which to approach faith development from that suggested by lifespan or cognitive developmental theories. They alert attention to the role of affect, imagination and human attachment in the development of faith. They focus awareness on the impact of the early years of childcare on an individual's later relationships, of which the relationship to God may be one. They suggest that religious symbols, narratives and practices will be interpreted and internalised by the individual not only through the cognitive structures available to that individual, but also through the dynamics of their attachments, both present and past, to significant others. They highlight the strongly relational orientation of women's thinking and identity, which is likely to have a profound influence on women's appropriation of faith.

Dialectical Theories

A final category of developmental theory may be distinguished by its overt attention to the dialectical interaction of the individual and society, and on the intersecting influence of biology, environment and history, sometimes described as dialectical theories (see Riegel, 1975; Fiske, 1980). Whilst earlier theories, such as the lifespan theories considered above, did pay attention to the interaction of the individual with their social environment, contemporary dialectical theories explicitly root the study of individual psychological development in an analysis of the power relations that profoundly shape development, and focus their attention deliberately on groups within society which have limited access to social power. Such theories represent in the psychological field the kind of 'bias to the poor' which we have become familiar with in liberation, feminist and womanist theologies. Such theories make an explicit commitment to the study of the development from the 'underside' of those who have been, up to now, neglected or marginalised in mainstream psychological accounts: women, working-class people, people with physical or other kinds of disability, and so on. These theories pay attention to the ways in which the life crises which such groups must navigate are rooted in unequal power distribution and conflict generated by such inequality of power. Development is understood as a conscious or unconscious attempt to overcome these inequalities through the acquisition of various competencies – cognitive, affective, behavioural, motivational, communicational, social – needed for specific race, gender, class and cultural contexts. As with liberation and feminist theologies, this theoretical approach is rooted in a commitment to social change, and challenges previous normative accounts of development.

Dialectical approaches represent a relatively recent innovation in developmental theory, and so there are no well-established models emanating from this perspective as yet. I therefore illustrate this approach via one or two research studies which have taken women's development as their particular focus and have utilised a dialectical framework in their analysis of female development. In a work which has become justly well known, Belenky, Clinchy, Goldberger and Tarule (1986) set out to study women's development of self, voice and mind – what they called *Women's Ways of Knowing* – in such a way as to pay careful attention to the interaction of environment, social class, gender, race and cognitive ability. They interviewed women students from a variety of academic institutions, as well as socially and educationally disadvantaged women. They identified a number of distinctive epistemological perspectives from which, they suggest, women know and view the world. These are not presented as developmental stages, though they hypothesise that they *may* be developmentally related.[5] What is significant about these epistemological stances is that they are contextualised explicitly in the presumption of women's social and cultural marginalisation. Thus they are not universally valid for all time, but reflect women's constructions of knowledge at a particular juncture in time and place, and are profoundly shaped by the particular social location of women. The five ways of knowing are first, *Silence*, 'a position in which women experience themselves as mindless and voiceless and subject to the whims of

---

[5] For ongoing debate about this study and its findings, see Goldberger et al. (1996).

external authority'; second, *Received Knowledge*, 'a perspective from which women conceive of themselves as capable of receiving, even reproducing, knowledge from the all-knowing external authorities but not capable of creating knowledge on their own'; third, *Subjective Knowledge*, 'a perspective from which truth and knowledge are conceived of as personal, private, and subjectively known or intuited'; fourth, *Procedural Knowledge*, 'a position in which women are invested in learning and applying objective procedures for obtaining and communicating knowledge' (two types of procedural knowledge are identified: separate knowing, in which knowledge is acquired through separation from the object and mastery over it, and connected knowing, in which there is an intimacy and equality between self and object); and fifth, *Constructed Knowledge*, 'a position in which women view all knowledge as contextual, experience themselves as creators of knowledge, and value both subjective and objective strategies for knowing' (Belenky et al., 1986, p. 15).

Whilst cognitive ability and educational opportunity are seen to determine to some extent which epistemological stance a woman adopts, Belenky and her colleagues also demonstrate how social, familial and cultural factors shape a woman's epistemological choices. All of the women who inhabited the epistemological stance of silence (admittedly numerically very small), and the majority of women who are categorised as received and subjective knowers, were from socially, economically and educationally deprived backgrounds, whilst the women who were able to achieve the more complex and nuanced forms of procedural and constructed knowledge generally appear to be those who made it to higher education and often tend to be those with more privileged backgrounds. The 'silent knowers' had all experienced some form of gross neglect and physical and/or sexual abuse, by one or both parents, and their families had been characterised by a lack of dialogue and play. 'Occasionally', they suggest,

> women of lower-class origins who grew up in families characterized by silence, hierarchy, and violence were able to find strengths elsewhere – from other relatives, neighbors, and excellent schools – that helped them transcend the epistemological atmospheres of their families. On the whole, however, when poor families fail their children, the society provides precious little help; while children of privilege are more likely to find rich sources of sustenance to promote their development elsewhere. (p. 160)

Judith Orr (2000) attends specifically to the shaping influence of class on women's development in her study of working-class women in Kansas City in the US heartland. Essentially a lifespan description, Orr's approach is dialectical in so far as it seeks to ground the description of the life challenges of these women within an economic and class framework, demonstrating how these women's developmental trajectories deviate markedly from previous standard accounts. Based on conversations with twenty adult women, Orr's model charts each major phase of the life cycle for these women. Their accounts of childhood are dominated by the pervasiveness of worry over factors such as shortage of money, keeping the peace, family fighting, illness and so on, whilst it is also the period during which working-class women 'learned a double consciousness' (p. 62) of existing both in their own working-class context and knowing how to operate in situations managed by those in power. Adolescence is marked by struggle over exclusion from mainstream middle-class culture, and a variety of strategies are employed to cope with the shame and rejection of this exclusion. In young adulthood, working-class women are likely to model themselves on the life choices of their mothers, marrying and parenting young, whilst also needing to bring in money by working outside the home. Survival is a key theme. In middle adulthood, as young children grow up and the demands of homelife decrease somewhat, working-class women articulate a strong commitment to helping others, not only those of one's own immediate family network, but also those within one's community more widely. This contrasts somewhat with the introspective focus of middle-class women at this phase of life, where greater economic security may admit of more extensive self-reflection than is possible for working-class women. It may also reflect the different values of middle-class and working-class communities, with a stronger emphasis on individual achievement characterising the professional middle-class women's environment. In old age, working-class women highlight the themes of learning and rest, 'providing the concluding dialectic to a working-class life that frequently lacked both' (p. 62). Reflecting on the patterns revealed by her study as a whole, Orr reflects, 'An examination of the lives of working-class women … helps us to understand the purpose of development as struggling through personal and systemic conflicts with race, class, gender, and culture to overcome intersecting psycho-socio-spiritual inequities to make possible mutually respectful life in community' (p. 63).

Where Orr focuses on working-class women's development, other researchers working from a dialectical approach have explored the developmental issues and challenges confronting abused and traumatised women and girls (Neuger, 2000; Cooper-White, 2000; Davis, 2000), analysing the ways in which the experience of abuse may subvert the 'typical' developmental trajectory traced by mainstream theories. Each of these accounts highlights the specificity of their particular contexts and the distinctiveness of the developmental pathways walked by women and girls in these contexts. Such accounts are critical correctives to the universalising tendencies implicit in lifespan, structural stage and even psychoanalytical relational theories. Each of the previous theoretical approaches tends to focus on the commonalities of development across a broad range of variables such as class, culture, gender and so on, flattening out difference and privileging a so-called 'normal' and thus normative model of development. Dialectical approaches, whilst limited in their generalisability, are valuable precisely because they do not attempt to universalise their findings. Their accounts are concrete and specific, politically and culturally biased in favour of the life situations of those groups of people who, up until now, have been invisible in psychological theory or, if visible, regarded as dysfunctional and exceptional, functioning merely to reinforce the hegemony of the mainstream accounts. Dialectical theories contribute a vital ingredient to our framework for thinking about women's faith development, for they remind us of the specificity of women's faith in any given context or situation, and encourage us to look for diversity and pay attention to context in our attempts to describe and account for the patterns in women's spiritual lives.

Faith Development Theory

The deliberate, systematic study of persons' faith development throughout the life cycle has been established in the United States by Professor James Fowler (1980, 1981, 1984, 1986, 1987, 1991a, 1991b, 1996), although the closely related work of Fritz Oser and his colleagues in Switzerland (Oser, 1980, 1991; Oser and Gmünder, 1991) is also significant. Fowler and Oser stand in the cognitive structural developmental tradition represented by Piaget, Kohlberg and others – although Fowler also draws more widely on lifespan theories such as those by Erikson – and share the principles and assumptions of that tradition. They have sought to map out in generalised, abstract stages, the development of faith across the lifespan. Grounded in mature theological reflection and considerable empirical research, and claiming universality of reference, the theories of religious development advocated by Fowler and Oser represent a qualitatively new stage in the psychology of religious development. They further the work of Goldman (1964) and other neo-Piagetians in a number of important ways: by extending research beyond childhood and adolescence into adulthood; by broadening considerably the earlier models of religious thinking to a much richer notion of 'faith' or 'religious judgement'; by developing empirical methodology in creative and more rigorous ways; by replicating findings across a broad range of empirical studies; by incorporating insights from other psychological traditions into the cognitive-developmental paradigm and thus enriching considerably the scope and significance of their theories; and by engaging in dialogue with a wide range of philosophical, theological, psychological and educational concerns in order to tease out the implications as well as shortcomings of their work. Although their theories have been subjected to sharp critique (compare Dykstra and Parks, 1986; Astley and Francis, 1992), including feminist critique (for example, Harris, 1986; Parks, 1990/1), and cannot be adopted wholesale for a study of women's religious development, it is inconceivable that such a study could bypass their work altogether. In vital and creative ways, they have established the study of religious development such that all future research in the field is compelled to orient itself in relation to their work, even if it is largely in opposition to it.

Whilst Oser's theory is significant, I focus the discussion in this chapter around Fowler's theory, since it has influenced my research more substantially than Oser's. In addition, Fowler's theory has been discussed more fully by feminists, and thus much of the secondary literature relates to Fowler's work.[6]

Faith, as Fowler understands it, is by no means confined to explicitly religious beliefs or practice. Drawing widely on the theological writings of H. Richard Niebuhr (1960), Wilfred Cantwell Smith (1963, 1979) and Paul Tillich (1953, 1957, 1964), Fowler has developed a model of faith as an active, dynamic, affective and cognitive process of meaning-making which is a human universal, engaging every human being from birth to death in the search for ultimate meaning. Faith, for Fowler, is 'the process of constitutive-knowing' which underlies 'a person's composition and maintenance of a comprehensive frame (or frames) of meaning'

---

[6] Other significant accounts of faith development are provided by Westerhoff (1976, 1980), Wilcox (1979), Powers (1982), Scott Peck (1993) and Stephens (1996).

(1986, p. 25). It 'gives coherence and direction to persons' lives, links them in shared trusts and loyalties with others, grounds their personal stances and communal loyalties in a sense of relatedness to a larger frame of reference, and enables them to face and deal with the limit conditions of human life, relying upon that which has the quality of ultimacy in their lives' (1996, p. 56). Whilst for many persons faith 'comes to expression and accountability through the symbols, rituals, and beliefs of particular religious traditions', many other persons in our time 'weave and paint their meaning-canvases in communities other than religious, and often with symbols or stories which have no direct relationship to traditions of group piety or religious worship' (1986, pp. 15–16). Faith is thus 'a generic *human* phenomenon – a way of leaning into or meeting life, whether traditionally religious, or Christian, or not' (ibid., p. 16).

In order to operationalise this broad model of faith adequately in psychological terms, Fowler draws upon seven different developmental theories or approaches (extended to eight from 1987) to create a kind of theoretical matrix within which faith can be studied. These eight theories concern eight basic dimensions or aspects of the structuring activity of faith: the development of logical thinking according to Piaget (1929, 1962); the construction of social perspective according to Selman (1980); the development of moral judgements according to Kohlberg (1981, 1984); the understanding of social reference points; the interpretation of what legitimates commitments; the ways of unifying meanings as found in Erikson (1980); the understanding of symbols, and the stages of self as elaborated by Kegan (1982).

Over many decades now, Fowler and his associates have been exploring individuals' constructions of faith by means of a lengthy, structured, semi-clinical interview (Fowler, 1981, Appendix A), exploring in detail their views, convictions and experiences regarding such topics as death and afterlife, the limits of knowledge, evil and suffering, the meaning of life, the future, loyalties and commitments. Out of the accumulated data from these interviews, Fowler gradually elaborated his six-stage theory describing the typical path of development for faith across the lifespan.[7]

Fowler's stages begin with *Primal Faith* (Stage 0), 'a prelanguage disposition of trust and loyalty toward the environment that takes form in the mutuality of one's interactive rituals of relationship with those providing consistent primary care' (1986, p. 28). We might think of this pre-conscious stage as 'nursed' or 'foundation' faith (Astley et al., 1991), in which the earliest foundations for faith are laid in an orientation of basic trust (or mistrust) in the world as it is. From about the time children start to learn language, *Intuitive-Projective Faith* (Stage 1, sometimes described as 'chaotic' or 'impressionistic' faith) emerges, characterised by an episodic, fantasy-filled construction of reality uninhibited by logical thought and dominated by powerful images and feelings. Whilst images of God are chiefly anthropomorphic at this stage, representations of the deity may mix anthropomorphic and non-anthropomorphic imagery. *Mythic-Literal Faith* (Stage 2) is born out of the emergence of Piagetian concrete operations and Kohlberg's instrumental exchange stage, and coincides with what Kegan calls the stage of the

---

[7] For Fowler's own accounts of the theory, see Fowler (1980, 1981, 1991b). A good basic introduction is to be found in Astley et al. (1991).

'imperial self', during which the self is embedded in its needs, wishes and interests. At this time, 'the person begins to take on for himself or herself the stories, beliefs and observances which symbolize belonging to his or her community. Beliefs are appropriated with literal interpretations, as are moral rules and attitudes. Symbols are taken as one-dimensional and literal in meaning' (Fowler, 1980, p. 69). Although persons during this stage cannot 'step outside the flowing streams of their stories and experiences in order to reflect upon them and draw overarching meanings from them', nevertheless, 'the narrative structuring of experience that emerges ... provides a central way of establishing identity, through the learning of the stories of those groups and communities to which one belongs' (ibid).

As a result of significant shifts in knowing and thinking between the ages of eleven and thirteen,

> ... identity and interiority, one's own and others', become absorbing concerns. *Personality* both as style and substance, becomes a conscious concern. Values, commitments, and relationships are seen as central to identity and worth, at a time when *worth* is heavily keyed to the approval and affirmation of significant others ... This stage holds together a vital but fragile dance in which we try to shape the movements of our life to give expression to a way of being forming from within, while at the same time trying to maintain connections and exchanges with all those to whom our becoming seems integrally connected. Beliefs and values which link us with them take form in a tacit, largely unexamined, unity. From within this stage, we construct the ultimate environment in terms of the personal. God is one who knows us better than we know ourselves – knows who we are and who we are becoming – and, in connecting deeply with others and with ourselves, we are somehow linked with the depth, or height, of ultimacy. (Fowler, 1986, pp. 29–30)

This is the stage Fowler names *Synthetic-Conventional Faith* (Stage 3), sometimes described as 'conforming faith' because it is so concerned with the approval of the peer group, and whilst it is normally achieved in adolescence, many adults remain in this stage for the rest of their lives, or for long tracts of their lives. For those adults who move on, a new stage becomes possible, which Fowler characterises as *Individuative-Reflective Faith* (Stage 4), in which the individual becomes more able to choose for themselves the faith that is theirs, even if this means standing out from the group or the tradition which has, until now, shaped one's convictions: 'In many respects this is a "demythologizing" stage. Creeds, symbols, stories, and myths from religious traditions are likely to be subjected to analysis and to translation to conceptual formulations' (1987, p. 70). At the same time, the self, previously defined and sustained by its roles and relationships, now struggles consciously with the question of its own identity, no longer content to be defined by social roles or the expectations of others and no longer prepared to take on trust the values and commitments which help to determine identity. As a result of these key changes, the self consciously constructs a worldview in an explicit system of meanings which is capable, for the first time, of translating symbols into conceptual meaning.

There is loss as well as gain in the achievement of Individuative-Reflective Faith. There is gain in clarity, precision and certainty of thought, but there is loss in richness, texture and openness of experience. For those who do not remain fixated in this stage, and who are willing to loosen the grip of control, there is a movement into *Conjunctive (or balanced, inclusive) Faith* (Stage 5): 'This stage arises from an awakening to polar tensions within oneself and to paradox in the nature of truth' (Fowler, 1986, p. 30). It seeks to find ways to rejoin or reunite what has been separated in Stages 3 and 4. The individual begins to recognise that, although symbols can be reduced and analysed in terms of abstract meanings, there is a deeper sense in which the truth they offer must be submitted to and allowed to take the initiative. Fowler goes on:

> Therefore, faith, in this stage, learns to be receptive, to balance initiative and control with waiting and seeking to be part of the larger movement of spirit or being. It develops a second or willed naivete, an epistemological humility in face of the intricacy and richness of mystery. Moreover, it comes to prize a certain givenness to life, as opposed to always choosing one's way or group. It comes to value the stranger as one by whom new truth – or liberation from self-deception – may come. It uses multiple names and metaphors for the holy. This is to avoid idolatry and to honor paradox. (1986, pp. 30–31)

Finally, some few persons move beyond the paradoxical awareness and embrace of polar tensions of Stage 5 to a new stage which Fowler calls *Universalising Faith* (Stage 6). Persons at this stage demonstrate visions and commitments which seem to free them for 'a passionate yet detached spending of self in love' (1991b, p. 41). Whilst they may still exhibit 'blind spots, inconsistencies, and distorted capacities for relatedness to others' (1987, p. 76), there is a new quality of faith and being such that they demonstrate a radical freedom: 'Such persons are devoted to overcoming division, oppression, and violence, and live in effective anticipatory response to an inbreaking commonwealth of love and justice, the reality of an inbreaking kingdom of God' (1991b, p. 41). The process of decentring from self that marks each successive faith stage achieves completion in this stage such that 'the self is drawn beyond itself into a new quality of participation and grounding in God, or the Principle of Being' (1987, p. 75). Empirical confirmation of this stage remains lacking, since Fowler has no examples of fully-formed Stage 6 persons from his interviews. Rather, he draws on exemplars from recent history and religious life such as Martin Luther King, Dietrich Bonhoeffer, Mahatma Gandhi and Mother Teresa of Calcutta to demonstrate the characteristics of this stage.

Fowler's theory has attracted a good deal of critical attention both in the United States and more widely (for example, Dykstra and Parks, 1986; Fowler et al., 1991; Astley and Francis, 1992). Enthusiastically adopted by some as a foundation for pastoral and educational ministry in the churches, welcomed by others for the general insights it affords into the nature and stages of development, it has also been the occasion of extensive critical debate.[8] Unlike some feminists, I do not wish to reject the theory out of hand. It offers a rich account of faith development which, at the present time, is unrivalled. We would be foolish to jettison it altogether. Yet there are a number of aspects of the theory which are problematic, particularly as they pertain to women. Although in more recent works, Fowler has given some attention to research on women's identity formation and development, he has not significantly

---

[8] See Parks (1990/1) and Streib (2002), for good summaries of faith development research and critique.

reworked his theory to reflect this work. His sources are overwhelmingly male theorists whose models of development are androcentric. Empirical evidence suggests that his stage descriptions are, in fact, biased against women – a number of studies show that women tend to score less highly on the Fowler scale than men and that men 'advance' to the 'higher' stages at younger ages than women (for example, Bradley, 1983; Bassett, 1985; White, 1985; Leary, 1988; Morgan, 1990). Fowler himself has admitted that he and his colleagues may have underscored some female subjects and overscored some of the men (Fowler, 1992, p. xiii). In the foreword to the German translation of *Stages of Faith* (Fowler, 2000), Fowler suggests a revision of Stage 4 to include a concept of relational knowing, although this has not been reflected in a wholesale reworking of the stage sequence. Thus, women's distinctive patterns of faith may not adequately be accounted for by his stages, particularly the middle stages where the movement is towards increased separation and autonomy – a pattern which may well reflect male norms more than typically female, relational ways of operating.

Feminists have critiqued, too, his ideal of faith as represented in Stage 6. Whilst there is much in Fowler's Stage 6 that is attractive as a model of mature faith – particularly the commitment to social justice, the radical freedom of selfhood and the global or universal dimension of faith – there are other features which are more ambivalent, and which appear to prioritise characteristically male patterns of development over female developmental preferences. As Parks (1990/1) points out, 'with the exception of Mother Teresa, all are males dead before their time, having in some way given up their life in the affirmation of a larger good' (pp. 108–9). These 'lonely male heroes' exemplify a selfhood achieved at the expense of community, including their relationships with women. They are all men who either willingly or unwittingly sacrificed their relationships with partners and/or families for the sake of some larger good, often cutting themselves off from their local communities at the same time. Such a portrayal of the ideal of faith in terms of 'lonely prophetic martyrdom' (Philbert, 1982, p. 122) is highly problematic for women. Parks suggests that the ideal of 'negation of ties' (Fowler, 1984, p. 73) which Fowler applauds in these male heroes is 'language which women do and *do not* identify with our deepest impulses towards faithfulness' (p. 114). It is also language with which many men feel uncomfortable (for example, Philbert, 1982).

All this suggests that Fowler's theory, whilst valuable in a number of respects, offers only a partial account of women's faith and its development. We need to turn to studies where women's faith has been at the centre of attention rather than at the margins in order to correct some of the omissions and distortions of the theories so far surveyed.

Research on Women's Faith Development

Whilst there are surprisingly few empirical studies of women's faith development as such, there is a flourishing wider literature of women's pastoral theology, popular spirituality and theology which has produced a plethora of personal testimony and narrative from women in the churches and on the edges of the churches speaking of their faith lives in the first person. With the explosion of feminism and feminist theology in the late 1960s and 1970s, women began to find their voices and tell their stories of struggle, of awakening, of conviction, of anger and protest, of solidarity and of experiences of the sacred. Whilst largely anecdotal and autobiographical, the emergence of such a literature in itself testifies to a new stage of consciousness in women's collective spirituality, at least in the West. The titles of some of these books bespeak the sense of daring as well as breakthrough represented by the simple fact of women talking about their own faith lives in the public sphere: *Walking on the Water: Women Talk about Spirituality* (Garcia and Maitland, 1983), or, more painfully, *Walking on Glass: Women Deacons Speak Out* (Treasure, 1991), or, simply, *Bringing the Invisible into the Light* (Quaker Women's Group, 1986). Critique of the church and other patriarchal institutions which have silenced and curtailed women's spirituality and development is evident in titles such as *Found Wanting* (Webster, 1995), *Not In Our Name* (Miles, 1994) and *Defecting in Place* (Winter et al., 1994). Whilst few of these writers are interested in development in any academic sense, their stories are fundamentally about the growth, change and transformation of faith and identity over time and through experience, and this developmental emphasis is reflected in the dominance of journey metaphors and metaphors of process and movement: *Pilgrimage to Priesthood* (Canham, 1983), *The Dance of the Dissident Daughter* (Monk Kidd, 1996), *Dance of the Spirit* (Harris, 1989) and *The Feminine Face of God: The Unfolding of the Sacred in Women* (Anderson and Hopkins, 1992).

Whilst most of this literature is personal and autobiographical (and none the less telling for that), a few studies have a wider significance in drawing on a larger corpus of women's witness and testimony than the author's own biography. Studies such as Alison Webster's *Found Wanting* and Rosie Miles' *Not in My Name*, though they do not claim to be empirically valid in a social scientific sense, nevertheless have significance in canvassing the views of groups of women whose stories are frequently not heard by the churches. Both are studies of women who, in different ways and for different reasons, find themselves on the periphery of the church or having been compelled to leave it, because of their sexuality and their personal relationships, because of the oppressive hierarchical attitudes and structures of the churches, and for myriad other personal, political and theological reasons. They are significant because of their commitment to 'hear into speech' (Morton, 1985) the voices and lives of women whose stories are frequently marginalised or suppressed.

A more ambitious attempt to gather the testimonies of women in and on the edges of the churches is represented by the American study, *Defecting in Place* (Winter et al., 1994), which canvassed the views of some 4,000 women – mostly white, highly educated and sympathetic to feminism – in small women's groups attached to the churches. The majority of the women made a distinction between religion and spirituality, and whilst many were critical of, and alienated by, the institutional churches, they were developing a new form of feminist spirituality characterised by the ritual naming of experiences in women's lives which are important to them, the sharing with other women to explore and nurture faith, the commitment to active involvement in peace and justice issues, the search for inclusive and non-hierarchical ways of relating to and being in the church, and an openness to multiple ways of experiencing and naming the divine. The primary stance of the majority of women, in relation to their churches, is expressed by the metaphor of 'defecting in place': 'To deflect in place means to leave and to stay – to leave the old way of relating and to stay on one's own terms, to be present in a whole new way' (p. 114). Although this study does not have an explicit developmental focus, it charts, at least implicitly, a typical journey of women in the churches through a process of awakening to patriarchal oppression and a claiming of responsibility for their own spirituality and the gradual evolution of new forms of faith and spirituality in solidarity with other women on a similar journey.

In my attempts to find previous empirical studies of women's faith development where development was a key concern, I found a few, mostly unpublished and fairly small-scale studies, based on a limited number of subjects, but nevertheless representing the beginnings of a research literature upon which my own study builds. I shall briefly review these studies.[9] Cooney (1985) interviewed twelve self-identified 'biblical feminists' about their understanding of faith, as well as the process of development which had led to their present faith stance. A number of themes emerged as characteristic of the transition into biblical feminism: spiritual depth, intellectual integrity, self-concept issues, the importance of relationships, social concern, and a commitment to the integration of biblical feminism with all of these life issues. Cooney identified an overarching theme within the interviews, which she names 'holistic relationality', an awareness of relatedness 'characterized by a commitment to connectedness with God, self and others' (p. i).

Anderson and Hopkins (1992) undertook a series of interviews with women across the United States and Canada, inviting them to reflect on their spiritual journeys. They identify a number of general themes which were dominant in the interviews, representing, they suggest, core aspects of contemporary women's spirituality. First, there was a profound emphasis on relationship and relationality, not only at the interpersonal level but at the cosmic level too: 'Relationship that does not separate and divide but connects and brings together spirit and flesh, human beings and other forms of life, God and nature, is precisely what women described to us as the heart of the spiritual in their lives' (p. 17). Second, there was a questioning of unexamined tradition and authority, a 'stripping away [of] the layers of encultured patriarchal values and beliefs' which was often 'a profoundly disruptive process' (p. 18). Third, there was a longing for wholeness, a 'desire to gather together what has been fragmented and lost', and, closely associated with this (the fourth general characteristic), a longing and need for women's community: a yearning for a spiritual refuge, place of gathering, 'a circle, a council, a society of women' (p. 20).

Devor's (1989) findings echo similar themes, and confirm both Cooney's and Anderson and Hopkins' thesis that women's faith is marked by a sense of 'holistic relationality'. An analysis of interviews with twelve women ministers established the essentially relational nature of faith for these women. Faith was experienced primarily as relationship with God, an experience of ongoing connection amidst the loss or threatened loss of connection in human relationships and amidst the uncertainties of human existence. Conversely, absence of faith was perceived as a

---

[9] Streib (2003) mentions also recent studies by Morgan (1990), Cowden (1992), Smith (1997) and Watt (1997), all utilising Fowler to examine women's faith development; the results of these studies seem inconclusive and do not add substantially to the review here.

disconnection from God, and sin and evil were described as actions or tendencies which disrupted or harmed human relationships. As a result of her findings, Devor reworked each of Fowler's stages, suggesting ways in which they need to be refined to take account of women's experience and bringing to greater prominence women's relational construction of faith. At Stage 1, where Fowler emphasises the power of unrestrained images to form the foundations of faith, Devor suggests that there are likely to be gender differences in terms of the images which will be formative: 'For boys, terror might arise with images of smothering relationships, whereas images of safety might arise from a growing sense of individual competency. For girls, images of terror might arise with a sense of being alone or isolated, whereas images of safety might arise from a sense of relationship' (pp. 268–9). At Stage 2, in contrast to the ethic of fairness and rules which Kohlberg expects to find, girls are more likely to exhibit an ethic of care and responsibility. It is Fowler's account of Stages 3 and 4, however, which requires the most radical revision. Where Fowler describes a process of growing separation and individuation, as well as a shift from external to internal authority and from a tacit belief system to an explicit system of meanings, women's stories reflect a very different pattern of development through ongoing relationship and responsibility. The women in Devor's sample described themselves again and again in relational roles, whether as pastor, mother, friend, wife or sister. Separation was a far less important theme, and when it did occur, it was within the context of relationship. At Stage 5, where Fowler speaks of the importance of learning from the 'sacrament of defeat', this is likely to be different for men and women: 'For men, it may be connected with the failure of dreams of success and individual achievement, and a growing desire to emphasize relationship. For women, it is likely to be connected with a conflict between care for others and care for self, in which women begin to incorporate themselves in the equation of care' (p. 272). Finally, at Stage 6, where most of Fowler's exemplars of Universalising faith seem to demand a withdrawal from community and human intimacy, one would expect women's faith to be expressed in an ever-widening circle of care and 'a deeper, more intensely emotional commitment to God and to others' (p. 272).

Leary's (1988) study focused on women as carers and the impact of such caring relationships upon their faith development. Leary interviewed 21 mothers of severely disabled children, all of whom were the primary caretakers for their children and each of whom had chosen to keep her child within the family unit, at least until early adolescence. All of her subjects thus exemplified, at least on the surface, a mature, self-conscious faith perspective and a strongly embedded, relational context. Leary's findings led her to conclude that Fowler's theory, whilst of some value, could not adequately account for the central aspects of these women's experience. In particular, she found major discrepancies between the coping strategies of the women and Fowler's description of Stages 3 and 4. Fowler's theory could not offer satisfactory criteria to account for the self-sacrifice chosen by the women which necessarily limited the scope of their responsibility and thus, on Fowler's criteria, implied a low level of faith. Nor could the theory hold together these women's movement from an outer to an inner locus of authority with their choice to remain embedded in a relationship of care. Because they had not made a clear move away from the significant other, they were scored at a lower faith stage, even though their relocation of authority within themselves led to a tested, rather than a naive and unreflective, commitment. Leary also found evidence to support Gilligan's thesis that the women operated on an ethic of care and commitment rather than the impersonal imperatives of law, rules and standards (which is characteristic of Fowler's Stage 4). Whilst all of these features tended to depress the women's scores to Stage 3, Leary found a high incidence of tolerance of ambiguity amongst her subjects – that is, 'a willingness to consider the multiple dimensions of reality and a more flexible adaptation to varying circumstances' (p. 133) – which, as she points out, is close to Fowler's description of Stage 5. These results led Leary, like Devor, to propose a redescription of Fowler's Stage 4 for female subjects.

Mader's (1986) study of faith development in older women, whilst only based on three subjects – all women in their fifties who were experiencing depression – is of particular interest in offering a more nuanced approach to the relational nature of women's faith. In this study, a loss of connectedness with their self-image and with the image of the God they had known and trusted throughout their lives precipitated a period of acute depression or loneliness in the lives of the women. They experienced a growing distance and separation between themselves and others, especially men, as they discovered that their generative caring was not valued or affirmed by society, and this distance extended also to their relationship with God, who had previously been the safe, dependable and life-giving source of their lives: 'Their agonizing loneliness was a longing for the reappearance of God in a form that would validate what they had become, and allow them once more to feel fully related.' The source of their depression seems to have been the threatening of the relational consciousness which we have seen is axiomatic for many women. Yet these women had to permit the separation from this life-giving connection in order to make the transition out of depression towards a renewed self-understanding and a faith less dependent on a felt sense of connectedness. Mader's findings raise the possibility that, contrary to some feminist claims, separation of self from others, including the God-image, *is* an important theme in women's development, though it may well happen later in women's lives than in men's, after rather than as the precursor to the generative stage of life, when women are likely to be rooted in caring relationship to others. Mader's study alerts one to the dangers of drawing conclusions too quickly about the patterns of women's development, and particularly to the dangers of overgeneralising gender distinctions which may, in reality, represent the experience of a particular class or age-range of women only. Gender differences are intimately related to other variables such as age, class and race, and are not likely to remain constant across these variables.

The danger of overemphasising relationality in women's development, or failing to differentiate between different forms of relationality, some of which may be less healthy or functional than others, is highlighted by Carol Lakey Hess in her fascinating study of girls' development in faith communities. Although Hess did not conduct her own empirical work, she does draw widely on the developmental theories and research of others, adapting and applying it to the issue of girls' and women's faith development. She speaks of development as a 'lifelong dance', in which there is played out a back-and-forwards rhythm created by the tension 'between our dual longings for *inclusion* and *independence*' (Hess, 1997, p. 58). Drawing on Kegan's account of the development of the self, she suggests that, for women, there is a particular danger in the middle stages of development, the stages described by Kegan as the 'interpersonal self' (corresponding to Fowler's Stage 3) and the 'institutional self' (corresponding to Fowler's Stage 4). The interpersonal self is characterised by the self's deep connection to others, and for women can take a variety of forms; one form that is very common across many cultures is the form of the 'Good Woman', the woman who is 'groomed for caring' (Wood, 1994) and so attuned to the needs of others that she 'loses the capacity to own and name her own interests, and she replaces her own motives with the needs and interests of others' (Hess, 1997, p. 63). Under the 'tyranny of the they' (Parks cited in Fowler, 1981, p. 158), the 'good woman' gives herself away sacrificially to others and can become unhealthily 'addicted' to relationships. Hess suggests that if the 'good woman' is to move to Kegan's institutional self – the stage of genuine self-authorship in which one is no longer defined by one's relationships but able to stand back from them and negotiate their demands in the light of some larger ideological commitment – she will need to 'kill the "angel in the house"' (Hess, 1997, p. 66), that is, to shatter or destabilise the interpersonal self. Women at this stage need to give up self-abnegation, to sacrifice self-sacrifice, and take up self-responsibility. It is then possible for the institutional self to emerge, a self that has a mind of its own, masters its own house, *has* relationships rather than *is* relationships; has a confidence in her own inner voice and is able to adopt a self-chosen ideology, even if it is not approved by significant others (Hess, 1997, p. 68). In describing this pivotal movement from the interpersonal (or synthetic-conventional) self to the institutional (or individuative-reflective) self, Hess warns against the error 'of making women's relationality definitive of women's being, and thereby reinforcing gender patterns that exist' (p. 61). Along with other commentators, she warns against a naive or uncritical embrace of relationality as the *sine qua non* of women's development, alerting us to the fact that relationality can be expressed in more or less healthy ways.

Alternative Models of Women's Faith Development

Some writers have proposed models of women's religious development which offer fruitful alternatives to set alongside Fowler's developmental model (and those revisions of it we have already considered), creating a broader framework for interpreting women's faith. Whilst these models are untested in any scientific sense, they are valuable in so far as they offer fresh perspectives upon women's faith development which can alert us to new insights and possibilities previously unconsidered. These models tend to envisage women's development through a process of radical *conversion* from a state which is characterised as dependent, passive and unknowing to a state of heightened awareness, initiative and empowerment. In doing so, they explicitly root women's religious development in a cultural context of patriarchy which is seen to distort and skew profoundly women's faith lives by its marginalisation and oppression of women. The models emphasise the significance of certain key *experiences*, usually of great intensity, which propel women into new consciousness and demand a reconceptualisation of past understandings of self, other and God or Ultimate Being. Although the language of *stages* or *phases* may be used, these concepts are used in a much looser sense than in developmental psychology, where a 'stage' designates a structurally patterned whole which exists in a necessary logical relation to other stages in a sequential hierarchy. Indeed, many feminists are wary of the language of 'stages' and 'sequential development', arguing that such categories are too restrictive to be helpful in making sense of women's varied patterns of spirituality. As Mary Grey (1989, p. 70) suggests, 'The feminist journey is as much about diving deep, spiralling, moving inward, as it is about moving upward and forward. A movement which seeks to recover and reclaim must seek alternative symbols and images.'

In her ground-breaking study based on women's fiction, Carol Christ (1986) examined the features of what she names 'women's spiritual quest', the process of 'a woman's awakening to the depths of her soul and her position in the universe' (p. 8). Although Christ acknowledged that this process might take place within the parameters of traditional religious practice and belief, it is a much wider, more universal process which, for the majority of women, she suggests, does not happen in relation to religion, but in connection with nature, significant relationships, political commitments or therapeutic practice. Christ turned to contemporary women poets, dramatists and novelists to seek both a legitimation and a description of the struggle for an authentic spirituality which she experienced within herself and recognised in other women. Christ detected a distinctive pattern in these writers' depictions of their heroines' quests for selfhood and significant relationship to 'powers or forces of being larger than the self' (p. 10).

The process begins, she suggests, in an *experience of nothingness,* in which women experience profound emptiness and powerlessness in their lives and a lack of fundamental meaning. This experience of nothingness often precedes an *awakening*, a kind of conversion experience, or mystical identification – often in relation to nature or in community with other women – in which 'the powers of being are revealed' (p. 13). This experience of awakening grounds a woman in a new sense of self and a new orientation in the world, and thus leads to a *new naming* that articulates the burgeoning sense of self and reality. This naming is often associated with a quest for, and a greater sense of, integration and wholeness, not only for the individual self but for the wider social realm in which women are set.

Christ explicitly disclaims any necessary linearity in this process. Whilst 'a woman's spiritual quest may proceed linearly from the experience of nothingness, through awakening, to mystical insight, and new naming', equally, 'sometimes awakening precedes awareness of the experience of nothingness, and mystical insight can intensify a woman's experience of the nothingness of conventional reality' (p. 14). What is important for Christ is the acknowledgement and valuing of each of these aspects of women's spiritual quest, including the most painful and apparently fruitless moments of nothingness. There is a kind of wholeness to the process which necessitates each element, no matter the order in which they appear: 'The moments of women's quest are part of a process in which experiences of nothingness, awakenings, insights, and namings form a spiral of ever-deepening but never final understanding' (ibid.).

Carolyn Osiek (1986) has described what she names as 'the process of awareness' by which women move 'toward claiming [an] identity as [a] Christian woman in the face of a tradition and community that have not generally been receptive to that journey' (p. 8). Whilst her concern is more narrowly focused on women within the church, her account of this process has some clear parallels with Christ's. Osiek suggests six steps in the movement towards feminist religious identity. First, there is a *fear of feminism* and a *rejection* of the challenges which pose the demand for a fundamental reappraisal of previously held beliefs and identity. This might be seen as the threat of nothingness which Christ identifies as pivotal to women's spiritual quest. If a woman permits herself to engage with the new challenge of feminism, she experiences a *turning point* as consciousness is raised, similar to Christ's description of awakening, which, itself, leads to profound *dissonance* within the self and an eruption of deep *anger* as she recognises the previous stunting of her growth and the *broken symbol systems* which are no longer adequate to her needs. This stage of the process seems to correspond to two of Christ's aspects: there is further experience of nothingness within the awareness of the brokenness of the past, but at the same time a profound awareness of the need for new naming. Yet for some time, short or long, women are held in a kind of *impasse*: the way back to old assumptions and beliefs is forever closed, but equally, there is no clarity about a way forward. Out of this painful time of 'stuckness' (similar to Bridges' [1980] notion of the 'neutral zone'), *breakthrough* is finally experienced as women discover a way to refashion sacred symbols and images that will sustain their emerging identity.

Using the metaphor of the dance, Maria Harris (1989) suggests that women's spirituality develops in a sequence of seven key 'steps'. Unlike the 'stages' of developmental programmes, these 'steps' are not hierarchical or uni-directional, but fluid, dynamic and rhythmic, even though, like the steps of a dance, they also have definite order and purpose. As Harris states:

> ... a more organic and human series of steps than the ladder and the staircase are those which like the dance can go backward or forward, can incorporate one another, can involve turn and re-turn, can move down as well as up, out as well as in, and be sometimes partnered, sometimes solitary. In the dance, we do not come to the next step by planning it beforehand, but by doing the bodily work from which the next step emerges. (1988, pp. 14–15)

Harris names the seven steps as awakening, dis-covering, creating, dwelling, nourishing, traditioning and transforming. In *awakening*, women start to connect with those aspects of their experience which are fundamental to the spiritual quest – mystery, love, sorrow, the hope for wholeness – and which lead to a rearrangement of normal perceptions and patterns, enabling newness to break in. Such awakening is often occasioned by transitions such as movement of job, relationship or home, or by critical life-events such as illness, accident or death of a loved one. The step of *dis-covering* flows naturally out of awakening, for it is that process of responding to, searching out and finding the hidden meaning implicit in the moment of awakening. In particular, the experience of awakening offers women opportunities to discover brokenness, power, community and divinity. Having awakened to their spirituality and discovered its main features, women move into the step of *creating*, in which they seek to give an original and authentic form to their spirituality, as creative artists give form to the stuff of their chosen medium. This is an experience of profound connection, according to Harris, in which the distance and separateness which are an inevitable part of daily life are for a time absorbed into a greater sense of unity and connectedness with the rhythm of the universe itself. The fourth step of *dwelling* is a step in which women pause, rest and linger, inhabiting the various spaces of their lives in order to make them sacred and holy. The fifth step in the 'dance of the spirit' is *nourishing*, the practice of spiritual disciplines, ranging from prayer, contemplation and fasting to embodiment, memory and justice, which sustain and fuel women's sense of self and rootedness in spirituality. *Traditioning*, the sixth step, refers to 'the action of handing on and handing over', 'the process by which humans communicate *ways* of knowing, *ways* of being, and *ways* of doing from one generation to the next' (p. 147). Women habitually 'tradition' spirituality by loving, teaching and mentoring others, in the family especially, but also in a range of other contexts. Finally, women's spirituality includes the seventh step of *transforming*, in which personal awakening and rebirth spread outwards to a passion for the renewal of social institutions and structures and the very face of the earth itself. Women practise such transformational spirituality in a variety of ways, but especially through listening, questioning, mourning, bonding and birthing new possibilities in the world.

Whilst none of these models is as fully developed as Fowler's, they are fruitful in widening out thinking about women's faith development, and, taken with the insights of diverse developmental traditions, offer a more comprehensive picture of women's faith. Thus, where Fowler describes faith development in primarily cognitive terms, these models describe a broader, more holistic process of development shaped by affect, imagination and relationship as well as by cognitive structures. Where Fowler describes the process of development in terms of linear, sequential and irreversible stages towards a highest level of faith, these models offer a more fluid and varied account of transition which, whilst demonstrating certain common patterns, can accommodate movement in different directions and can allow for regression as well as the anticipation of prospective growth. Above all, where Fowler asserts that faith development is uniform across diverse contexts, feminists insist that women's religious development is shaped profoundly by the cultural context of patriarchy which is antithetical to women's full personhood and spirituality. In contrast to the cognitive developmental paradigm which would render invisible the distinguishing cultural context within which faith development takes place, feminist models insist that the socio-political context of gender oppression and socialisation must be given priority in the analysis of women's faith lives.

Summary and Conclusions

The literature review in this chapter has identified a range of broad developmental frameworks which may be helpful in understanding women's faith, and has subjected to particular critical scrutiny the structural stage theory of James Fowler. Whilst Fowler and others working within this paradigm offer valuable insights into human faith, the over-reliance on a cognitive model of faith and on previous androcentric theories of development skews their theories *vis-à-vis* women's faith, tending to undervalue women's characteristic ways of knowing and operating. In order to compensate for these limitations, a range of resources needs to be drawn upon to set alongside the faith development paradigm. This chapter has identified some available resources in psychological studies of women's development as well as in the literature of feminist spirituality which, together, provide a broader canvas upon which to paint the richness of women's faith lives.

Chapter 3

Developing a Feminist Research Methodology

No one told us we had to study our own lives, make of our lives a study, as if learning natural history or music.

Adrienne Rich[1]

Whilst I do not think that feminist methodology is unique, I think feminists do uniquely contribute to social science by seeing patterns and interrelationships and causes and effects and implications of questions that nonfeminists have not seen and still do not see.

Judith Lorber[2]

Introduction

In undertaking this study, it was important for me not only to employ feminist sources for the elaboration of a conceptually adequate model of faith but also to ground the methodology within feminist principles of research so that the process of the research itself was consonant with its avowed feminist orientation. This involved the consideration of basic questions about the ethics and power dynamics of empirical research, as well as the philosophical principles shaping methodology. How is it possible to research with integrity and sensitivity the hidden spaces of women's faith lives which, until recently, have been largely absent from public accounts of religion? How does one approach the gaps, the fissures in the standard accounts of faith, the absences and omissions? How may women's truths be 'heard into speech' (Morton, 1985)? How may women's 'unstories' be heard and narrated (Bons-Storms, 1996)? What sort of methodologies are appropriate for bringing into visibility women's faith lives, women's concerns, women's meanings? In this chapter, I attend to these questions, describing how I developed my research methodology and explaining the basic principles undergirding it, before giving a detailed account of the different stages of the research.

The Debate About Feminist Research Methodology

Questions concerning the development of an appropriate feminist methodology in social science research arose out of a wider feminist critique of the social sciences

---

[1] Rich (1978), p. 73.
[2] Lorber (1988), p. 6.

which began in the early 1970s and has continued vigorously since (for example, Smith, 1974; McCormack, 1975; Roberts, 1981; Bowles and Duelli Klein, 1983; Bell and Roberts, 1984; Harding, 1986, 1987; Stanley, 1990; Fonow and Cook, 1991). Whilst this debate has ranged widely, and has demonstrated a plurality of perspectives, it is possible to identify a number of broad approaches which are loosely allied to the chronological development of the debate.

The first phase of the debate, which we might call the critical stage, developed in the late 1960s and early 1970s as a result of women's entry into higher education after the war and their growing presence in higher-level research. Women developed a critical awareness of the sexist bias built into the theories and methods of the social sciences which resulted in women's experience being systematically excluded from consideration or else included only as a 'problem' or aberration in an androcentric frame of reference. In practice, the critique was focused particularly upon quantitative methods within the social sciences. Such methods were widely regarded as alienating and inimical to women's experience, rooted in a positivist empiricism which reified objectivity and philosophical neutrality whilst masking its own commitments to such culturally conditioned (and male) values as autonomy, separation, distance and control (compare Keller, 1978; Oakley, 1981; Unger, 1983).

Awareness of the biases against women inherent in social scientific methodology led on to a second, constructivist phase in feminist research characterised by the commitment to researching women's experiences, worldviews and meanings using methods grounded in their own social practices. In order to reform social science, it was argued, it was insufficient merely to 'add women' to the range of issues already being addressed by research, since this would leave the basic assumptions, values and methods of the science unchanged. Rather, what was needed was the creation of an entirely new paradigm: a social science not simply *about* women, but *by* and *for* women; that is, a social science in which women are the subjects and not the objects of analysis. Feminists widely advocated a 'participatory model' (Reinharz, 1983) which would aim at producing non-hierarchical, non-manipulative research relationships with the potential to overcome the separation between researcher and researched, and to allow the subjectivity of both to be placed centre stage in the research enterprise. In practice, what this meant for the majority of feminist researchers was the adoption of qualitative methods as the only ones capable of yielding such mutuality of participation (for example, Oakley, 1981; Duelli Klein, 1983; Finch, 1984; Graham, 1984). Ethnographic and interview methods were favoured because they were capable of taking account of the social contexts within which research is conducted; allowed subjects to speak of their experience in their own words and thus to have some measure of control over the research process and its content; permitted some degree of mutuality in the relationship between researcher and researched; and encouraged an inductive approach to the development of theory which took seriously subjects' experience as the starting point for arriving at explanations, instead of imposing prior categories on that experience.

At the same time, feminists made significant amendments to existing qualitative methods, developing a more interactive approach to research. This is evident in the friendship model of interviewing advocated by Ann Oakley and others (Oakley, 1974, 1976; Finch, 1984; Segura, 1989); in the use of collaborative strategies which involved subjects in discussing the meaning of the data collected, or at least being offered the 'right of reply' to the researchers' conclusions (for example, Kelly, 1988; Gregg, 1991); and in the sharing of research findings with the non-academic community of women through public meetings, consciousness-raising groups, media presentation and popular forms of writing (for example, Reinharz, 1983; Mies, 1983; Scanlon, 1993). There was a deliberate attempt to reinstate research as a meaningful human activity which exists on the same plane as the rest of peoples' (including women's) lives, and to deconstruct the elaborate strategies practised by scientists which mystified the research process and reified it in abstract, universalist terms, beyond the reach of 'ordinary' women's lives.

The third phase of the debate about feminist research methodology can be identified as a stage of diversification and self-reflective critical sophistication. This more recent phase is marked by a broadening out and a deepening of the discussion beyond a concern with methods and procedures narrowly conceived, to a proper consideration of fundamental epistemological issues underlying the practice of method (for example, Smith, 1974, 1977, 1979, 1988; Harding, 1986, 1987) as well as by a calling into question of earlier simplistic conclusions (Cotterill, 1992; Jayaratne, 1983; Shields and Dervin, 1993) and an insistence upon plurality and diversity within feminist practice (Cannon et al., 1991; Etter-Lewis, 1991).

As a result of such widening of the debate beyond a narrowly methodological focus, a general consensus seems to have emerged in recent years that the pursuit of a specific feminist methodology *per se* is doomed to failure for at least two reasons. On the one hand, methods in and of themselves only take on meaning within a particular social location which itself is defined by many complex social, political and epistemological constraints. On the other hand, feminism is not reducible to an agreed set of beliefs, values and practices, since feminists exhibit as much diversity of perspective and practice as one finds in any other academic or political grouping. Thus, Stanley and Wise (1983) assert that 'the idea that there is only "one road" to the feminist revolution, and only one type of "truly feminist" research, is as limiting and as offensive as male-biased accounts of research that have gone before' (p. 26). They argue that 'methods in themselves aren't innately anything', and although 'positivist methods and world views are objectionable, sexist even, ... what should be objected to about them isn't quantification or their use of statistical techniques' (p. 159) so much as their abuse of power and the illusion of neutrality they attempt to maintain. Likewise, Harding (1987) points out that, since 'feminist researchers use just about any and all of the methods, in [the] concrete sense of the term, that traditional androcentric researchers have used ... it is not by looking at research methods that one will be able to identify the distinctive features of the best feminist research' (pp. 2–3). Harding suggests that what is fundamentally at issue is the basic epistemological commitments that underlie particular methodologies, and it is these to which feminists must first give their attention. On the question of method *per se*, there is thus a call for a more inclusive perspective which 'promote[s] the value and appropriate use of both qualitative and quantitative methods as feminist research tools' (Jayaratne and Stewart, 1991, p. 91) as well as deliberately broadening the range of women's experience which is included in research (Cannon et al., 1991; Opie, 1992).

Principles Informing the Research Design

Rejecting the idea that there are discrete research methods which are intrinsically feminist over against others which are not, the pursuit of a feminist methodology needs to be grounded in basic epistemological principles which can then inform the research design. At the same time, it needs to be recognised from the outset that research is always a compromise between principles and pragmatics, and that one's principles will be tempered by practical constraints such as the limitations of time, resources, and so on. Nevertheless, even if one cannot fully live up to one's ideals, they provide a vision to aspire to and a set of criteria against which to measure the validity of the research. In this section I outline the principles which informed my own research design and indicate how I attempted to put them into action.

The Grounding of Research in Women's Experience

The first principle was that the research should be explicitly grounded in women's experience, deliberately foregrounding and giving priority to women's faith narratives. The feminist critique of traditional social science called it to account because its analyses were grounded only in male experience of the world, and therefore addressed only issues which were deemed to be significant or problematic to men, yet masked its own ideological commitment under the guise of its claims to objective, universal truth. In rebellion against a tradition which has grounded all truth-claims in the limited and privileged experience of white, middle-class adult males, feminist research explicitly avows women's experience as the source of knowledge: 'It generates its problematics from the perspective of women's experiences. It also uses those experiences as a significant indicator of the 'reality' against which hypotheses are tested' (Harding, 1987, p. 7). In other words, women's experience is called upon as both *source* and *norm* in feminist theory. It is the substance, material and evidence upon which theory is developed and built, on the one hand; and it is the norm against which theories and claims are judged on the other. Thus, in my study, the deliberate choice was taken for a woman-only study, rather than a comparative one, on the grounds that the faith experiences, needs and patterns of women have been largely neglected for centuries and require study in their own right, in order to generate the concepts and terms within which that faith can adequately be addressed.

A good deal of discussion has centred around the notion of 'women's experience' in recent feminist writing (for example, Hogan, 1995; Graham, 1995). The notion of a global, undifferentiated women's experience has been discredited in favour of a much more nuanced and critically aware understanding of different women's *experiences*, which includes attention to differences of race, class, culture and social location. Pamela Dickey Young suggests:

> 'Women's experience' is a complex and multi-faceted term that includes women's bodily experiences, women's socialized experiences (the messages of society about being a woman), women's feminist experiences (feminist analysis and critique of women's socialized experiences), women's historical experiences (the records we have of women's writing), and women's individual experiences. (1996, p. 61)

Whilst much critique has been brought to bear upon the notion of 'women's experience', it is difficult to do without some such hermeneutical principle to call attention to the marginalisation and exclusion of women from scientific enquiry in the past and to highlight the ongoing need for the rigorous and painstaking study of women's lives in all their diversity. However, it is important to recognise the need to ground feminist analysis in a much more sophisticated, nuanced understanding of women's experiences than has often been the case, which explicitly acknowledges and welcomes diversity and brings to bear what Linda Hogan calls 'a hermeneutic of difference' (1995, p. 166) upon all our theorising.

Listening and Looking for Difference

The need to extend the notion of 'women's experience' beyond simplistic assumptions of a common, undifferentiated unity of experience led to the formulation of the second principle, which explicitly welcomes and seeks to highlight difference and diversity within the research account. This has become a prominent commitment within recent feminist theory,[3] rooted in the assumption that no matter how much like another human being one person may be, there is always difference present and usually along a multiplicity of axes. Such differences exist between and among women, and thus, as Sandra Harding puts it, 'There will be many different feminist versions of "reality", for there are many different realities in which women live, but they should all be regarded as producing more complete, less distorting, and less perverse understandings than can a science in alliance with ruling-class masculine activity' (1986, p. 157).

As Elaine Graham points out, in her book *Making the Difference* (1995), the notion of 'difference' itself is by no means a straightforward, unproblematic one, and is used in a variety of ways by feminists to signal rather different meanings and for different ends. Graham distinguishes three usages of the notion of 'difference', which we might term difference as female distinctiveness, difference as fragmentation of feminism, and difference as deconstructive praxis. The first usage posits the distinctiveness of women's experience over against normative, androcentric understandings of human experience predicated on men's experience, as the platform upon which to advance feminists' demands for justice. The second usage runs somewhat counter to this first usage, repudiating the notion of a singular difference between women and men in favour of multiple differences among women. The third usage, rooted in a post-modern deconstructionism, 'sees difference itself as unstable and enacted, the process by which social interests are entrenched' (p. 172). The second and third understandings of difference run counter to the assumption of a monolithic, singular difference between women and men, and, whilst they might be seen as dissipating feminism's original project of liberating women, this need not be so. As Harding (1986) has argued, a post-modern feminist epistemology which rejects the assumption of a commonality of women's experience can still find 'a political and epistemological solidarity in our oppositions to the fiction of the naturalized, essentialized, uniquely "human" and to

---

[3] For a recent discussion of taking difference seriously in feminist theology, for example, see the essays in *Feminist Theology* 21 (1999).

the distortions, perversions, exploitations, and subjugations perpetrated on behalf of this fiction' (p. 193).

Whilst the three usages arise from distinctive philosophical and political commitments and exist in tension with each other, they have each informed my own research design in an attempt to pay attention to difference along three different axes. First, there is a broad question underlying my research about differences between men's and women's constructions of faith and their differing developmental pathways. Whilst my study is not a comparative one, and therefore cannot establish conclusive differences between men and women, it seeks nevertheless to exercise an attentiveness to what might potentially be distinctive characteristics of women's spirituality against the background of existing models of faith which purport to describe universal patterns, but are actually based on male experience. Second, and running somewhat in tension with this first aim, there is an attempt to be alert to differences among women of faith by deliberately talking to a range of women from different backgrounds, settings and cultures, and by looking for differences along lines of race, age, sexuality and relational status. The extent to which one person can engage with difference in this second sense is inevitably limited. As Griffiths (1995) suggests, the attempt to listen to others in all their particularity and individuality is time-intensive and laborious and requires 'making the effort to understand the context in which they speak' (p. 44), if it is not to be mere 'cultural tourism':

> On the one hand, a creation of a theory which is not blind to difference requires me to be able to hear those who speak from the margins ... On the other hand, the more marginal someone is, if they are on a different part of the margin from oneself, the harder it is to listen to them, and engage with them. This is a continuing tension. (Griffiths, 1995, p. 44)

The limitations of my own ability to pay attention to and read difference became very evident as the research proceeded, as I will discuss below. I also experienced a constant tension, particularly at the stage of analysis of my data, between the pull to find common patterns *across* each of the interviews, and the requirement to highlight differences *between* the women's accounts. Finally, there is an attempt in my study to attend to the differences *within* each woman's account, on the basis of the shifting, unstable and potentially contradictory meanings present within any narrative account. It is important not to make the assumption that the interviewee speaks with a coherent and consistent voice; the self in dialogue is likely to be constantly situating and resituating itself in shifting relation, both to the other person and to its own rehearsed and retold meanings. Paying attention to differences, tensions and contradictions *within* the one narrative is a means of identifying those places where thought and identity are in transition or crisis, and thus likely to be of particular interest or significance. As Josselson (1995) suggests:

> We must find those places within narrative where the self is most clearly in dialogue with itself. These moments of crisis represent nodes of change in which the individual becomes other than who he or she was ... In these dialogic moments, where the planes of self meet, the challenge to empathy and to our capacity to narrate is greatest and is also where our learning about the other is maximized. (p. 37)

Commitment to Liberating and Empowering Women

This is sometimes known as the 'advocacy' or 'standpoint' position (Harding, 1986), or the 'praxis' or 'empowerment' principle (Ortner, 1984), and is defined by Acker, Barry and Esseveld as 'a commitment to a social science that can help change the world as well as describe it' (1983, p. 424). What makes research feminist according to this principle is not merely the subject matter or content (research *about* women) or the gender of the researcher (research *by* women) but the commitment to conducting research with the specific goal of empowering and liberating women (research *for* women). Fonow and Cook (1991) express this in terms of a necessary 'action orientation' to feminist research, but this seems to me too narrowly activist; the broad aim of women's liberation can be served by a wide range of research, from studies aimed overtly at changing policy to those with a much more obvious theoretical slant. Thus I prefer to maintain a broader definition of the emancipatory intention of research such as that suggested by Acker, Barry and Esseveld (1983), who propose the goal of a commitment to

> the eventual end of social and economic conditions that oppress women and the achievement of a free society ... The ideal is that women should be self-emancipating and our conviction is that social scientists can contribute to this process [by] provid[ing] women with understandings of how their everyday worlds, their trials and their troubles, were and are generated by the larger social structure. (pp. 424–5)

Anne Opie (1992) considers how, in a more immediate sense, participants can be empowered through taking part in research. First, the socially marginalised can be empowered by being taken with radical seriousness such that they come to experience that they can contribute significantly to the description and analysis of a social issue. Second, there is 'an inbuilt therapeutic dimension to the process' (Opie, 1992, p. 64) of being involved in research which can be empowering; participants are offered the opportunity to reflect on and re-evaluate their experiences as part of the research process, and this may well empower them to act upon their experience in new ways. This was confirmed by my own study, in which the vast majority of the interviewees expressed a sense of the value of the interview in helping, not only to clarify their understanding of their own faith perspective, but also to affirm and empower them in significant ways.[4] Thirdly, research which incorporates the experience of marginalised groups has itself the potential to be subversive of established meanings and thus to destabilise the *status quo* which maintains unequal power structures.

The commitment to a social science for women entails a radical epistemology which both stands in sharp opposition to the implicit goals of mainstream social science and calls into question the so-called 'objectivity' of research as it has been conducted in the past, since this can now be seen to be every bit as ideologically committed as feminist research, only frequently its commitments were not openly declared. Harding points to this when she asserts:

---

[4] See Chapter 4, pp. 63–4.

> The goal of [feminist] enquiry is to provide for women explanations of social phenomena that they want and need, rather than providing for welfare departments, manufacturers, advertisers, psychiatrists, the medical establishment, or the judicial system answers to questions that they have. The questions about women that men have wanted answered have all too often arisen from desires to pacify, control, exploit, or manipulate women. Traditional social research has been for men. In the best of feminist research, the purposes of research and analysis are not separable from the origins of research problems. (1987, p. 8)

In my research, the empowerment principle was worked out in a number of ways, both in relation to the participants in the study and the wider community of women to whom I hold myself accountable. For the participants, the interview was designed with the intention, not only of gathering the data I required, but also of being an empowering experience for the women in offering them an opportunity to tell their stories and reflect on their experience. In terms of my commitment to the empowerment of a wider audience, there was an intention to bring to greater visibility the faith developmental needs and experiences of women, to challenge the marginalisation of women within the churches, and to prompt deeper consideration of educational and pastoral praxis which will further the liberation of women.

The Use of Non-oppressive Research Methods

In order to be liberating for women, it was axiomatic that the research methods employed should not, themselves, be oppressive. Whilst there are no specifically feminist methods *per se*, there is a range of ground rules which ensure the use of methods consistent with the feminist principles already adumbrated above. In my own study these included transparency with my interviewees about the aims and methods of the research; making my own personal agenda and experience available to critical scrutiny; negotiating ownership and control of the material shared by interviewees in such a way as to respect the confidentiality and integrity of the women's stories; keeping in touch with interviewees beyond the original interview so as to feed back how the research was progressing and to communicate key findings, and offering to my participants the opportunity to take part in a series of seminars in which I shared the findings of the study and invited critical response and discussion.

Whilst such procedures are not specifically or exclusively feminist, they arise from feminist values and they represent concrete ways in which to work out the accountability of the researcher to the researched and seek to ensure that the research process is a humanising and liberating exchange for the participants. Having said this, it must be acknowledged that it is never possible to guarantee the outcome of the research experience for one's 'subjects'. There is an inevitable gap between the researcher's philosophical commitments and the actual reality of the experience for the participant which cannot be dictated or predicted. Particularly where the research involves the elicitation of personal material, there is always the possibility of causing distress, bewilderment or pain to the interviewee. Again, where the difference between the interviewer and the interviewee is very marked, especially where the power relations between them are markedly unequal, there is a risk of engendering misunderstanding and even of reinforcing oppressive power relations. In my own study, despite the intention to use non-oppressive research methods, and the attempt to conduct the interview as far as possible on the woman's own terms, I was not able to 'read' how a few of my interviewees were experiencing the exchange, and had some misgivings that, due to my inability to respond aright to the material they were offering me, their experience of the interview may well have been less than helpful, even alienating and disempowering – though this was never explicitly articulated. This sense occurred a few times, and almost always in relation to women from cultures alien to my own, whose first language was not English and who had limited experience of British culture. This experience raises for me important questions about the difficulties of creating research methods which are genuinely cross-cultural (compare Riessman, 1987).

The Practice of Reflexivity

A final principle underlying the research methodology is the practice of reflexivity. This is defined by Fonow and Cook (1991) as 'the tendency of feminists to reflect upon, examine critically, and explore analytically the nature of the research process' in such a way as to 'gain insight into the assumptions about gender relations underlying the conduct of inquiry' (p. 2). For Harding (1987), the principle of reflexivity demands that the researcher is located in the same critical plane as the overt subject matter, thereby recovering the entire research process for scrutiny in the results of research (p. 9). Similarly, for Stanley (1990), the principle is stated in terms of the requirement that 'written accounts of feminist research should locate the feminist researcher firmly within the activities of her research as an essential feature of what is "feminist" about it' (p. 12).

The practice of reflexivity as it has been developed by feminist social scientists challenges established understandings of 'objectivity' and 'subjectivity' in the research process. It eschews an 'objectivist' stance that renders the researcher's cultural beliefs and practices invisible while simultaneously throwing the spotlight on the beliefs and practices of the objects of research. Rather, feminists insist that the beliefs and behaviours of the researcher are part of the empirical evidence for (or against) the claims advanced in the research. This evidence too must be open to critical scrutiny no less than what is traditionally defined as relevant evidence. Drawing on Marxist analysis, Stanley speaks of this as making transparent 'the modes of production' (1990, p. 4) of academic knowledge, as a way of demonstrating the essential unity of research processes and products and demystifying the results of research. Research, like every other social commodity, is situated within a market place and is a material product of particular processes; it is part of the responsibility of the researcher to make available to public scrutiny the processes of production so that 'the power differential between the researcher/writer and the consumer/reader can begin to be broken down' (Stanley, 1990, p. 120). Introducing this 'subjective' element into the analysis in fact increases the objectivity of the research and decreases the 'objectivism' which hides the processes of production from the public (Harding, 1987, p. 9).

In practice, the principle of reflexivity has much to do with transparency about the research process, and is evident in the way in which research is both conducted and written up, bringing to visibility the commitments of the researcher and the conditions under which knowledge is constructed. It is expressed in such practices as writing oneself in the first person into the research account; being honest about aspects of research traditionally rendered invisible such as mistakes, 'errors' or dead-ends, and building them into the research so that they become avenues for further enquiry; showing how the research evolved and changed during the process of the research project, including ways in which the researcher's convictions changed or the evidence contradicted her ideological commitments or hunches; and being honest about one's feelings within the research enterprise, not as self-indulgence but as a way of insisting upon affectivity as a major resource in knowing. In these, and other ways, feminists seek integrity within the research enterprise and work to establish a new set of conventions in the world of scholarship which will demand, and not merely allow, the statement of the conditions of production under which knowledge is pursued.

The Research Design

I applied these basic principles to the design of a qualitative study using open-ended interviews. My design is broadly informed by a grounded theory approach (Glaser and Strauss, 1967; Strauss and Corbin, 1990) which works inductively from the 'ground' upwards towards the development of theory, but also draws eclectically from other qualitative approaches such as the oral history method (for example, Gluck, 1979; Gluck and Patai, 1991) and narrative analysis (Josselson and Lieblich, 1993; Lieblich and Josselson, 1994; Josselson and Lieblich, 1995). In what follows I describe each stage of the research design, beginning with the constitution of the research group before going on to describe the main features of the interview and the various stages of transcription and analysis of the data.

The Research Group

A research group of thirty women self-designated as Christian or previously Christian formed the subjects of the study. The women ranged in age between 30 and 67 and were drawn from a variety of cultural backgrounds, with approximately one-third from contexts other than British; the group included women from Asia, South America, the Antipodes and Eastern Europe, as well as the United Kingdom and Ireland. Single women, women religious and women in partnerships, both with and without children were all represented. Although the majority of the women described themselves as heterosexual, four described themselves as lesbian and one as bisexual. Eight women were ordained ministers within their denomination, the remainder were lay (including religious). There were twelve Anglicans, seven Roman Catholics, five Methodists, one Quaker, one Presbyterian and one woman with joint Anglican and Methodist membership. Four of the women maintained only very occasional contact with a church congregation, whilst two had ceased attending church altogether. In terms of educational attainment, the women represent an 'elite' since all were either graduates or of equivalent status. This was not a deliberate policy, but the desire to interview women who could articulate and reflect upon their faith with a certain degree of competence manifested itself in a bias towards more highly educated women. The majority of the women described themselves as middle-class, with six working-class women.

The choice of women on the margins of Christian tradition as well as those, such as clergy or religious, whose roles placed them at the centre of church life, was deliberate, not only to represent a range of theological views but in order to take soundings from the liminal edge of Christian belonging. I was motivated to include such women by the conviction that the boundary of any group or tradition is often a place of both creativity and insight, where significant questions are being asked and issues wrestled with which those more bound up with the preservation of the tradition ignore at their peril.[5]

The research group evolved over the period of 18 months during which the interviews were conducted. At the outset, a number of women were contacted via local women's groups. Other women were suggested by individuals and contacted directly with the request for an interview. Approximately a third of the interviewees were known by me before the study began, although only two were well known;[6] the rest I had not met before. At a certain point in the study, after I had conducted perhaps a dozen interviews, I made the decision to include myself as a subject in the study, and invited one of the women I had already interviewed, and whom I knew well, to interview me. This decision was taken for a number of reasons: partly because I wanted to have the experience of being interviewed so that I could reflect at first hand on the process which my research subjects were experiencing; and partly because I wanted to include quite explicitly my own faith experience as data within the study, to be analysed and critiqued alongside the other women's material.[7]

In accordance with the practice of transparency, I need to be honest about the limitations of the research group. There is an overwhelming bias towards middle-class and highly educated women. Despite the attempt to include cultural diversity, the group ended up being less diverse than I would have liked or originally intended. One or two black women I approached refused to be interviewed by a white woman because of their fear of being subjected to racist attitudes and/or behaviour or their unwillingness to take that risk. I respect their decision to decline the invitation to participate in the study, and their response compelled me to ask searching questions about the power relations between me as a white, middle-class woman, who enjoys a position of relative privilege within the church and the educational establishment in comparison to those of my interviewees who were black or Asian.

Equally problematically, a number of interviews conducted with women from countries outside the western setting were, in the end, not included in the analysis

---

[5] For an insightful analysis of liminality in women's religious experience, and the significance of liminal groups for the life of the church, cf. Ward and Wild (1995a).

[6] At the start of the interviews, when I was feeling my way, I made a deliberate decision to interview women I already knew so as to minimise my own anxiety and enable me to develop confidence and skill in the interviewing process.

[7] Clearly, my own situation as an interviewee was qualitatively different from that of any of the other interviewees because of my location as the researcher. I chose to include myself as a subject in my own study as a way of seeking both to be honest about the shaping effect of my own religious experience upon the research, and in an effort to contextualise and relativise this impact.

because of my inability to 'read' the meanings within them and make sense of what the women offered me. The difficulties experienced by these women in communicating sensitive material across linguistic and cultural barriers were exacerbated by my ignorance of the cultural customs, speech patterns and taboos operative within the interview, such that I could not find an appropriate hermeneutical key to unlock the meanings which were undoubtedly present within the woman's story. Where the choice was between misrepresenting the stories of these women and not representing them at all, the lesser evil appeared to me to be the second option; but I am well aware of the resulting impoverishment to the research. In addition, there were two interviews with white women where the tape-recorder failed and so again, these interviews were not able to be included. Although they were not included in the formal analysis, I like to think that none of these conversations was wasted. They all contributed, in some way, to the formation of the research either in terms of raising questions about the methodology and cross-cultural intention of the study or in helping to form my wider sensibilities and understanding of women's faith lives.

From this account it will be clear that the research group did not constitute a representative sample. Rather, it should be seen as a highly specialised population of religiously and educationally developed women, who, between them, focus some of the characteristics of women's faith within one religious tradition at a particular historical juncture; and yet with sufficient diversity of background and experience to enable at least some differences to become evident.

The Interview

The women were interviewed using an open-ended, loosely focused, semi-structured interview of one-and-a-half to two hours. Along with many feminist researchers, I felt that there were strong reasons for adopting this approach. Chief amongst these was the commitment to the creation of an environment in which the women would feel at ease, would be able to tell their stories in their own words and offer their own meanings, unhindered, as far as possible, by a predetermined format. The choice of an unstructured interview also meant that the unfolding process of the interview itself, being amenable to shaping by the interviewee, could become a significant feature of analysis.

After an initial contact explaining the aims of the research and negotiating the parameters of the interview, including permission to tape-record the interview, the women were interviewed at a time and location to suit their circumstances – usually in their own home. Although there are some disadvantages in using the home setting, such as distractions and interruptions, the sense of naturalness and ease provided by being on the woman's own territory outweighed these. At the beginning of the interview, care was taken to negotiate confidentiality, the right of the interviewee to refuse any questions she did not wish to answer, or to request further information about the study. I made a clear commitment to the open-endedness of the interview, encouraging the woman to take responsibility for what we discussed and how far she wished to go in talking about issues in her life. I also stressed my own willingness to answer questions, discuss issues of concern or share aspects of my own experience and understanding. I contracted with the interviewees to send a copy of the transcript as near to the interview as I could manage, so that they could make any corrections or indicate any parts of the transcript they were not willing for me to quote. I also offered to send a summary of my research findings at a later date.

After these preliminaries, the women were asked to reflect on their present understanding of faith, significant events or influences upon their faith from childhood onwards and the significance of their particular context upon their faith (that is, of being single, religious, married or living in partnership, of having children, belonging to a particular cultural community, and so on). After setting out these three basic areas of interest, it was emphasised that the woman herself should choose where she wanted to start and what she wanted to say and that I would respond to her initiative, asking follow-up questions as necessary. This was a deliberate strategy, not only to honour the woman's ownership of her own story and to place as much control of the interview situation in her hands, but also because I felt that the choices the women made about what they wanted to say, where they chose to start, and how they conducted their own narratives, would itself provide valuable clues to their understandings of faith. The majority of women seemed comfortable with this approach, and although some needed encouragement to take the initiative and exercise ownership of the situation, most were able to do so as they relaxed into the interview. Some women seemed unwilling to adopt such an initiative and requested me to take the lead by asking questions. Where this happened, I tried to help them to identify issues and experiences which had been significant in their faith lives and attempted to use open questions to elicit this material. Most women chose to proceed by telling a chronological narrative of their faith lives, beginning with childhood and working up to the present, but some started with their present experience and then looked back over their lives retrospectively.

An important aspect of the conduct of the interview was to honour and support, as far as possible, the woman's own preferred style of self-expression, to 'hear into speech' (Morton, 1985) her meanings and narrative, and not to dictate my own agenda or style. This required a particular kind of listening which was attuned both to the distinctiveness of each woman's pattern of communication and to the difficulties which many women experience in bringing their own meanings into language. Much standard research methodology, including interview techniques, has tended to mirror male patterns of oral communication, disadvantaging women subjects.[8] According to Kristina Minster (1991):

---

[8] A substantial body of research exists which establishes clear gender differences in the patterns of speech and communication employed by men and women, and boys and girls, in single-sex settings and certain patterns in mixed group conversation. Cf. Spender (1980, 1988), Kramarae (1981), Edelsky (1981), Maltz and Borker (1982), Fishman (1983), Treichler and Kramarae (1983), Mitchell (1985) and Stewart et al. (1986). See Cameron (1992) and Coates and Cameron (1988) for a review and discussion of this research. Generally speaking, women's conversational style is cooperative and supportive in contrast with the more competitive ethos of male conversation. Maltz and Borker (1982) suggest that girls and boys learn these different conversational patterns early on, in single-sex peer groups. Boys tend to play in large groups organised hierarchically where they learn direct, confrontational speech. Girls, by contrast, play in small groups of 'best friends', where they learn to maximise intimacy and minimise conflict. Research has also established some key

the standard oral history frame topic selection determined by interviewer questions, one person talking at a time, the narrator 'taking the floor' with referential language that keeps within the boundaries of selected topics denie[s] women the communication form that supports the topics women value ... Women who do not participate in the male sociocommunication subculture do not usually want to talk about activities and facts, and they are unused to developing topics without a high degree of collaboration from other women. Without abundant collaboration from other women, they are rendered nearly speechless in a situation demanding speech. (p. 35)

The interview situation thus needs to be reframed with women's communication patterns in mind. Practically, this means that women should always do the interviewing of other women, they should pay particular attention to the establishment of nonhierarchical relationships of mutuality and empathy, and they will not expect women subjects to take the lead in initiating topics or offering fully formed or well-polished accounts of events. Because women's speech is more likely to exhibit 'an unfinished or incomplete quality and will not conform to the plot and action structures of publicly performed pieces', the interviewer needs to be ready to offer 'verbal intersupport work' in the form of 'frequent overt and nonverbal expressions of understanding' (ibid., p. 37) in order to support and sustain the woman's talk. They also need to 'hold in abeyance the theories that [tell them] what to hear and how to interpret what [the] women [have] to say' (Anderson and Jack, 1991, p. 18):

When women talk about relationships, our responses can create an opportunity to talk about how much relationships enriched or diminished life experiences. When women talk about activities or events, they might find it easy to take blame for failures, but more sensitive responses may also make it possible to talk about feelings of competence or pride, even for women who do not consider such qualities very womanly. When women talk about what they have done, they may also want to explore their perceptions of the options they thought they had and how they feel about their responses. We can probe the costs that sometimes accompany choices, the means for accommodating and compensating for such costs, and how they are evaluated in retrospect. We can make it easier for women to talk about the values that may be implicit in their choices or feelings. When women reveal feelings or experiences that suggest conflict, we can explore what the conflict means and what form it takes. We can be prepared to expect and permit discussions of anger. If our questions are general enough, women will be able to reflect upon their experience and choose for themselves which experiences and feelings are central to their sense of their past. (ibid., p. 17)

As I have already indicated, for many, perhaps the majority, of the women, the interview was an emotionally powerful experience which evoked strong memories, feelings and associations. Some women were moved to tears as they shared painful experiences and many expressed a sense of awe and mystery in the face of their own

---

patterns in mixed-sex conversation, demonstrating that women do not talk as much as men in mixed company and girls do not talk as much as boys in mixed classrooms. Males also exert more control over talk, determining the topic of conversation and interrupting females more. Girls and women listen more, tend to support others' conversation and work at sustaining it through offering more verbal and non-verbal feedback than men do.

unfolding life-stories, articulated often in reflective silences and pregnant pauses. There was also a good deal of laughter, as well as occasionally more uncomfortable feelings of awkwardness or uncertainty or unwillingness to share some aspects of their experience, although such responses were the exception rather than the rule.

The Analysis

In a qualitative study of this kind, the purpose of data analysis is to elicit and reveal, as far as possible, the meanings for the subjects of their experience. The process of data analysis is in many ways akin to the process of interviewing itself, and requires a continuation of the same skilled listening processes, so that the underlying meanings implicit in the women's accounts can be brought to light and articulated. Such a process 'requires the detailed accessing of the participant's world' (Opie, 1992, p. 57), and each of the different stages of analysis evolved as a means towards this end.

Following each interview, and as close to it as possible, initial impressionistic notes were made, recording my immediate reactions to the meeting, noting themes or issues which seemed dominant, identifying questions the encounter raised in my mind and recording any particularly significant features of the process. The next task was to transcribe the interviews in order to render them amenable to more detailed analysis. Because my study was concerned to take into account *process* features of the interview situation as well as the content, I needed a method of transcription which would allow something of the process to be visible yet without detracting from, or overwhelming, the content. Drawing on a variety of available approaches, but particularly the method modelled by Chase (1995), I evolved a means of transcription which involved setting out the interview in units of 'speech spurts' (Chafe, 1980), rather than prose sentences, with each line of text representing one unit of speech, so as to reflect the nature of the interview as a speech act, with its many stops and starts, intricate dynamics and interactive flow between speakers. Para-linguistic features, such as pauses, so-called speech 'fillers' (such as 'um's and 'ah's and 'you know's), laughter, tears or other strong emotions were also recorded.[9] This method of transcription created a vast bank of qualitative data. Each interview, when transcribed, was rendered into between 30 to 100 pages of text, with the majority somewhere in the region of 50 pages. In total, this amounted to between 1500 and 2000 pages of transcript to be analysed.

The transcripts were then analysed using several different methods which were aimed at working from the data itself 'upwards' in order to identify themes and relationships, rather than coming to the data with pre-defined constructs (such as the application of stage criteria). Although I broadly espouse a grounded theory approach, in practice, the relation between theory and data is more complex than can be captured by a straightforward inductive or deductive model. The method I evolved allowed for a kind of free-flowing dialogue, characterised by a constant backwards and forwards movement between the data on the one hand, and my own precommitments, hunches, questions and insights on the other, which, themselves,

---

[9] I have, however, eliminated many of these para-linguistic features in this account for a greater ease of reading, unless they have seemed crucial to the meaning.

had been shaped by my reading of the literature, as well as by my own experience. Essentially, the method involved a series of 'readings' of the data, informed by the texts and traditions of faith development theory, the psychology of women's development and the literature of women's spirituality. This graduated series of readings allowed for an increasing refinement of the data into more and more manageable units and a gradual sharpening up of the main issues and themes which became the focus of the study. This method attempted to honour the integrity and richness of the data without denying or obscuring the subjectivity and selectivity of my own shaping of it.

The first level of analysis involved an extensive and detailed reading and re-reading of the transcripts, in order to absorb the material and to allow the themes and issues from each transcript to interact and inform each other. At this stage, detailed notes were made on each transcript, paying attention both to content and process features and bearing in mind my original research aims and questions. I noted dominant or recurring issues for the woman, significant relationships or events, major turning points or crises, as well as prominent images and metaphors of faith, the feeling content of the interview, and key characteristics of the process such as the nature of the dynamic between me and the interviewee, the para-linguistic features, and so on. This generated another vast amount of secondary material, almost equivalent in quantity to the original data. Although this stage of the analysis raised many more questions and issues than could possibly be pursued in one study, it also allowed for a sharpening of the focus of the study as some of the basic themes began to emerge. In particular, the focus around issues of relationality and connectedness, the experience of alienation and powerlessness and women's ways of resolving such experiences began to crystallise at this stage, although not in any fully formed way.

Following this stage, a summative analysis of each transcript was prepared, dividing each into several major sections, identified both by theme (that is, subject matter) and form (that is, whether narrative, analysis, reflection, and so on). This brought to visibility the overarching shape and structure of each interview, as well as a further categorisation of the most salient themes and issues. From this process, a second summative analysis was prepared, this time focused around a number of key questions which had been gradually refining themselves in previous stages of the analysis. In practice, not all of these questions were given equal weight or attention in the next, and final stages of analysis, largely due to the sheer limitations of space and time.

During each of these stages of analysis, I called upon a wide range of criteria to enable me to attend both to the content and to the process of the interviews, although none of these criteria was applied in a thoroughly systematic fashion (for example, by coding all the data). In relation to the content of the interviews, I paid particular attention to the following features:

- the images, metaphors and symbols the women used;
- the narratives the women chose as significant in speaking of their faith lives;
- the themes, issues and questions which were dominant for them;
- the underlying models of mature faith implicit in their accounts.

The various models of women's spirituality considered in Chapter 2 were used to help to identify key themes and patterns. I was looking in particular to see whether some of the characteristics of women's spirituality which have been claimed to be distinctive of women's experience – such as the claim about the distinctively relational pattern of women's faith – would be mirrored in the women's accounts.

In terms of the process of the interviews, I called upon a number of criteria identified by feminist researchers, including:

- the metastatements in the interview ('places in the interview where people spontaneously stop, look back, and comment about their own thoughts of something just said' and which provide one with privileged access to valuing and interpretative activity in the making [Anderson and Jack, 1991 p. 21]);
- the logic of the narrative, the sequence and structure which the subject imposes upon or discerns within her own experience (ibid.);
- the intensity of the speaking voice which indicates the emphasis with which the speaker makes a point and the value and meaning with which she invests it (Opie, 1992);
- contradictions, paradoxes and uncertainties in the woman's account, features which are likely to indicate where meaning is fluid and currently under threat or in the process of revision (ibid.);
- the emotional content or tone of the voice which contributes significantly to the implications of what is said, alerting attention to the finely tuned layers of emotional significance which speakers may invest in different events and interpretations (ibid.);
- the extent to which the participant uses whole sentences, rather than the more usual recursive speech patterns, as a powerful indication of significant moments of control, lucidity and conviction which by their very scarcity demand particular attention when they do happen (ibid.).

From these series of readings of the data, a number of *faithing strategies* and *generative themes* were identified which formed the core of the theoretical models proposed in the chapters which follow. The final stage of analysis was then to re-read the transcripts once again in the light of these developed theoretical constructs, to test out how far they 'fitted' the data, and to note exceptions, differences and contradictions to the hypothesised models, so as to build these into the reporting of the findings and to allow the limitations of the theoretical models proposed to be as transparent as possible.

Summary and Conclusions

The foregoing account of the research methodology may suggest a rather more systematic process than, in fact, was the case. Whilst the principles underlying the methodology are capable of clear enunciation, their translation into specific research practices was by no means straightforward. Ideals had to be balanced against the constraints of time and other practicalities. In addition, it was only as a particular stage of the research process was tried out that I discovered whether or not it worked, what data and meanings it was capable of eliciting, and what its limitations were. Thus, in reality, the process of research design was more one of trial and error than a systematic application of principles. As Judi Marshall (1986, p. 206) puts it, 'Research is not the linear activity in time which most texts suggest. It is at least cyclic.' This is not a weakness of design so much as an inevitable feature of any research project, especially where the area of study or the methods used are new. Often the phases of the research process which prove the most problematic are precisely those which yield the most fruit.

Notwithstanding the above, I am certainly aware of the limitations of my own research design. At a practical level, the study was hugely time-consuming, requiring far more time for the conduct, transcription and analysis of the interviews than I had originally anticipated. The method also generated far more data than could possibly be analysed with any degree of comprehensiveness; and I am aware that many significant features of the women's faith lives have been neglected or superficially treated in the account which follows. Nevertheless, in spite of the limitations of the methodology and analysis, the research yielded an enormous richness of data which it is the task of the following chapters to describe.

Chapter 4

The Processes of Women's Faith Development

Lifelong faithing necessitates each of us taking the responsibility for his or her own faith journey. It means the recognition that an individual's faith is always 'in process' of becoming fully whole. Faithing never ends. It is always dynamic.

Kenneth Stokes[1]

Now this is what I want: I want to hear your judgments. I am sick of the silence of women. I want to hear you speaking all the languages, offering your experience as your truth, as human truth.

Ursula Le Guin[2]

Introduction

The data yielded by my research are both extensive and rich, and, in the chapters which follow, I can only elaborate some of the most salient features: much of the detail of individual case stories will remain hidden and many intriguing lines of enquiry will not be pursued. Nevertheless, I hope to be able to highlight dominant themes, trends and possible developmental paths, whilst also uncovering some of the qualitative depth, distinctiveness and 'thickness' of the women's first-person narratives. In mapping out these narratives, I make a basic distinction between what I name the 'processes' and the 'patterns' of the women's accounts. In this chapter, I offer an overview of the *processes* of the women's faith revealed by analysis of the transcripts: that is, significant and recurring linguistic strategies which the women used, within the context of the interview, to shape and pattern their faith experience. In the chapters which follow, I uncover what emerged from the data as three overarching and recurring generative themes which, together, constitute some kind of *pattern* or model of women's faith development.

The Processes of Women's Faithing[3]

Analysis of the transcripts revealed a number of distinctive faithing strategies employed by the women by means of which they discerned and embodied shape,

---

[1] Stokes (1989), p. 80.
[2] Le Guin (1989), p. 159.
[3] I prefer to use the verbal form 'faithing', rather than the noun 'faith', to highlight the

pattern, meaning and coherence in their life experience. Because these strategies all emerged from the interview context, they are largely linguistic or, at least, para-linguistic, arising out of and around the edges of language and conversational speech. These are not the only faithing strategies available to women. Indeed, many of the women referred to other, non-linguistic methods of faithing which were significant to them in their lives: ranging from wordless, contemplative prayer to creative activities such as painting or sculpting; from physical pursuits such as walking, gardening or dancing to a wordless being with others or the tactile, intimate bonding with child or lover in which meaning took tacit shape; from attentiveness to pattern and beauty in the natural world to involvement in social activism and political reform. Nevertheless, whilst the faithing strategies revealed by an analysis of the interviews by no means provide an exhaustive account of the ways in which women pattern their faith, they are still important ones. Indeed, the linguistic faithing strategies described below may mirror, in significant ways, women's non-verbal and non-linguistic faithing, and, to the degree that this is so, may be understood as representative of wider ways of faithing available to women beyond the conversational context.

Six basic faithing strategies were identified. Whilst it is not possible to claim, nor is it indeed likely, that these strategies are unique to women, they nevertheless emerged as significant ways in which the women in my study engaged in the dynamic patterning process of faith. They are not presented in any hierarchy of developmental ascendancy, nor are they mutually exclusive. Most women, at one time or another in the course of the interview, called upon all or most of the strategies, though some showed a marked preference for one or two. On the whole, these strategies did not appear to represent distinctive developmental ways of structuring faith, although it was possible, in some instances, to distinguish between different developmental levels in the ways the different faithing strategies operated (see the discussion of apophatic faithing, for example).

Conversational Faithing

The setting of the interview itself provided a conversational context for the expression of faith which, for the majority of the interviewees, was significant. As Fowler has remarked:

> Conversation as a hermeneutical enterprise helps persons bring their own meanings to expression. With sensitive, active listening we 'hear out of' each other things we need to bring to word but could not, and would not, without an *other*. This is Martin Buber's 'I-Thou' relationship with its dialogical transcendence; this is Reuel Howe's 'miracle of dialogue. (1981, p. 37)

Fowler has noted how many of his interviewees comment on the positive impact of the interview experience in articulating and revealing the meaning of faith to themselves, and this was echoed by the women in my study too. Sally[4] commented,

---

dynamic and active process of meaning-making with which we are concerned in the study of faith development.

[4] Pseudonyms have been used throughout, and any identifying features changed to protect, as far as possible, the anonymity of my interviewees.

'I found the interview helpful; articulating my own faith journey led me to see how it has developed and shifted over the years.' Rachel 'enjoyed it immensely', finding it 'a source of reflection to have the chance to relate the story of my life journey from the beginning through to the present day all in one go'. Pam found it 'very challenging to be going over my life and making an evaluation of it in terms of my faith'. Marion described the interview as 'surprisingly rich', a process which helped her to 'recall and assess something of the past, whilst reminding me that I feel "on the brink" of a new discovery'.

A number of the women reflected on the way in which the interview had enabled them to become aware of aspects of themselves or their faith in qualitatively new ways. Sue spoke of the interview enabling her to 'make links' between parts of her story which she had not previously seen as connected, whilst Elizabeth felt that she had 'touched upon some things which have been neglected and unexpressed within me' and Hannah felt the interview had 'prompted some glimmerings of truth about critical aspects of faith'.

The capacity of the interview for opening up sensitive areas and powerful emotions has already been noted, and was commented upon by a number of the women. Sheila became aware that the conversation had 'opened up issues which are not resolved', whilst Kerry was left feeling 'vulnerable', Ruth 'shaky emotionally ... [and] taken by surprise by my own feelings' and Elizabeth 'feeling somewhat exposed and uncertain of what to do with the things I have touched upon'. These reactions highlight the power of the one-to-one conversational context as a means of revealing depths which may not often be touched upon in more informal or diffused everyday discourse. At the same time, they reinforce the need for responsible pastoral care within the context of feminist research (as well as other educational and pastoral contexts), if women are to feel empowered by the process of talking about their faith rather than exposed and endangered.

Whilst conversation is a significant catalyst of faith for both women and men, the conversational context of faith may be particularly important for women. If it is the case, as we have considered in Chapter 2, that women's identity and faith are embedded in relationship, then the conversational context may be a peculiarly appropriate means for women to articulate and shape their faith, in relation to an attentive and welcoming other. The power of such a process of naming oneself and one's reality in a relational setting becomes even more significant when one places it over against the cultural silencing of women which has denied them the right to speak out their own meanings, and obliterated or at least relegated to obscurity such public expressions of meaning which they have managed, against the odds, to articulate. Within a context of the patriarchal silencing of women, the invitation to women to voice their life stories in the presence of a validating other, may become a profoundly empowering act.

As well as providing a context within which to articulate meaning, the open-ended nature of the interview also provided an opportunity for a dynamic patterning to emerge within the conversational flow of speech itself. In a structured interview or questionnaire, the shape of a person's narrative or thought-sequence is largely determined beforehand by the researcher. This makes for ease of analysis, but it does so at the cost of imposing the researcher's own frame of reference on the interviewee. In my study, I made a clear commitment to the open-endedness of the interview, both so that the women had the freedom to speak about their faith lives in their own words and ways, and so that the shape and dynamic of the interview would, itself, be amenable to analysis. Each conversation took on its own distinctive shape, structure and dynamic, arising out of the nature of the interviewee's faith story and the interaction between interviewee and interviewer. Analysis of the structure of each interview suggested that often, an unconscious mirroring or matching of process with content was taking place within the interview such that the pattern of the interview itself reflected, in significant ways, the larger shape of the woman's faith development. This mirroring of life-story in the micro-narrative of the interview itself can best be elucidated by describing a few examples.

In the meeting with Lesley, there was a striking contrast between the first hour of the interview in which she reflected in a highly analytical mode on her upbringing and faith journey, and the latter part of the interview when she moved into narrative mode to tell about going on pilgrimage with a group of disabled adults. The move to narrative mode was marked by a much greater immediacy, emotional vulnerability and abandonment of control. This seemed to mirror a wider movement in her life from an analytic, cerebral and rational mediation of faith to faith experienced as radical vulnerability, gift and grace mediated through the poor and the socially powerless. *Both* modes of faith were important for Lesley – the analytical and conceptual, on the one hand, and the experiential and emotional on the other. She saw her present journey of faith as concerned with the integration of these two modes, which, for much of her life, had been polarised. The interview itself, with its clear demarcation between the two styles of faithing – cerebral and narrative – demonstrates her ongoing efforts to integrate these two sides of herself and her faith.

Where Lesley's interview divided neatly and clearly into two halves, representing two sides of herself struggling to come into closer relation, the pattern of Alice's interview was much less clear-cut. There was the sense of a dense and many-layered narrative, in which it was frequently difficult to decide which part of the story to tell next, reflecting Alice's struggle throughout her life to hold together a number of equally important but competing vocations as an academic, a wife and mother and a person of prayer. Throughout the narration, Alice returned again and again to the monastery she has visited for some twenty years and which, for her, incarnates the sense of a core holding all things together and in balance. As her story moved this way and that, she seemed to be drawn back to this centre again and again, as if to a touchstone. This narrative circling and recircling back to the one stable point of the monastery mirrored precisely her sense of her spiritual journey as a repeated 'turning' and 'returning to the centre' from which she is constantly deflected and yet to which she is constantly drawn. It was only by 'returning to the centre', to the presence of God at the centre of all things that she was able to keep everything else in balance. The micro-story of the interview again encapsulated and mirrored the macro-story of the woman's life.

A third example is Ruth's interview which, in both structure and dynamic, mirrored the centrality of relationship to the male in her faith formation and the crisis precipitated by the death of her father. Following an initial description of her early upbringing and family relationships, Ruth's story unfolded through a sequence of narratives about relationships with a variety of male clergy, before coming to speak about the defining relationship of her life, her relationship with her father, and how this relationship had set the tone for other relationships with men. Stepping back from the narrative briefly, Ruth then summarised her faith development in the image of a slowly rising line throughout her childhood, adolescence and early adulthood, progressing evenly until her father's death, which she described as 'a precipitous cliff', at which point her faith 'vanishe[d] down into some chasm somewhere'. Not only did she *describe* this image of a gradually ascending line which suddenly broke off mid-stream and descended into meaningless chaos; she also *acted out* this metaphor in the process of the interview itself. At the point in the interview where she began to talk about her father's death, Ruth broke down, weeping, and was unable to continue with the narrative for some time. Her story came to an abrupt halt as she was overcome by emotion and grief, just as, in the larger story of her own life, her father's death precipitated a crisis in which the continuity of her life was ruptured by the 'chasm' of his absence. After some minutes, Ruth was able to continue with her narrative, which was dominated in the later stages by a mood of realism, as she spoke of coming to terms with her father's death, taking responsibility for her own life and faith, and integrating the different relationships in her life with her most fundamental convictions. This shift in the tone of the interview corresponded to a shift in Ruth's wider life-story, in which her father's death marked the major division of her life, bringing to an end her childhood and compelling her to grow up and live life more responsibly, with open eyes and an awakened awareness of grief, limitation and loss. Again, the unfolding process of the interview reflected the larger patterns within Ruth's faith narrative.

These examples – and more could be given – demonstrate how paying attention to the dynamic shaping of the interview can provide clues to the larger pattern of the women's faith lives. They illustrate how conversation which gives women the freedom and space to tell their own stories in their own way, can be not only a liberating space for women to find a voice but also a means of revealing and bringing to light the larger shape and structure of a woman's faith. The process of the conversation can illuminate and reflect the content and dynamic of the woman's faith-life. Conversation with an attentive other can then become a place of epiphany and discernment, revealing something of the larger meaning of a woman's life as she tells her story and listens for its shapes and patterns to be worked out in the flow and pattern of the conversation.

Metaphoric Faithing

Metaphor, analogy and image are amongst the most basic linguistic tools by which human beings seek to make meaning out of experience; they provide a way of shaping what can otherwise appear inchoate, insignificant or potentially threatening events. Linguistic philosophers argue about the precise nature of metaphor,[5] but there are good grounds for the assertion that metaphor is more than a mere ornament of speech or even a device for the expression of affective meaning (though it is

---

[5] Cf. Soskice (1985) for a review of different theories of metaphor.

certainly that), and is capable of capturing and expressing genuine cognitive truth (Soskice, 1985). On such an account, metaphor is a primary means of cognition, in which the juxtaposition of unexpected and unlike leads to novel insight. Such philosophical accounts are paralleled by psychological studies of metaphor which draw attention to the way in which metaphor functions cognitively as a means of meaning-making (for example, Genter, 1977; Gardner et al., 1978; Gardner and Winner, 1982; Reynolds and Ortony, 1980).

It is thus not surprising that metaphor and imaging emerged as a dominant means of faithing for the women in my research. The interviews revealed an extraordinary metaphoric potency amongst the women as they called upon a wide range of images, similes and analogies to articulate their experiences of faith – although there was also a wide degree of variation in the extent to which individual women employed metaphor, ranging from some who offered only a few images or metaphors to others – the majority – for whom metaphors were sprinkled liberally throughout the interview. Natural and geographic images were drawn upon to speak of faith as landscape, frontier, weather, growth, harvest, the flow of a river or a bottomless well and a cultivated garden. Sensual, physical metaphors were used to speak of faith as energy, electric current, fire, warmth or light, and spirituality was likened to physical passion, sex and music. Faith was compared to the creative processes of painting, writing and sculpting; as a way of seeing, apprehending and shaping meaning; or to a therapeutic process of becoming aware, discovering self and other, learning to be real. The realm of the ordinary and everyday provided metaphors of faith as food, nourishment, hospitality and home-making, whilst female bodily experience provided images of faith as mothering and being mothered, birthing and being birthed. Relational images were dominant (cf. Chapter 7), with faith being conceived as relationship to, or dialogue with, the Other – named in a wide variety of images as Father, Mother, Lover, Friend, Mentor, Midwife, Child, Sister, Brother, Stranger and so on. Closely connected to such human relational imagery, metaphors of connectedness were powerfully present, in which faith was spoken of as a process of meeting, bridge-building, relating across difference, and the interconnectedness of all things was expressed in metaphors of the web, weaving or tapestry. Journey imagery provided metaphors of faith as the quest, search, pilgrimage or voyage towards God, reality or death; but several women also used the polar opposite metaphor of faith as dwelling, inwardness, stillness at the centre, holding all things at the core. Such images of inwardness and centring were closely related to metaphors of depth and dimension, in which faith was spoken of as the larger reality, the deeper dimension which is the bedrock of all experience, or as the transcendent otherness permeating all things. Even when faith was spoken of in darker terms of struggle or survival against overwhelming alienation, oppression and paralysis, an enormous richness of metaphor was called upon to wrest significance from such apparent threats to meaning (cf. Chapter 5). Indeed, one of the most striking features of the women's metaphor-making was the way in which experiences of extremis pushed them to a level of metaphoric creativity which more mundane experience did not elicit.

Such a catalogue of the women's metaphors of faith hardly does justice to their originality, nor to the variety of *ways* in which they were employed: in striking juxtapositions, or elaborate development (even when conventional metaphors were used, they were often developed in unusual ways), or even apparently contradictory readings. It must be left to the chapters which follow to elaborate in more detail the subtlety and novelty of these metaphoric usages. What can be noted here is the theological and psychological significance of this creative naming *per se* for women's faithing. As many feminists have argued, one of the key struggles for women in our time is to find a voice and a language to name our experience in terms which are authentic and empowering, against a patriarchal culture in which women's silence and invisibility have been normative, women's experience systematically occluded, and where the only language available for naming has been codified in terms of male meanings. As Mary Daly has expressed it, 'Women have had the power of naming stolen from us. We have not been free to use our own power to name ourselves, the world, our God' (1986, p. 8). And Ursula King writes, 'Women have almost been like a dumb and deaf person, enclosed in a world of their own, separate from that of most others, with no public voice to express their feelings or communicate their thought' (1989, p. 2). Riet Bons-Storm (1996) writes of the 'incredible woman' whose stories are not taken seriously or even believed, and are frequently misunderstood by those to whom they tell them.

Against such a reading of women's silence, the very act of naming becomes revolutionary, the fundamental act which at once breaks the silence of oppression and breaks open a new power of being in women's souls. It is the beginning of women's claiming of consciousness, power and subjectivity. It is the 'new naming' (Christ, 1986) which falsifies the androcentric 'false naming' (Daly, 1986) typified by Adam's naming of the world in which Eve became an object of his world rather than a subject capable of her own linguistic self-definition. The women in my study can be seen to be engaged, to greater or lesser degree, consciously or unwittingly, in this process of 'new naming'. Struggling to overcome the stultifying effects of silencing or false naming which renders their experience and meanings impotent, they reach out for images, metaphors and combinations of metaphor which can evoke the reality of their lives. The potency of their metaphoric language is testimony to their linguistic creativity and to the ownership of their lives towards which they aspire. Even when their words assert a sense of spiritual powerlessness, the originality of the images they use to describe this reality gives the lie to its ultimate thraldom. By its very presence, metaphoric creativity – when it is not merely the repetition of stock imagery or unthinking assent to 'dead metaphor' – is indicative of women's spiritual vibrancy and engagement in the claiming of experience and the naming of the powers that be.

Narrative Faithing

Story, like metaphor, is one of the most basic linguistic means of meaning-making available to humanity, and seems to represent a fundamental human need, as well as proclivity. Like metaphor, story gives shape, significance and intentionality to experience, but, unlike metaphor, its linear unfolding over time implies a historical perspective on experience which is capable of capturing the dynamic movement and flow of human experience. Where any single metaphor is limited in the range of its reference, story can encompass the totality of experience, weaving together the many disparate images and metaphors which capture different aspects of experience into a patterned whole.[6]

More than any other style of faithing, narrative emerged from the women's interviews as a primary and fundamental mode of patterning experience. There was no woman who did not use story as a way of reflecting on her faith journey and her present experience of faith, whereas all the other modes of faithing, even the use of metaphor, were far more variably employed. Stories were large-scale and small, simple or complex in structure, featuring one or more narrative lines, few or many characters, with considerable or very little development, and covering a wide range of themes; what remained constant was the ease and spontaneity with which women told their stories. Perhaps more than any other faithing strategy, story represents the mode nearest to experience, most concrete and accessible, and yet at the same time most capable of capturing the complexity, dynamism and nuanced nature of lived experience. This is not to deny the artfulness of story, which by no means provides direct access to unmediated experience. In the process of story-telling, the selection and patterning of events dictates that much is left out of the account, and certain elements are highlighted and accorded significance over others. What emerges from the story is not so much a descriptive account of 'what actually happened' as the speaker's construction of events and the meaning they hold for her in the present: a meaning which can and does change over time, leading to reworkings and retellings of the tale, sometimes radically transformed ones. Like metaphor, story can, however, also fossilise into unreflective, rigid forms such that it fixates at a particular level of understanding and ceases to develop. One then becomes conscious of hearing a rehearsed version, in which the story has assumed a certain form, usually repeated in a variety of contexts, and has lost the spontaneity and vividness which is characteristic of story in its original telling. Story may then function as a protective screen or a polemical device behind which the speaker can mask or camouflage dangerous and unacceptable feelings, presenting an 'authorised version' which will not curry disfavour or opprobrium. This more rigid and rehearsed use of story was apparent in several of the interviews, particularly with women clergy or others who had been required through formal processes of selection or training to tell their faith stories on successive occasions over a number of years, often to those in authority with the power to thwart or sanction.

Whilst the transcripts contained a huge variety of different types and styles of story, it was possible to identify several major categories. A dominant type centred around issues of identity. Identity was worked out, typically, through narratives of affiliation or separation from primary social institutions such as family, school, church, and, to a lesser degree, land and/or culture. Stories of positive identity formation were characterised by a sense of belonging to, welcome within and inclusion in groups where the women received affirmation, acceptance and a clear role or identity as a member of the group. Most fundamentally, this was rooted in

---

[6] The nature of narrative has become a prominent concern in recent theology. For accounts of the significance of narrative in faith construction, cf., for example, Navone (1977), Stroup (1981) and Cupitt (1991). The significance of narrative in women's identity construction is highlighted by Laird (1991), Bons-Storm (1996), Josselson and Lieblich (1993, 1995) and Lieblich and Josselson (1994).

the family and the relation to the parents, but it was also shaped by a sense, often so axiomatic as to be unconscious, of belonging to the dominant culture, social class or ethnic grouping. In contrast, stories of identity loss or confusion were marked by a painful sense of exclusion, rejection and difference, located either within the family or the social setting of the school, or within the wider culture within which the child was a representative of a marginalised minority, where such difference was evaluated negatively as a lack or failing, leading to the woman's sense of a neglected and disapproved self, lacking value and affirmation.

For most women, their stories of identity formation were charted as a dialectic between such positive and negative inclusions and exclusions, neither wholly negative nor wholly positive, but a mixture of the two, in which there was an interplay of belonging and feeling on the edges of various groups. Religious identity may be formed as a reinforcement of the basic affiliations in which the child is embedded, or as an alternative to them. In the first case, the network of loyalties and affiliations of the family, school, church and culture all interweave and create a cohesive unity within which the identities provided by each group are reinforced by the others. In the second case, the religious community provides an alternative, corrective or salvific identity, over and against the confused or painful identity offered by family or culture, marked by separation out from, and cancellation of, prior loyalties. Thus, where the child has not experienced the sense of belonging and affirmation in relation to the family group, and particularly from parental figures – whether through the death, absence or neglect of the parent – the religious community, embodied in a particular minister, priest or Sunday School teacher, may provide an alternative locus of affiliation. In addition, a precocious religious identity may form around a symbiotic relationship to the divinity which functions to meet the child's needs for parental intimacy and bonding. This was the case for a number of the women in my group. Such an alternative religious identity was often achieved at the cost of rejection or suppression of parts of the child's identity which were not deemed acceptable by the religious institution, or a 'splitting' of different parts of the child's world – home and church, secular and religious – with the former negatively evaluated as 'bad' and the latter as 'good'.

Another cluster of narratives, also centring around identity issues, were stories of significant persons in the women's lives, whose lives and exploits enshrined core values for the women and offered a clear marker against which to work out their own developing identity. These narratives will be considered in more detail below, as they appear to represent a distinctive mode of faithing; but for now, I simply note that, like the stories centring around affiliation to, or exclusion from, social groups of various kinds, these stories represent a typically relational means of identity construction, in which connection and affiliation to a significant other provides the nexus for achieving a satisfactory religious identity.

Just as narratives of heroic exemplars focus in a particular way the core values esteemed by the women, so a number of other narratives served to illustrate or concretise such core faith values. These might be incidental stories describing occasions of apparently little moment, such as typical family activities or patterns of conversation with friends, or some concrete example of worked justice or compassion that the woman had experienced; or they might describe more momentous occasions such as major cultural upheavals or political transitions in the life of a nation. Whether small or grand, incidental or pivotal to the overall narrative of the woman's life, what is significant about these stories is that they capture in a concrete, accessible and historicised form the core values and ethical/religious commitments which are central to the woman's notion of faith. They represent the lived quality of faith-in-action to which the woman aspires but which is not always achieved; they are reminders for her, talismans, of that which she holds most dear, concretisations of the values which hold her life in place and invest it with ultimate meaning.

Other categories of narrative dominant in the women's interviews were narratives characterised by conflict, struggle and choice, in which major decisions were faced and resolved or continued to be struggled with, resulting either in a clarification of core identity or a continued challenge to it. These narratives, like the others, centred around identity, but offered a means of wrestling with core tensions or unresolved dilemmas in the women's faith lives. Often focusing around major transitions in the women's lives or key marker events, they crystallised basic choices faced by the women and provided a means of articulating and analysing those choices. Such stories might deal with conflict and struggle over commitment to a particular relationship, choice of vocation, sexual awakening or orientation, crises such as death, illness, loss or grief of other kinds, or the conflicts encountered between the competing needs of self and other, work and creativity, personal values and social constraints. For many, but not for all, of the women, narratives of conflict led to narratives of resolution, in which the tension was resolved by some choice or commitment, or by an altered perception which enabled the woman to live with the situation in a new, less conflictual way. Such stories of resolution may be related to religious conversion or awakenings (cf. Chapter 6) or may constitute episodes within an ongoing trajectory of faith development.

As with metaphoric faithing, the very fact of telling stories about their own experience, the act of narrative shaping of their own lives, is itself of fundamental significance for women's faith development, over and beyond the diversity and artistry of the narratives themselves. For a woman to tell her own story in her own words, when that story may well go against the grain of dominant religious and cultural plots, is to claim a narrative agency, an ownership of her story, which, in effect, proclaims 'This is my life; this is my story; this is who I am' and, at the same time, challenges and subverts standard or traditional cultural narratives and widens the repertoire of available texts by which women can 'read' their own lives. It is to become a rebel self refusing the 'proper roles' which the dominant patriarchal discourse assigns women (Bons-Storm, 1996, pp. 46ff). When women refuse to 'fit into' existing narrative plots that do not describe adequately their lives and experience, they find themselves impelled to new narrative creativity, to construct a narrative identity which can speak more truthfully their lives' shape and texture. Such a 'telling of women's stories' and 'naming of women's spiritual quest has the power to transform our lives and our relation to the world in which we live' (Christ, 1986, p. xxiii).

Personalised Faithing

Closely related to the use of narrative but distinct from it, personalised faithing refers to the way in which faith was articulated by reference to human exemplars. These heroes or heroines of faith seemed to function for the women as personalised symbolical representations of faith, a concrete incarnation of an ideal around which the person's core values crystallised and cohered. As Hannah expressed it in her interview, these are people who are 'gift to you', 'a great encouragement', who 'communicate [an] integrity' in which 'their spiritual life and their working life and their domestic life ... all have a oneness', are 'all of a piece'. In ways analogous to the God representation, these symbolic representations appeared to serve a multiplicity of psychological functions for the women, offering a point of coherence, security, acceptance and a sense of relatedness to the imaged exemplar which offset the threats of isolation, fragmentation or meaninglessness.

Parental figures served for a number of the women as exemplars of lived faith, 'the expression of God's love for me', as Judith put it; with a rather more marked dominance of the father figure, not only in terms of the number of women for whom the father was the dominant parent (either positively or negatively), but also in terms of the intensity of the relation to the father figure (and to subsequent male friends, partners, mentors and/or offspring) and the emotional emphasis upon the father.[7] Dala spoke of her father as 'my example' 'throughout my life', representing 'the love and care of Christ', illustrated in many stories, of an almost hagiographic quality, which told of his devotion to prayer, sacrificial suffering, wisdom, compassion for others and spiritual insight. For Mary, her father was the one who, pre-eminently, exemplified what it means to walk on the journey towards death with faith, generosity, courage and an abiding sense of the 'fear of God'. Rachel learnt what faith was from her father, too, imbibing from a young age qualities of 'openness and acceptance of other people and their different ways as equally valuable'. For Ruth, her father was the exemplar of worldly wisdom and intelligence – he was 'the person who knew everything/ who could tell me all about history/ and about art and culture' – and, at the same time, an example of stoical suffering and endurance, as he bore the pain of a physical disability which left him vulnerable and dependent. For these women, the father-figure exemplified what had become for them axiomatic in the relation to the divine, and the ongoing internalised relation to the father continued to mediate the love and presence of God, such that the presence of the human father and the presence of the father-God were inextricably compounded.

Although the relation to the mother generally appeared less significant in my interviews, for some of the women the maternal figure was the chief exemplar and mediator of faith. Elizabeth treasured early memories of her mother praying with her and a sense of 'spirituality ... being every day and part of ... the domestic experience', a sense which survived the loss of her evangelical faith and remained basic to her radically reworked spirituality. Hilary rooted her childhood experience of the love of God in the reality of her mother's faith, for whom the abiding presence and love of God was unquestioned, and who 'was very committed to bringing up her children in the Christian faith ... to walk in the ways of the Lord'. For a significant number of the women, it was the grandmother rather than the mother who provided that strong early maternal presence. Lorna's earliest memories of religious faith

---

[7] Perhaps the dominance of the relation to the father in my interviews is not surprising, given the patriarchal context both of family life and of religious identity in which the father remains for many women the primary source of authority, power and affirmation.

were of shared chapel-going with her Welsh grandmother; the powerfulness of sharing in this 'adult mystery' 'beside my grandmother' provided the foundations for her later sense of faith as mystery, presence and connectedness to the source of life. Similarly, Lolita's grandmother 'was very important in my life' because she still practised the faith that Lolita's parents had abandoned, and Lolita found herself drawn to the church by her early church-going experiences with her grandmother, with whom she felt a strong bond.

After parents and grandparents, the next most significant category of exemplars were those who might be described as mentors: teachers, ministers, spiritual guides, counsellors or therapists who, at various stages of the women's lives, had provided guidance, direction and encouragement and had modelled, in compelling ways, a quality of faithfulness which mediated hope, healing and acceptance. The women's stories were full of such mentors: teachers who 'kind of half adopted me', who gave 'approval' and enabled Meg to feel 'safe' in ways which were not true at home; a local parish priest who was 'a small man in a big, loud, horrible place/ but somehow he transformed/ anybody who came in touch with him' and, above all, 'stuck with it ... he would never leave the people'; an elderly priest who 'was gifted in seeing/ what people could offer/ and developing their gifts' and who nurtured Sue's vocation to priesthood, acting as a 'midwife' who brought her vocation 'to birth'; a therapist who, after years of lonely struggle with a sense of vocation to the ministry in a church which did not accept women ministers, listened with respect and attention to Lolita's vision and entered into dialogue with it; a counsellor who offered unconditional acceptance and, through his patient acceptance of Anne's confusion and pain, enabled her to experience the reality of 'being loved' by God and thus to 'begin to accept myself'. Over and beyond any particular qualities, these mentors represented for the women a faithful, attentive presence of availability, encouragement and unconditional regard which compensated for the shortfall in what parents or siblings could offer. Rather more of these mentors were men than women, partly reflecting the unequal gender distribution of leadership rôles within the church, but also perhaps indicating the significance of male affirmation of a woman's faith and vocation which, because it may not be assumed, has a double impact when it is freely offered.

Friends and partners represented a distinctive category of exemplar in so far as the emphasis was on a mutual rather than an asymmetrical relation, a kinship of equality and partnership rather than one of discipleship or dependence. Friends were those who, perhaps more than any other, represented a freely chosen commitment of love and availability and thereby exemplified the free, spontaneous and mutual love of God.[8] Friends were seen as those who are 'there for us' unconditionally, who provide a 'safe' but 'completely open space', who offer 'really good support' and thereby 'keep us sane'; they are ones with whom there is 'no tension', 'it's just total relaxation', you can be yourself, 'just hang out' without being anxious about being judged or judging. They are 'people that I share deeply with/ about the things that matter to me/ and the explorations that I'm making and/ people that I can talk to about spiritual things'.

---

[8] For recent accounts of the theological significance of friendship, cf. Hunt (1991) and Stuart (1995). Both studies draw on the earlier philosophical study of Raymond (1986).

Partners and lovers similarly represented the freedom and spontaneity of love, but with the added dimension of sexual intimacy and a quality of passionate embrace. These exemplars reflected and incarnated for the women the sense of being partnered by One who knows the self intimately and yet remains always mysteriously elusive and unknown. Several women spoke of the way in which the relationship with a lover provided the context for experiencing in a qualitatively new way the power and passion of divine desire. Sarah expressed this when she described sexual love with her partner and the feeling they both shared that, 'If human love is like this/ what must the love of God be like?' For Lesley, the love and acceptance of her husband, who did not share her Christian commitment and yet affirmed in a generous way her own vocation as a minister, was enormously important, a way of 'being embraced by God', 'of being able to receive God through him'. In contrast to her father, whose love seemed to impose impossible demands, her husband was 'utterly non-judgemental', and characterised by 'so many qualities of/ humanity and human living', with a 'deep respect for difference' which had been freeing and affirming for her in ways she would never have expected at the outset of their marriage.

Other women chose as their exemplars those with whom they had had only fleeting contact, but who, nevertheless, had captured for them some essential quality of faithfulness which made such an impact that it had abided with them, and been internalised and reinforced by repeated recall and reflection. For Anna, a chance meeting with Mother Teresa of Calcutta formed a turning point in her spiritual search, which she received as a great gift, something so 'special' she 'can't describe it' yet which had a dramatic impact upon her, breaking into her 'darkness' and 'loneliness' with love and hope. What seemed 'exceptional' and 'saintly' about Mother Teresa was her capacity to pay absolute attention to each person, to express in her very being and quality of availability to others her conviction that 'every single person matters': qualities which stood in stark contrast to the fear, suspicion and distrust Anna remembered as characteristic of the 'culture of silence' in which she was raised. For Stella, it was not so much a famous personage who was the exemplar of faith, but the ordinary, common 'little people' whose unsung heroism inspired admiration and emulation. Stella's time in the Philippines working with base Christian communities provided many examples of courage, when, in the face of a brutal political system, ordinary people made a stand for justice and dignity. By doing so, they not only demonstrated their own basic humanity, but also publicly shamed the cowardice and cruelty of those who sought to overcome them by force.

Whilst there is great variety in the exemplars the women chose, what is common is the tendency and the apparent need to enshrine faith in a human other or others who can incarnate for the woman the qualities of commitment, compassion and conviction by which she seeks to live. Even or perhaps especially in times when the woman herself feels her own life to be far from such faithfulness, the ongoing relation to the idealised faith-figure preserves for her a sense of the enduring reality of faith. In a context in which women frequently feel themselves to be isolated and unsupported in their struggles towards an authentic spirituality, the human exemplar, whether living or dead, famous or unknown, represents in a powerful way an assurance of connection, continuity and relationship to that which transcends the struggles and hardships of faith in the present. Interestingly, across the interviews as a whole, rather more of these exemplars were men than women, suggesting both the ongoing dominance of the male within women's religious consciousness and the psychological need of many women for affirmation from the male.

Conceptual Faithing

Despite the high level of education and intellectual ability of the women in my study, it is notable that abstract, conceptual forms of talking and thinking about faith were not dominant. However, they were by no means absent altogether. Typically, analysis and reflection were woven into the larger narrative of the woman's life-story, so that they took the form of a kind of running commentary on the story.

In drawing upon conceptual forms, the women called upon both psychological and theological concepts in order to interpret and analyse their experience. A number of women, in telling their stories, explicitly called upon the notion of stages or phases to account for major changes in their lives and used the strategy of episodisation in order to divide, arrange and highlight qualitative shifts in the events of their lives. At the beginning of her interview, Anne spoke of the development of her awareness of God in 'three obvious phases' and went on to tell her story in terms of three major stages, the first representing the inherited faith of her family and upbringing, the second her evangelical conversion and the third the critical reworking and emotional integration of repressed elements of her past with her evangelical faith. Although Anne did not reflect directly on the stage metaphor after her initial use of it, it was clear that the three 'phases' of her life represented qualitatively distinct experiences and understandings of faith, and these were highlighted in the narrative itself. Similarly, Rachel used the language of psychological 'stages' to organise her narrative, but also employed the 'journey' metaphor, speaking of 'milestones' and 'major turning points' interchangeably with the language of 'stages'. Unlike Anne, she did not clearly demarcate the stages at the beginning of the interview, but they emerged as the narrative unfolded, so that, at several key points, she would highlight one 'stage of development' ending, or another one beginning, in order to emphasise the major changes in her life. As with Anne, the stage metaphor seemed important to Rachel less for any substantial psychological content than for its ability to demarcate significant transitions in her life.

Other women, especially those who had experience of therapy, counselling or spiritual direction, related events in their adult lives back to pivotal events in their childhood or to the dynamics of relationships within the family, and saw meaningful patterns in the relationships between present and past experience. Thus, a good deal of Lesley's account of her own faith was explicitly related to the spiritual and psychological legacy she had inherited from her parents, analysed in terms of a tension she experienced between her mother's religious emotionalism and her father's highly rational approach to faith. Similarly, Ruth analysed early family patterns of the sublimation of suffering and the channelling of feeling into intellectual debate, and explored their impact on her own ambivalence towards emotion and the way in which this expressed itself in her religious commitment. Many women recognised psychological 'patterns', some healthy and others more destructive, which they had learnt in early life, and which continued to inform their present spirituality. Thus Janet articulated a pattern of constantly putting herself in impossible situations, both professionally or personally, and thereby setting herself up to 'fail'. This pattern she recognised as rooted in her relationship with her father, whom she experienced as impossible to please, and whose judgementalism she had internalised.

Where some women called upon psychological concepts as a means of accounting for patterns and dominant issues in their lives, other women employed theological constructs as a way of naming order and significance. Theological notions of providence, grace, salvation, redemption, forgiveness, testing and so on were employed to speak of the larger meaning of events which, perhaps at the time, had seemed random or absurd. Thus, Elizabeth contrasted her early evangelical faith, in which she could never find the connection between the 'external' God who was presented to her and her own experience, with her emerging spirituality rooted in a new sense of herself brought to birth through a period of psychotherapy. She described this as an experience of 'grace' and 'being born again' in which, 'without trying', all the 'crap' and 'anger' which she had been 'carrying around' from her family suddenly 'dropped off' and 'lost its significance'. Only such theological language seemed capable of capturing the mystery and gift-like quality of Elizabeth's experience of release: a theological language which she had both inherited from her evangelical past but also reworked, remapping the concepts which had originally had a somewhat limited reference to the religious realm narrowly conceived, onto a broader, wider canvas of the whole of her life.

Lolita, a theological teacher from South America, gave several examples of how, for her, theological beliefs had a strong political and social grounding. She spoke of her passionate belief in the resurrection, not as a historical assertion of what may or may not have happened to the body of Jesus after his crucifixion, but as God's commitment *now* to the 'vindication of the poor', a preferential option for those whose lives are cheap. In a context where 'life is very cheap', resurrection 'is the focus of faith' because it declares, against all evidence to the contrary, that 'there is future hope'. The meaning of resurrection is a declaration by the living God that 'I am not with the powerful ... I am not with the liars/ the rich [or] the dead' but rather 'with the prostitutes [and] the marginalised'. 'Resurrection is the vindication of the poor'; it is 'God's last word' which stands to inspire and encourage all who work against the cheapening of life. Here again, we see an adaptation and extension of religious vocabulary which the woman has inherited from her tradition, onto a broader canvas, this time the socio-political reality of public life.

A number of the black women called upon notions of God's love and deliverance as the foundation of their existence, which alone gave meaning to a life of personal struggle. For Hilary, the presence, activity and deliverance of God were the primary realities whose veracity is not dependent upon particular historical outcomes but which stand as eternal verities over and against empirical evidence to the contrary. Her allegiance was to the God who is 'on the side of the oppressed' and who will 'bring deliverance', even if it is not possible to say how or when. This sense of faith as 'the assurance of things hoped for, the conviction of things unseen' (Hebrews 11:1) was shared by Pam. She articulated faith as 'believing in God/ whom you have never seen/ you have never heard ... and obey[ing] what he's saying', a conviction that 'things will get better', a 'hope/ that your hopes and your realisations can be fulfilled', despite all evidence to the contrary. Such a notion of faith over against the empirical experience of oppression, struggle and apparent defeat, was articulated strongly by several of the black women, as well as by some women from working-class backgrounds, and seemed to represent a tradition with its roots in slavery and class oppression, which Delores Williams has named the 'survival/quality of life tradition of African-American religion' (Williams, 1993, pp. 6–7).[9] For these women, theological concepts of providence, deliverance and salvation were not subjects of abstract speculation or intellectual conviction so much as concrete realities upon which they depended, on day-to-day terms, for their survival. Such terms were called upon, in their narratives, in order to explain the resilience, endurance and survival of faith in a hostile territory.

In the women's conceptual thinking, both psychological and theological concepts stayed close to personal experience, to image and to narrative, demonstrating a typically contextual and relational form of analysis and reflection. Conceptual thinking emerged in an inductive fashion out of the telling of story or the reflection upon a metaphor or image which was important for the woman. It was also used in creative ways by the women, reappropriated to wider or different contexts than those in which it had been originally learned, adapted beyond the confines of the narrowly religious to personal and sexual identity, to public and social issues, to the women's own culture and community.

Apophatic Faithing[10]

Finally, some women employed a means of shaping faith typified by its negative, denunciatory or contradictory quality, in which faith was named, not explicitly or directly in terms of positive qualities or images, but in implicit, indirect, negative or contradictory terms. In Christian tradition, the apophatic way (literally, against or away from the light) refers to spiritualities of negation rooted in a mystical awareness in which language and conceptual thought are deemed incapable of expressing the truth of faith. The ultimate reality of God or Being can only be named as 'not this, not that', or through a series of paradoxical and apparently contradictory images and symbols; it can never be described or denoted directly.[11] In similar ways, for some women in my research group, faith could not be named directly, in straightforward referential or even metaphorical terms, but had to be indicated indirectly through a 'via negativa' which denounced false namings of faith and spirituality and, by implication, pointed towards more adequate namings. For these women, it was possible to say what faith and spirituality are *not*, and to name

---

[9] In this tradition, according to Williams, 'emphasis is put upon God's response to black people's situation rather than upon what would appear to be hopeless aspects of African-American people's existence' (1993, p. 6). Cf. also Blassingame (1972), p. 206 and Wilmore (1984), p. 223. A similar emphasis on survival and preparing children for a hard life is noted by Judith Orr (2000) in working-class women's narratives of faith, particularly in young adulthood, in contrast to the dominant themes of personal achievement in comparable middle-class women's accounts.

[10] For a somewhat fuller discussion of women's apophatic faithing, see Slee (2001).

[11] For summaries of the apophatic tradition, cf. Egan (1978), Jones (1985) pp. 25–7 and Sheldrake (1995) pp. 199–206.

what must be denounced and rejected for the sake of wholeness and justice, but not to state positively what faith *is*.

Three categories of women seemed to use this strategy as a primary means of faithing: first, women who had experienced religion as a predominantly negative and oppressive force in their lives, and who were still struggling to see beyond such negative forms of faith and unsure how to frame faith in positive terms; second, women who were in transition from old patterns of spirituality, and for whom the old metaphors, narratives and exemplars of faith were no longer adequate, but for whom new, more satisfying terms had yet to be discovered; and third, women whose journey of faith had brought them to a point where paradox, the holding together of apparently contradictory opposites, was of the essence of faith and for whom, therefore, apophatic language seemed the most appropriate means of expressing the mystery of faith. Whilst apophatic faithing would appear to represent a transitional phase for the first two groups, for the third one it represents a more permanent way of faithing.

Sheila and Sarah are typical of those whose experience of religion had been so negative that it could only provide a counterpoint or foil against which to construct a new sense of spirituality. For such women, the traditional religious language and concepts they have inherited can no longer serve as a medium for spiritual truth, leaving them at a loss for language with which to describe their fragile but burgeoning sense of spirituality. For Sheila, 'faith' was an almost wholly negative term, something she had 'lost', and yet 'something which has stayed with me/ and sort of crippled me', throwing up 'a tremendous amount of anger/ and resentment and so on', and bearing virtually no relation to her sense of herself as 'a spiritual person'. Her spirituality came 'from other sources' to do with creativity, reflection and inner exploration, but, whilst she could name the sources – poetry, writing, dreams, therapy – and even offered one striking metaphor of spirituality as 'a bottomless well' (the only significant metaphor in the entire interview), the interview was dominated by a denunciation of what must be left behind, with only hints and guesses at an alternative way of framing faith. Sarah likewise could no longer make positive use of the traditional religious imagery which had dominated her upbringing:

> I don't want the religious language
> it's not helpful
> it doesn't mean anything
> it gets in the way
> in a great big way it gets in the way

Elizabeth is typical of those in a transitional phase from an externalised, conforming faith to a subjectively appropriated, critically owned faith (the move from Fowler's Stage 3 to Stage 4); but being in the place of transition, such women are unable, as yet, to frame their new awareness of spirituality in positive images or concepts. Rather, they fumble and feel their way towards something new in paradoxical, contradictory and apophatic language. So Elizabeth expressed 'a sense of myself as being a spiritual being' 'but I don't quite know what I'm meant to do with the spiritual' – 'or', she added, laughing, 'what it's gonna do to me!' None of the old patterns of religious observance would serve any more, but she had yet to find new patterns. The sense of being caught between old and new meanings was reflected in her struggle to reconcile her new sense of an 'internal' spiritual reality with her old sense of an 'external', authoritarian God. She admitted to still 'hankering after' 'the external God', wanting 'to believe there is something external' [beyond my own experience] – 'I wish God would reveal themselves, you know, come out, come out, where/whoever you are!' – yet she was unable to embrace what she considered the pre-packaged theologies of particular religious traditions, making it 'very difficult to link in' or to know 'where to put it' (that is, her inchoate awareness of the God within). Even her grammar belied the paradoxical, contradictory nature of her theological understanding, as she mixed second- and third-person references ('themselves', 'you'), at one moment naming God as personal ('they', 'you'), then as impersonal object ('it'). She recognised that, in order for a new, more satisfactory understanding to emerge, she must 'live with all the uncertainty and doubt', 'actually experiencing/ you know living through the doubts/ and the questions', and allowing 'my relationship with/ with a God/ my sense of a God ... to heal'. In the working-through of this process, old and new concepts and experiences jostled around in her consciousness together, and were held in uneasy tension, giving rise to the contradictions, negations and speech struggles characteristic of apophatic faithing.

In contrast to those women who used apophatic faithing strategies as a means of working through a transitional phase, other women seemed to have embraced this way as a more conscious choice arising out of an owned awareness of paradox at the heart of things and the need to hold apparent opposites in tension. These women, who demonstrated some of the characteristics of Fowler's Stage 5, held an apophatic faith as a more permanent and secure faith stance which alone was deemed adequate to hold the mystery and transcendence of faith. Lorna, for example, spoke of her present experience of faith as characterised by 'a state of unknowing' in which 'I don't have anything to hold onto' and 'I don't need to be held quite so tightly' [by God] as in the past. At the heart of this unknowing, in which previous certainties had been shorn away, there was a 'knowing' which was more than a matter of faith: it was an unshakeable conviction of 'God's faithfulness' and that 'all will be well', which allowed her to 'hold things' in prayer and in her work of painting, not only for herself, but for others who found themselves fragmented or torn apart by conflicts. It is significant that, for Lorna, the most characteristic expressions of faith were silent prayer and abstract painting, both forms of knowing which move beyond the limitations of words and concepts and capture the apophatic nature of her knowing.

Mary, in rather different but equally paradoxical terms, spoke of faith as 'mystery' always eluding her grasp, a bigger dimension of which she is a part yet which always extends beyond experience and understanding, and which can only be hinted at in paradoxical 'both-and' kind of language. God's ultimate reality was affirmed as beneficent, even when experience appeared to contradict such a conviction:

> even when God isn't
> when things aren't good
> God is still good

Even when, on a day-to-day basis, there was an overwhelming sense of loneliness and struggle, or the institutional structures of the church seemed hopelessly oppressive or irrelevant, these contradictions did not cancel out the fundamental reality of belonging and connectedness which characterise the ecclesial nature of Christian faith. In similar language, Kate struggled to express her conviction of the ultimate goodness and love of God without minimising the terrible pain and injustice in the world whose reality appears to contradict faith in a God of love. Holding together the twin realities of good and evil without lapsing into an ultimate dualism on the one hand, or an easy idealism on the other, stretched at the very limits of understanding and language, as well as her own personal integrity:

> I'm crazy and chaotic and awful sometimes
> you know I just don't understand any of it really ...
> but within all that
> that God is good
> I do believe that there is a goodness
> and I can't define that ...
> I just know that in the end it is not evil
> and it is not malicious

For women struggling to bring faith to authentic expression in a patriarchal context in which the dominant thought forms continue to reflect and serve the needs of men, apophatic ways of faithing may well represent a particularly potent means of movement away from limiting forms of faith, towards more adequate understandings. Whilst the inability to name faith in positive, explicit terms may be experienced by women as a lack, a disempowerment, a void, the negative naming of apophatic faithing is nevertheless a powerful means of shaping the meaning of things. Even a negative naming is still a naming, a claiming of voice and agency. When it is not possible to announce, there is still a power of denunciation which can be surprisingly liberating. To resist and protest against what is inadequate or oppressive is already to pave the way towards fresh and more adequate forms of faith.

Summary and Conclusions

A number of general features characterising the women's faithing strategies described in this chapter are worthy of note. First, there is a dominance of concrete, visual, narrative and embodied forms of thinking over propositional, abstract or analytical thought. Whilst conceptual thought was not absent from the interviews, there was a marked preference amongst the majority of the woman for a more concrete language of metaphor, story or exemplar as the vehicle for the expression of their faith experience. This seems particularly significant, given that the women in my study were an educational 'elite' and had ready access to more conceptual and analytical discourses, but nevertheless chose, on the whole, not to employ them. Second, there is a dominance of personalised and relational forms of appropriating faith over abstract and impersonal means: faith was worked out in relation to the other, and this is demonstrated in the preference for metaphors emerging from personal life and relationship, the use of exemplars drawn from personal life and narratives centred around issues of inclusion and exclusion from communities of belonging, as well as in the conversational nature of the interview itself, in which faith was articulated in dialogue with the presence of the other. Third, each of the faithing strategies is rooted in a dynamic context of meaning-making in which the *process* of the interaction between interviewer and interviewee is as significant as the content. It was not only *what* was said, but the *way* in which it was said, and the para-linguistic features that surrounded and supported the narrative, which indicated the nature and style of the women's faith. This has implications both for future research, in which the shape and dynamic of the interaction between interviewer and interviewee is a rich source of knowledge, as well as for pastoral and educational encounters with women, where paying attention to the underlying dynamics of women's speech is as important as the overt content.

Chapter 5

The Patterns of Women's Faith Development: Alienation

More and more frequently the edges
of me dissolve.

Margaret Atwood[1]

The greatest hazard of all, losing the self, can occur very quietly in the world, as if it were nothing at all. No other loss can occur so quietly: any other loss – an arm, a leg, five dollars, a [spouse], etc. – is sure to be noticed.

Søren Kierkegaard[2]

This becoming who we really are requires existential courage to confront the experience of nothingness.

Mary Daly[3]

Introduction

In addition to identifying the *processes* the women used to give shape to faith, analysis also identified three major generative themes which, I suggest, reveal core *patterns* in women's faith development. This chapter and the following two map out these themes in detail, following a similar format. I begin by setting the theme within the wider framework of the literature on women's spirituality and faith development, then illustrate from the transcripts the variety of ways in which the theme was elaborated by the women, before ending with summary reflections on the significance of the findings.

Alienation in Women's Faith Development

One of the major generative themes to emerge from the interviews was women's experience of alienation, a profound loss of self, of authentic connection with others, and of faith. This experience of alienation goes by many names, yet shows certain similarities of form and significance for the women. For some, it marked a definite phase of their faith lives out of which they had passed; for others, the

---

[1] From 'More and More' in Atwood (1998) p. 49.
[2] Kierkegaard (1980), p. 32.
[3] From Daly (1986), p. 23.

experience remained a present reality with which they struggled or of which they appeared largely unaware. In a sense, this phenomenon seems to represent a challenge to notions of development *per se*, for it concerns precisely a *lack* of movement, a sense of being stuck, the inability to grow and move forward; yet it appears to be a highly significant feature of women's spiritual lives which pastors and educators must take with fundamental seriousness.

Several feminist writers have drawn attention to the experience of lack of authentic connection with self, other and God of which I am speaking. Carol Christ (1986) has charted the loss of self and connection as a prevalent theme in contemporary women's fiction. She describes it as an experience of 'nothingness', an emptiness, a self-hatred or self-negation which manifests itself in feelings of inadequacy, anxiety or dis-ease, amnesia and loss of feeling, an inability to act, a sense of being imprisoned or trapped, a lack of meaning and of sense of self, a vicarious living of the self through some other person or project (often a male partner), and a giving away of the self to be absorbed by the other. Similarly, Sue Monk Kidd (1996) speaks of the 'deep sleep' which may afflict women, characterised by a kind of unconscious state in which the woman 'seems unaware or unfazed by the truth of her own female life' (p. 18). She describes it thus:

> Although outwardly appearing stable and satisfied, inwardly we may feel silenced, afraid, stuck, self-doubtful, unable to carry through with things, angry but unable to express it directly. We may grow perfectionist and driven, but strangely at the same time we may feel powerless, without boundaries, overwhelmed with the roles we are expected to carry out. Morevoer, we may harbor fears of being left alone, of risking ourselves, of conflict. (p. 22)

Yet, painful and destructive as this experience of nothingness always is, neither Christ nor Kidd see it as ultimately hopeless. When women bring the experience of nothingness to consciousness, they have an opportunity to make a fundamental choice about their lives and to initiate a new awareness and direction: 'Experiencing nothingness, women [may] reject conventional solutions and question the meaning of their lives, thus opening themselves to the revelation of deeper sources of power and value' (Christ, 1986, p. 13). Thus the experience of nothingness may precede an awakening in which the powers of being are revealed and there is the grounding in a new sense of self and a new orientation to the world.

Alicia Suskin Ostriker (1987) has elaborated the theme of nothingness in modern women's poetry. 'In a sense', she writes, 'contemporary women's poetry commences with the dread of nonexistence' (p. 60). At the heart of this poetry, she argues, is the experience of a divided self, and a quest for authentic naming of the self against marginality, inferiority and inadequacy, and against the fear of punishment if the poet dares to assert herself as her own subject in a male-defined culture. She highlights the prevalence of images of the self as nonexistent, invisible, mute, dissolving, deformed and divided in women's poetry from the 1960s onwards. In particular, the image of the split self is axiomatic in contemporary women's poetry: the wild self is divided from the tame self, the strong rational self from the weak emotional self, the perfect external selves from the ugly internal selves; and this self-division 'is culturally prescribed', both reflecting and reinforced by 'our culture's limited images of feminine personality' (ibid., pp. 83, 84).

What Christ has done for fiction and Ostriker for poetry, Carolyn Heilbrun has done for women's biography. In her ground-breaking study, *Writing a Woman's Life* (1989), Heilbrun shows how, until very recently, traditional biography and autobiography confined the narratives of women's lives to the norms of romantic love or religious vocation, both of which constructed female identity in terms of relation to the male other. Safety and closure were held out as the ideals of female destiny, and to the extent that women internalised this cultural norm, they experienced powerlessness, passivity and imprisonment, and a culture of silence about the realities of their own lives. The 'unthinkable facts' (p. 29) of anger, ambition, accomplishment or the insistence of a right to one's own life were not given voice, thus reinforcing women's experience of nothingness. Riet Bons-Storm's (1996) analysis of 'women's silences' in a church context coheres with Heilbrun's analysis of the limited roles available to women in mainstream patriarchal culture. Such roles all have in common the defining relation to the male, whether as father, partner or deity, in relation to whom the woman's desires and quests are always secondary. Bons-Storms calls on Jean Laird's (1991) notion of the 'unstory', 'the story that is not there' (Laird, 1991, p. 437) to describe the self-narratives that women attempt to articulate which do not 'fit' the accepted narrative forms provided by patriarchy. Where women's self-narratives do not conform to these expectations, they are highly likely to be misunderstood, denied or rendered invisible. Not infrequently, women whose stories break out of the limitations of the 'proper roles' are considered abnormal, neurotic, immoral or even mad. The effects upon women of such reactions includes depression, a profound sense of powerlessness, an inability to take meaningful action, anger, fear and self-hatred.

Several psychological studies resonate with these literary and theological analyses. Mary Field Belenky and her colleagues (1986) found that the experience of 'silence' or absence of voice was a significant one for many of the younger, and socially deprived women in their study. These women described themselves in terms of feeling 'deaf and dumb', a profound lack of confidence in their ability to learn, an experience of disconnection, a passive and dependent obedience to wordless authorities, a compliance with extreme sex-role stereotypes and an inability to describe the self. Women who employed the epistemological stance of 'received knowledge' also demonstrated an acute dependence on the views and opinions of others in the acquisition of knowledge, a living out of the self through relationship to the other, a failure to recognise, utilise and develop their own intellectual powers, and a markedly literalistic and dualistic worldview which values predictability, absence of ambiguity, closure and 'being right'. Rubin (1979) interviewed 160 professional women between the ages of 35 and 54 who were also mothers, and noted the difficulty the women had in answering the question 'Who am I?' Twenty-five per cent of Rubin's sample could not answer the question at all, and the remaining 75 per cent answered in terms of physical attributes, stereotypical feminine personality traits, such as 'sensitive', 'caring', 'kind', or relational roles such as 'wife' or 'mother'. Typically, the women's sense of identity was rooted in female stereotypes and role functions, and many of them were unable to posit a sense of themselves as subjects of their own lives with an independent identity.

In her extraordinary book, *Women Who Run With the Wolves,* Clarissa Pinkola Estés (1992, pp. 11–12) describes some of the feeling manifestations of women's experience of powerlessness which she has observed in her work with clients as a Jungian analyst:

> ... feeling extraordinarily dry, fatigued, frail, depressed, confused, gagged, muzzled, unaroused. Feeling frightened, halt or weak, without inspiration, without animation, without soulfulness, without meaning, shame-bearing, chronically fuming, volatile, stuck, uncreative, compressed, crazed.
>
> Feeling powerless, chronically doubtful, shaky, blocked, unable to follow through, giving one's creative life over to others, life-sapping choices in mates, work or friendships, suffering to live outside one's own cycles, overprotective of self, inert, uncertain, faltering, inability to pace oneself or set limits.
>
> Not insistent on one's own tempo, to be self-conscious, to be away from one's God or Gods, to be separated from one's revivification, drawn far into domesticity, intellectualism, work, or inertia because that is the safest place for one who has lost her instincts.
>
> To fear to venture by oneself or to reveal oneself, fear to seek mentor, mother, father, fear of caring for another or others, fear one will run on, run out, run down, cringing before authority, loss of energy before creative projects, wincing, humiliation, angst, numbness, anxiety.
>
> Afraid to bite back ..., afraid to try the new, fear to stand up to, afraid to speak up, speak against, sick stomach, butterflies, sour stomach, cut in the middle, strangled, becoming conciliatory or nice too easily, revenge.
>
> Afraid to stop, afraid to act, repeatedly counting to three and not beginning, superiority complex, ambivalence, and yet otherwise fully capable, fully functioning.

What are the origins of such powerlessness? A number of studies highlight the period of adolescence as a crucial developmental period when girls experience this loss of self and of voice (for example, Brown, 1989; Brown and Gilligan, 1992; Gilligan et al., 1988; Gilligan et al., 1990; Hess, 1997). The results of this research are helpfully summarised by Maria Harris (1993). Prior to age twelve, suggests Harris, girls speak with confidence and authority about their experiences and expect others to listen to them. Somewhere around age twelve, however, their awareness of society's gendered expectations grows, and so the seeds of a divided self are sown. A terrible choice presents itself to girls at this point, summarised by Harris as follows:

> (a) either to stop or hide one's own voice in order to become, or be thought of, as a 'nice girl', and so become alienated from oneself; or (b) to refuse to be silent and take the risk, perceived and real in this society, of becoming alienated socially and politically, of being ostracized as, for example, 'brash', 'loud', 'aggressive', 'outspoken', 'bossy'. (p. 56)

Carol Lakey Hess speaks of this pivotal point of development as the 'perilous divide' (1997, p. 126), the threshold from girlhood to womanhood during which girls can 'give themselves away' and lose touch with their own authority and identity. This dilemma may be experienced differently by girls in diverse social and ethnic settings. For working-class girls, the transition out of childhood may come much earlier with earlier patterns of marriage and parenthood, and the loss of self may be experienced as an absorption into such roles (Orr, 2000, pp. 55ff), but, at the same time, the transition may be less clearcut as ongoing connection with the girl's family of origin preserves childhood expectations and ties. Crises of identity may also be experienced as more continuous for working-class girls, rather than focused in a particular transition point, as their options are curtailed by economic and class constraints which are less amenable to resolution. For some black girls, the developmental crisis may be less intense because of the way in which black communities may value female voice and offer solidarity to the growing girl (Neuger, 2000, p. 78). Beverly Jean Smith (1991, pp. 144–5) suggests that African-American girls do not fall prey to the rules of femininity which dictate the adoption of passivity as often as do European-American girls. Speaking of her own upbringing, she says, 'As an African American, I grew up within a particular cultural context that values voice.' But this voice is not simply the lonely voice of the individual speaking out against the crowd; it is a voice that speaks out of and on behalf of the wider community which gives it more than an individual strength and significance: 'African American culture demands that individual voices be connected to the whole and not just to go solo and fly off somewhere.'

It is, then, important not to generalise white middle-class young women's experiences to all adolescent women, whilst remaining alert for the signs of a developmental hiatus. Nor should we assume that the developmental crisis, when it does occur, is resolved in early adulthood. Whilst this may be the case, alienation and voicelessness is still a pervasive experience for many adult women, as the testimony of my own interviews demonstrates; and for women who belong to the church, the church itself may be one of the chief sources of their alienation and paralysis, as the large national study conducted in the United States by Miriam Therese Winter and her colleagues confirmed. The majority of women in this study, both ordained and lay, Protestant and Catholic, felt profoundly alienated from the institutional church: 'Many women feel let down by their churches. They feel deprived, discounted, and stifled in areas of significance to them' (Winter et al., 1994, p. 45). They experience the church as exclusive, inward-looking, oppressive and out of touch with major social issues.

Particularly insightful analyses of the phenomenon of alienation within a religious context are provided by Carolyn Osiek (1986) and Constance FitzGerald (1986). Osiek's account of the journey of women within the church to feminist awareness highlights the particular impasse experienced by women who, as they begin to engage with the challenges of feminism, experience a dissonance between their own loyalty to the institution of the church and their experience of oppression. This leads to a 'profound sense of crisis', including a 'religious crisis of severe proportions' in which the religious tradition which has nurtured and shaped one is perceived to have betrayed and abused one (pp. 16–17). This realisation can erupt in enormous anger, or be turned inwards leading to depression and sadness, loss of energy, zest and a taste for life, an inability to pray or to worship or even to trust and believe in God. There is a breakdown of symbol systems, as 'the woman who allows herself the full awareness of what is happening realizes that her whole religious symbol system is disintegrating'; the 'sense of loss and collapse of meaning which comes from this faith crisis can be acute, even paralysing' (pp. 21, 22). The experience is characterised by 'depression, emptiness and joylessness', the 'sense of having been abandoned', with 'all forms of support ... pulled out ... It is a death experience, a dark night ..., a spiritual crisis of enormous proportions' in which 'the forces of creation and destruction, of consolation and desolation seem to come from the same source and to be at war within the person'. A way out of this predicament 'must be found ... but it can only be found by remaining in the darkness, *with* the sense of impasse ... The way out is the way through' (pp. 23–4).

Constance FitzGerald (1986) characterises impasse as an experience of imprisonment marked by despair, hopelessness and loss of meaning, as well as powerlessness and disintegration. She identifies the peculiar impasse of women in our time as that of being 'stuck' in an inherited patriarchal religious tradition with no going back and no going forward, so that women 'are imprisoned in a night of broken symbols' (p. 304). She nevertheless proposes that, paradoxically, 'a situation of no potential is loaded with potential, and impasse becomes the place for the reconstitution of the intuitive self' (p. 289). Drawing on the literature of medieval mysticism, she reads the contemporary experience of alienation through the lens of John of the Cross's analysis of the 'dark night of the soul', and thereby offers a creative account of the potential generativity of the apparent sterility of impasse. Although the experience of paralysis is not automatically redemptive,

> ... impasse can be the condition for creative growth and transformation *if* the experience of impasse is fully appropriated within one's heart and flesh with consciousness and consent; *if* the limitations of one's humanity and human condition are squarely faced and the sorrow of finitude allowed to invade the human spirit with real, existential powerlessness; *if* the ego does not demand understanding in the name of control and predictability but is willing to admit the mystery of its own being and surrender itself to this mystery; *if* the path into the unknown, into the uncontrolled and unpredictable margins of life, is freely taken when the path of deadly clarity fades'. (pp. 290–91)

For women in our time, the experience of 'dark night' is both a 'critique of religious consciousness' (p. 301) and the 'crucible in which our God images and language will be transformed and a feminine value system and social fabric generated .... Impasse is a call to development, transcendence, new life and understanding' (p. 305).

Metaphors of Alienation

The women in my study manifested extraordinary creativity, insight and a powerful sense of voice in the manifold and vivid images which they used to describe the experience of alienation and paralysis. They called upon landscape imagery, metaphors of deadness and loss of self, disconnection and alienation, being stuck or blocked, images of the quest or search for what is out of reach; they spoke of the abdication of the self and more violent images of the attack or rape of the self, to describe their struggles against powerlessness and impasse. Other women seemed to represent a state of faith more akin to Belenky and her colleagues' stance of 'silence' marked by an absence of voice and language with which to name the reality in which their lives were so deeply embedded (Belenky et al., 1986, pp. 23ff).

Silence and Linguistic Deprivation

I have already spoken of a kind of apophatic faithing demonstrated by some of the women I interviewed in Chapter 4, and tried to offer a positive reading of this more paradoxical and denunciatory style of faith. Nevertheless, there was also what appeared to be a more problematical, passive and oppressive form of silence for some of the women in my study, closer in nature to Belenky and her colleagues' epistemological stance of silence. A number of the women in my study exhibited a similar inability to articulate the sense of themselves as subjects of their own history or to name the shape and significance of their faith stances in any kind of meaningful way. These women's inability to name their experience seemed to go beyond momentary linguistic occlusions to a more fundamental epistemological silence and unknowing. They were stuck in some place of paralysis, passivity and muteness and seemed not to know it. In contrast to the women who were, at least to some degree, *aware* of being in such a place and able to offer images and metaphors of it, these women seemed fundamentally cut off from some part of themselves, or else were unable to speak openly and truthfully to me about some aspect of their story or experience, perhaps for fear of judgement or rejection. Only one or two women seemed to exhibit this more profound epistemological silence and powerlessness, and even then, none of them demonstrated such total or extreme epistemological silence as Belenky and her colleagues describe, but it was none the less present, in a muted form.

Other women did not so much exhibit this speechlessness in the present as describe previous times in their lives of cultural and social silence and taboo which had forbidden them, either explicitly or implicitly, to name their experience and their struggles. Women's 'linguistic deprivation' (Ruether, 1985, p. 4) is, of course, not simply a feature of their own psychological well-being (or lack of it), but is always socially and culturally located. Rachel, a woman in her mid-forties, described the culture of silence prevalent in the religious community to which she belonged during the years before Vatican II inaugurated sweeping changes in the Catholic religious orders. In particular, Rachel's struggles to come to terms with her own intellectual, emotional and sexual needs could not find expression within the community because there was an unspoken taboo against naming such feelings: 'There wasn't any *space* ... or any avenues ... to ask these kind of questions'; 'there was nobody to talk [to] about it'; 'it just wasn't thought of'; 'nobody talked of sex'; 'it was never articulated.' She tried once to talk about her attraction to another woman in the order, but 'there was just no way ... this was taboo'; 'I never felt I could talk about this with anybody'; and anyhow, 'I really didn't have the *words* for it.'

For Anna, a middle-aged academic brought up in a Communist Eastern bloc country, the epistemological silence was virtually absolute, politically dictated and enforced. She described vividly her experience of growing up in a culture where religion was a strictly taboo subject, an object of fascination and danger, and yet where the residue of centuries of deep Christian devotion was still somehow mysteriously alive and potent. Even without being aware of it, her family 'behaved as Christians' so that she could describe them as 'anonymous Christians', those who had imbibed and transmitted a 'set of values and ethics' which had been bred into their bones, somehow imparting to her a dim, inchoate awareness of the spiritual realm, for which she had no language but a growing longing and curiosity.

Anna described an early memory which evokes the combined fascination and forbiddenness woven into her experience of silence. When she was about ten, she went with her grandmother to a monastery in St Petersburg that had been converted into a museum. Leaving the child outside, the grandmother went into the church and came out:

> and when she walked out
> I noticed that her eyes were red
> and I was so you know stupid
> I sort of ran after her saying you know
> 'Why are you crying? Wh' wh' what's wrong?
> what did you do there?'
> and she said something like
> 'Oh you're you're you're too small
> you know you wouldn't understand
> but maybe one day you will understand something'
> but you know people just you know
> wouldn't talk about it

Silence for Anna represented danger, fear and taboo, a denial of inwardness, beauty and God:

> Everything was hush hush
> especially not a word to to the children
> and the parents you know
> you have to be silent ...
> you always had to be quiet
> quiet and silence –
> silent? –
> you know be because that was dangerous
> you never knew who the people were
> yes and who was listening

Yet silence also exercised its own allure, drew her by its power and mystery and fed a longing for something she could hardly name. Silence could also function as a form of covert resistance, a refusal to play the game or join in the 'culture of lies': 'You know for us very often truthfulness/ was equal to being silent ... because being silent was an opposition to/ to just join in and praise'.

Anna's very voice, throughout the interview, mirrored something of her double-edged experience of silence. She spoke for some two hours in a lowered, hushed tone of great intensity, as if she still hardly dare name the reality of faith, or rather, as if to do so were an act of great daring, in which she waged combat against the unseen hand threatening to close her throat. Her speaking had all the intensity of a ritual naming, a performative speech act (Austin, 1975),[4] conducted with great solemnity, in which she not merely described but also exorcised the powers of oppression. Anna's experience demonstrates how even the stultifying silence of fear and deception which can paralyse women so profoundly can be subverted so that it

---

[4] Austin (1975) coined the notion of 'performative' speech acts to describe statements which performed certain actions in their utterance, such as the making of a promise, bet or vow, or the naming of a child or ship.

generates the seeds of its own destruction and gives way for another reality to be born within it. Anna's story went on to reveal how she had come to faith and finally been able to break the stranglehold of spiritual speechlessness against which she had struggled for many years. In her long search for the something for which she had no name, it was her introduction to Quaker silence, whilst staying with an English family, which provided a healing experience of silence as grace, welcome, openness and freedom and enabled a breakthrough to new self-awareness. In a culture of previously imposed silence, the democratic silence of Quaker worship – a silence which may be freely broken at any time – was profoundly transformative for Anna.

Wilderness and Desert, Confinement and Enclosure

Whilst the women locked within the place of silence could find no words with which to name it, others had found a tongue to speak that reality. The images the women used to describe the experience represent what Ostriker calls 'signals of crisis, signs of a fragmented being unable to unify itself, unable to tolerate some part of itself that is necessary for its wholeness, yet unwilling to remain scattered' (1987, p. 88). Like all living metaphor, these images do not merely describe; they effect genuine cognitive insight and, by their potency, disrupt the state of paralysis they denote, forging a kind of psychological fissure in which women may find the space and courage to move on from the place of silence to language, renewed selfhood and faith.

Some used spatial and landscape metaphors to describe their experience of alienation. It is a 'desert experience' or 'wilderness time' of barrenness, heat and dryness, without trees or soulfriends, where one's spiritual life and prayer 'withers'. It is a 'hell on earth' in which the sense of the self is 'of something fragile and dried up and ... lots of leaves ... peeling away'. There may be 'oasis experiences' but they are few and far between, and 'the desert is a heck of a long journey' which threatens to 'break' or even 'kill' one's spirit. Nothingness is a 'vast continent' of 'immense spaces' which goes 'on and on and on'; it may even be beautiful, but it is also 'empty', with 'something missing'; 'an enormous hinterland of unexplored material'. It is a place of 'humbling' and 'stripping' in which 'you can't hide from God'; ultimately, therefore, a place of confrontation and disclosure, if one can face the challenge of unearthing what is there to be revealed.

For others, rather than being a wide open space, powerlessness was a 'dark place', a confined space 'penned and enclosed' where they feared being trapped, stifled or suffocated; a 'narrowness and restriction' from which one longs to escape. It was 'being underground' and wondering 'when is this bulb going to emerge?' or 'all closed up inside', 'living in an ivory tower' which 'completely screened you off from real life'. It was like 'living under siege' where there is 'no place of safety' into which to retreat. It was being enclosed 'in a convent garden' and 'held in by walls' or being stifled by oppressive forces which threaten to overwhelm or, as in one woman's dream:

> it was like being on a cliff
> on a ledge in a cave
> and trapped on that ledge

and the tide rising and me unable to move
unable to do anything about it
or lying absolutely flat
spread-eagled on the wet sand
pinned by I don't know what force to the sand
and watching the tide rise
unable to do anything about it

These metaphors of enclosure and suffocation are reminiscent of what Mary Mason describes as 'the autobiography of imprisonment', represented in women's writings from Charlotte Perkins Gilman's autobiography to Sylvia Plath's *Bell Jar*, in which is charted 'the grim tale of a woman's claustrophobia when she cannot get out of the prison of the self or of her nightmare when she is kept from coming into her own self through the proximate existence of another or others' (Mason, 1980, p. 234).

In contrast to either expansive images of desert or the confined spaces of imprisonment, some women named the place of powerlessness apophatically, in negative terms, as a no-place, a kind of existential placelessness of lostness and homelessness. 'I was nowhere really spiritually', says one, 'I just had got nowhere', says another. 'I was rootless', 'in a foreign land', says a third; or, again, another described it as 'feeling like the alien', 'not belonging'. Although these images are cast in negative terms, they evoke an arid wasteland of empty space, a kind of unrecognised no-woman's-land, a refugee camp outside the official boundaries of belonging.

Deadness, Loss of Feeling and Reality, Not Knowing the Self

Whilst geographical metaphors suggest the physicality of women's religious experience, another set of images convey the opposite impression, namely the *lack* of feeling and bodily awareness which characterise spiritual impasse. These women spoke of feeling 'dead' or 'unreal', of being 'out of touch' with themselves, of being only 'half-awake' or 'half-alive' or being 'submerged ... for long periods', of 'losing a sense of' themselves or their sense of identity 'evaporat[ing]'. Such feelings are commonly recognised descriptors of depression (cf. Nairne and Smith, 1984), and seem to be all too familiar to women living in or on the edges of the church.

Jane, a young mother in her late thirties, described her struggle with feelings of unreality which finally led her to seek therapy:

one of the things I said to the therapist
when I first negotiated why I wanted to go
was I felt that I wasn't real ...
that that
I I wasn't
I just didn't feel like I was real
and that's about not being alive
or or being stuck

Sheila, an older woman in her late fifties brought up in a large Catholic family, looked back on a long struggle against the sense of being unreal, excessively passive or dead which had its roots in childhood. She described the experience of being a middle child of a large family and lacking any sense of individuality or uniqueness: 'You know/ going around the town and that/ people would stop and say/ "Well which one are you?" ... because we actually all looked alike ... I just never felt that um ... / I was unique in any way.'

Marion, a religious sister in her sixties, described a similar life-time's journey against feelings of unreality, being half-awake or locked in an ivory tower. Her early childhood experience of intense connection with the natural world and a sense of the presence of God was 'arrested' by some event in late childhood or early adolescence to which she alluded but did not spell out, although it was clear it had some connection with her father and his 'black moods where he wouldn't speak to anyone in the family for several days on end'. Marion described a long stretch of her life during adolescence and early adulthood as a time of 'arrested development', a 'missing out' on the teenage years of 'wearing lovely clothes and experimenting' which left her 'terribly immature' and living vicariously through books and daydreams, unable to reflect on herself and her surroundings, obediently compliant to the dictates of her superiors and unaware of her own desires or will. Although she had subsequently experienced many moments of 'awareness' and 'breakthrough' to fuller life, she acknowledged that

> I'm still battling with the ...
> unresolved things of my life ...
> well I still feel that I'm only half awake um
> ... uh I still feel I'm struggling with
> I suppose we do this till we die
> but I'm still struggling with a
> a hinterland of
> of stuff in my life
> which should be creative but
> but has somehow
> hasn't got there yet

For Sarah, a woman in her late sixties brought up by emotionally distant parents and inculcated with religious teaching from an early age, religion was associated with 'duty' and 'accepting what you were told', as well as with an absence of emotion, a passivity which literally sent her to sleep when she said her prayers at night. Although she sensed a longing for something she couldn't name, religion as she experienced it always lacked reality and meaning: 'God was never a reality for me ... however much I joined in all these services and said these prayers, that didn't seem to have much meaning in it either ... I couldn't relate to [it] at all.'

Some women described the loss of feeling or awareness in startlingly physical, even sensuous terms, as a kind of sensory deprivation. For Lorna, an artist in her mid-fifties, faith had always had a physical element to it, experienced as a 'tingling' of the hands during prayer, an increase of the pulse as though the blood is racing round the body, and a physical sense of 'blessing' manifested as feelings of peace and ecstasy. Conversely, the absence of faith was experienced as the deprivation of this physical awareness, the loss of intense feeling, what she described as 'dead praying' and lack of connection to self or God. Similarly, for Ruth, a vibrant and highly energetic woman in her forties, religion was strongly connected to the realm of imagination, feeling and creativity, as well as sexual passion, and a loss of selfhood and spirituality was experienced as a loss of connection to these centres of energy. The death of her father, occurring at the same time as the ending of a stormy sexual relationship, precipitated a cataclysmic crisis of faith for Ruth. At a stroke, she stopped going to church, stopped listening to music, stopped functioning sexually and 'God just dropped out of the equation'. Shutting off from feeling and religion and sex and music was almost a conscious decision for Ruth, a way of blotting out the grief and pain of her father's death. She described it as 'sitting on top of a sort of small volcano' and 'banging shut the door on my inner workings ... leaning against it heavily ... and piling up the furniture and stuff on the outside'.

Disconnection, Fragmentation, Division, Alienation and Breakdown

Another series of images revolves around women's feelings of disconnectedness, cut-off-ness, alienation, fragmentation, being out of balance with some fundamental part of oneself, and, where the disconnection is acute, breakdown or disintegration of the self. Women spoke of failing 'to make the connection' between different aspects of experience, being unable to 'fit' or 'bring together' perceived opposites, of receiving 'contradictory messages' from their families or religious communities which they were unable to reconcile, and of being unable to 'relate' to religious teaching or ritual. They experienced religion and life in 'separate compartments', 'not really related', as 'separate issues' or even 'two very separate stories'. There was a profound sense of 'split' or 'divorce', not only a cognitive but also an existential dissonance between mind and emotion, the needs of self and the demands of others, sexuality and spirituality or spirituality and politics, which could be so total that it was as if they are 'truly irreconcilable'. It was like 'living between two cultures', being 'on the edge'. Where the disconnection and contradiction became so acute that they could no longer be sustained, there was a 'falling apart' of the person, a 'folding up' or 'falling to bits', a 'collapse', 'breakdown' or 'burn-out'.

Sarah experienced a pervasive sense of contradiction and 'split' for years in her practice of religion which left her feeling disconnected and alienated from it, and yet somehow not able to let go. She received many 'contradictory messages' about faith from her upbringing which she 'couldn't make sense of'. Religion was very definitely not about 'emotion', and she received many warnings about the 'dangers' of excessive emotion, yet you were supposed to 'love God' and how could you do that without emotion? Religion was supposed to encompass the whole of life yet she experienced it as something separate, a compartment, 'something different and separate ... from the other parts of life'. In particular, she experienced a profound split between physicality and spirituality:

> I mean God is pure spirit
> no physical parts to God
> physical things
> particularly sex
> are sinful
> they're the sort of sinful part of human nature

we're actually *meant* to be spiritual
and you can't be
but this was the aim you see
this was the ideal
to be spiritual
and the physical
you've got to look after your body properly
but really it's rather despicable somehow
all physical functions and that sort of thing ...
em so there was always this sort of split
kind of 'be ye perfect as your Father in heaven is perfect' em
in spite of the incarnation you know
God hasn't really got anything to do with the world
and we *really* need to
be out of the body [*chuckling*]
kind of thing
em and be spirit

For Jane, there was also a difficulty in being able to 'connect' different aspects of her religious heritage, only in her case, it was a tension between the realm of ideas on the one hand and emotions on the other. Like Sarah, she imbibed many contradictions from her family, who were strongly committed, liberal-thinking Protestants; yet they never talked about religion, politics or feelings, even though these forces had so clearly shaped their lives. Jane found it difficult to 'connect' personal spirituality and the commitment to justice on the one hand, or to differentiate between personal spirituality and emotion on the other: 'I don't know how to fit it all together/not at all.' This was graphically illustrated in the following story:

I went to a conference in about 1985
where we did a
a guided meditation ...
the conference was about politics and spirituality
we did a guided meditation where we went to a
a safe place and we had to pick up some
some object to
symbolise spirituality and some object to spin
symbolise political activity
and then to put them together
and I picked up um
I went to a garden
a walled garden
and I picked up a butterfly
to represent spirituality
and a clenched fist to represent politics ...

And when I put them together
the clenched fist squashed the butterfly

The violence of Jane's fantasy, in which the fragile, delicate butterfly of spirituality was completely obliterated by the brutal clenched fist of politics, suggests not only the radical dichotomisation in Jane's religious worldview but also the cost to her own embryonic spirituality of this dualism: violence and even extinction of all that was fragile and delicate within her own religious consciousness.

The sense of an immobilising contradiction in one's experience of faith and selfhood was particularly acute for women whose sexuality or ethnic identity put them into uneasy relation to the mainstream culture or religious tradition. Elizabeth demonstrated the 'split' she experienced between her lesbian identity and her spirituality not only in what she said, but in the process of the interview itself. She began the interview by narrating what she described as her 'spiritual history', tracing the origins of religious belief and practice in childhood and their later development. Pausing and reflecting on the story she had just been telling, she commented: 'there are lots of stories that almost run simultaneously, aren't there?' She then began to narrate the story of her discovery of her sexual identity as a completely separate narrative line, before again pausing to reflect:

> You know ...
> I feel like I'm telling a different story
> which feels divorced from
> other things I've said
> but I think they were just
> you know lots of different issues
> separate issues going on ...
> and I certainly felt that
> at that time that sort of
> being gay and
> and being Christian were
> were truly irreconcilable ...

The separation between her sexual and her religious identity was so complete that she could not articulate them in relation to one another; they represent 'two very separate stories' which 'run simultaneously' but hardly seemed to interconnect. At the time of the interview, Elizabeth was still struggling to connect these two story-lines and to work out what it might mean to reconstruct her identity as a person who is both lesbian and spiritual, and what relationship to God might constitute in these terms. The sense of contradiction could still be very powerful and the internalisation of religious rhetoric so deep that she could still be 'easily drawn into thinking that ... I'm wrong' or even 'that I'm possessed' and 'in need of healing'. Although she had rejected these ideas with her mind – 'your head can say "it's not true"' – she knew that she had 'internalised all those things' at a deeper level, and still had 'a long way to go' before achieving integration of thought and feelings.

Black women living in a white-dominated culture can also experience the sense of divided selfhood and faith. Hilary, a second-generation British-born woman of Caribbean parents exemplified this sense of 'splitting' and the profound alienation resulting from it. Her story illustrates the oppressive constraints experienced by a young black girl growing up in a white culture which militate against a positive sense of self. She described early experiences of going to bed and praying she would wake up white because all the images of being black were so negative. She imbibed from her mother at an early age the message that 'if you want to get on you have to be as good and twice as good as the white person.' She experienced explicit and implicit racism at school, university, work, and the white-majority church where 'most white men would not be happy to take home someone who was black.' More pervasively, Hilary described her acute sense of 'not belonging', of 'living between two cultures', of being 'on the edges as normal, strange'. She felt she belonged neither to the British culture into which she had been born and where she had lived all her life, nor to the Caribbean society where her familial roots were but which she experienced as strange and exotic:

> You're in between
> you belong to neither
> because people there won't accept
> they would call me a foreigner
> I was in a foreign land ...
> I found I was in a place where I was accepted by neither
> and I always say it was living between two cultures
> so in a sense you didn't know who you were
> you were rootless

Whilst such cognitive and emotional dissonance can be creative and lead to the disequilibrium of the existing faith stage and the gradual emergence of a new, more satisfying one, this did not always seem to be the case for the women in my study; or, if it was, it was not achieved without high psychological cost. Where the lack of connection was acute, it was experienced more strongly as a fragmentation or even a total breakdown or collapse of the self. Meg described the upheaval to her faith and identity that took place when, shortly after her marriage, she moved from her working-class origins to a university town, as she encountered the totally new environment of academic culture, at the same time as trying to adjust to married life. Whilst this experience was ultimately creative, pushing her to construct a more secure and flexible selfhood and spirituality, it was initially frightening and confusing, leading to a radical loss of self. Meg spoke of 'not knowing who I was', losing or failing to recognise herself in the 'whole role thing of being somebody's wife and being labelled somebody's wife'; the difficulty of 'finding myself' in a place where 'it was almost like ... everyone speaks a different language.' She described the process of reconstructing a faith identity as 'a kind of dramatic internal refocusing' and a 'huge reappraisal' in which her different 'selves' – self as student, wife, working-class northerner, pious believer – were all up for grabs, jostling together in confused competition. This seems to correspond, at least to some measure, to Fowler's description of the movement from Stage 3, in which one's sense of self is largely shaped by one's roles in relation to others, to Stage 4, when one constructs a sense of identity that moves beyond role configuration. Yet for women such as Meg, where the self has resided almost entirely in caring roles oriented to the needs of the other, this is a fearful movement. In an extraordinary image, Meg spoke of 'pinning' herself onto 'things' in her environment 'that were safe and good' in order to 'make it OK', as if her self were so fragile and so disoriented that it was in danger of evaporating or disintegrating totally.

Alice, an academically successful woman nearing sixty, described a crisis of identity in adolescence when she went to university and 'folded up completely from 'overwork', driving herself and being driven until she experienced a 'physical and emotional collapse', and was 'wrecked', no longer able to complete her studies or to write effectively. Rachel described a breakdown which, like Alice's, was both physical and emotional, the climax of bearing within her body and her psyche for many years the warring tensions between her mind 'which was highly analytical and quite developed' and her emotions 'which needed to be accepted'. She experienced acute conflict between obedience to religious authorities and charity to others, between her sexual attractions and her commitment to celibacy, between the safety of the life she had chosen and the sense of a wider, freer life beckoning her from beyond. Finally, the tensions became unbearable, demanding resolution; she became ill and experienced a kind of 'burn-out' or 'break-down', literally 'falling' and 'collapsing' as her body refused to continue functioning and her divided self made its irresistible demands for attention and reconciliation. Such narratives of breakdown and burnout are potent reminders that there is nothing automatic or easy about women's faith development, and that the trajectory of a woman's life can descend into some fearful places in which the unmaking of the self may or may not be the precursor to some larger liberation.

Paralysis and Impasse

Images of paralysis, being unable to move, act or to complete a particular project, being 'stunted' or 'arrested' were common in women's descriptions of their struggles to come to authentic selfhood and spirituality. Participants spoke of getting 'locked into a situation', being 'stuck, in a rut, going nowhere', of being 'entrenched' in a 'double life'. There was a feeling of being 'trapped' and 'unable to move, unable to do anything about it'; 'I felt I couldn't go back and I couldn't go forward'; 'there's no way of moving on'. The place of impasse was described as a 'dead-end', a place of 'complete standstill', from which the women 'couldn't seem to break out'. There was often a desire to break away but a sense of being unable to do so, being 'held back' or 'controlled', 'forced' by powers and feelings beyond one's own agency. Many women described a sensation of repeating 'old patterns' and 'old behaviour' learnt from their families of origin, a feature especially common when speaking of their relationships with their own children. Being in the place of impasse, where one cannot go forwards or backwards, led either to feelings of extreme tension and conflict or, where the conflict was suppressed, to depression and despair, a sense of hopelessness which is itself paralysing, compounding further the sense of impasse.

Jane spoke of her current struggle to 'untangle some of the dead ends' that she constantly seemed to run into, recognising a repeated pattern of 'feeling stuck', 'ways of behaving that have been just not getting anywhere really'. This 'stuckness' was reflected in a number of dilemmas Jane was experiencing with regard to her faith which, at the time of the interview, she could not see how to resolve. Having been brought up in the church and trained as an accredited lay minister, she no longer found the theology and ritual of her church meaningful and she even had the feeling that her spirituality might blossom if she were to leave the church, yet she remained on the edges, with one toe still in, unsure whether to stay or to go. She wanted her child to belong to some kind of community providing ritual, a language for mystery and otherness and the resources to address important global issues. She did not think the church provided this kind of community, yet she was not sure where else she would find it. She strongly wanted some kind of public naming ceremony for her child, yet she was stuck between creating one of her own, on the one hand, or adapting the ritual offered by her church, on the other. Jane's struggle against 'feeling stuck' and getting tangled up in 'dead ends' was mirrored in the process of the interview, in which she often seemed to 'run out' of language, feel uncertain where to go next or how to follow through a particular topic or theme, appealing to me: 'You'll have to help me about where to go next 'cos I'm sort of a bit stuck really.'

Writer's block is a classic symptom of impasse. Helen, a woman in her late thirties, both academically and professionally 'successful', described her experience of the drying up of the writing voice and her inability to complete an academic piece of research to which she had committed herself:

> I think you know a lot of my confidence went ...
> well *certainly* in my work
> ah em very frightening experience really
> I couldn't do it
> first time in my life
> I mean I'd just always been successful at school
> without really trying
> and my degree you know
> I'd just been very successful
> and then suddenly I couldn't do it
> I couldn't –
> didn't *really* know what I was supposed to be doing
> and I and the writing just went
> and I would sit at my desk for hours
> and cover sheet after sheet of paper
> but it I kept getting stuck
> you know screw it up and throw it in the bin
> and that was just desperate really
> and very *frightening*
> very frightening.

Janet recognised 'strong patterns in [her] life' whereby she 'set up for [her]self situations' in which she was doomed to fail, in which she 'required of [her]self the impossible' – situations such as falling in love with unattainable men or accepting jobs for which she was not well suited and which made her unhappy. This pattern, as Janet recognised, was rooted in a negative God-image, itself modelled on her father, a remote, angry and judgemental man. Whilst, rationally, she had rejected the image, for years she experienced the demands of God as harsh, punitive, impossible, shouting at her to 'Get out there and get on with it!' as her father had; and the less congenial and more difficult the particular project was, the better.

Although the experience of being 'stuck' or 'blocked' may have roots in negative parenting, it is frequently reinforced culturally by societal expectations about women's roles. Thus, Lolita's childhood sense of vocation to ordained ministry was blocked consistently by her church, which did not admit of women's ordination, and she had to wait many years before her personal sense of calling could be tested and, finally, affirmed. Whilst Lolita demonstrated remarkable resilience and strength of purpose during these years, the costs were high: a sense of loneliness, depression and rejection, and great frustration at the waste of her talents. Hilary's vocation to ordained ministry was not blocked overtly, but had to overcome repeated racist prejudice. From early childhood, when her primary headmaster channelled her into the local comprehensive school rather than the grammar, to her early years in ministry, when her training incumbent would not allow her to use her doctorate in her title, Hilary had repeatedly had to struggle against the assumption that 'it's impossible for a black person ever to achieve.' For these women, psychological and spiritual impasse is both compounded and generated by structural injustices endemic to patriarchy and racism.

The Quest or Search for What is Unknown

The journey image is a common one in the literature of spirituality, and has been associated particularly with the heroic quest of the lonely male separating himself from his community and setting out on some voyage or adventure in which he proves his mettle and wins reward for his courage and bravery. In my interviews, whilst the journey image was not a central or defining one for many women, it was used in a particularly striking way by a number of participants to name their experiences of powerlessness and disconnection. Central to their use of the image was the paradox of being on a quest or search for something, but being unable, not only to *find* that which they desired, but being unable even to name or know what it was they were searching for. They were 'searching' and 'looking for something' but not 'clear really what [they] did want and where to look for it'. They may have had a dim sense that they were searching in the wrong place or the wrong *way* or on the wrong track, so that there was a resulting sense both of frustration and of lack of reality about the journey. 'I never lost the faith', says one, 'but I could find no way, I could find no path'; 'I just had got nowhere' says another.[5]

Sarah was brought up by strict Anglo-Catholic parents and, later, trained as a religious education teacher. For years she experienced the sense of being on a 'search', 'just searching, trying to find something', 'looking for something deeper and something that would have more reality in it', a 'something' she could never find or recognise, a longing which never seemed to be met by her experience of the church, even though she found tantalising glimpses or echoes of it there. Her search was associated particularly with a longing to pray:

---

[5] The women's paradoxical use of journey imagery finds parallels in contemporary women's poetry (Ostriker, 1987, p. 224), where there is an attempt to recast traditional masculine quest imagery and suggest an alternative female quest in which the heroine is 'engaged in a quest for wholeness at once spiritual, psychological, and social'. 'Unlike the epic hero, however, [the female protagonist] does not know her own goal in advance and must discover it through fluid and nonlinear psychic processes which constitute her real adventure – meditation, memory, prayer, questioning, and associative weavings ... And, unlike the epic hero, her role is not to support but to unravel and rewrite the already-written drama or script of religion and history' (ibid.).

... for really many years
I have been wanting to learn to meditate ...
I can see that for years and years and years I've been
searching for that
and I think I
seems as if I've always been thinking that em
there must be a way to discover
there must be a kind of technique to discover
'I don't know how to do this thing'
so as if
not that it was
necessarily going to be a *difficult* thing to learn but
I thought of it as something you had to learn
not as something that's just there as a natural thing
and I couldn't find the right way for me
different ways I tried
ugh like using biblical words or
meditating on biblical parables or events or whatever
didn't seem to do anything for me
so either I was doing it wrong
or there was some other way and so on
and really that's been the case til very very recently
still thinking 'I must learn to meditate'
'cos if I try on my own
I don't even know what I'm trying to do

For Sarah, 'part of the problem was/ that I wasn't clear really what I did want/ and where to look for it':

I have said over and over and over again
for the past
quite a number of years now
em uh uh sort of things like
'I want something more spiritual'
but I don't know what I mean by this word 'spiritual'
but I know that's sort of what I'm looking for
but I you know
I don't really know what 'spiritual' means
I don't know how to define it em
but I know it's something I'm wanting

Sheila, a woman who shared with Sarah a strict and devout religious upbringing, echoed this same sense of longing and hunger for something unnamed, elusive, always 'around the corner', 'somewhere else', out of reach. She employed much the same language of 'searching' or 'thirsting' for 'something deeper' yet not knowing or being able to 'get there'. This longing was manifested in a deep attraction to the village church, where she would go and sit alone for hours, a love of the mystery of Catholic ritual, especially the Latin requiem masses, a 'great feeling for nuns and convents', a hunger for reading and for education, and a rich inner fantasy world. Yet none of this was ever quite 'enough'. She described a 'repeated pattern of trying to get *away* to something better': wanting to 'get away ... from the narrowness and restriction' of her rural Catholic environment and wanting to 'get *towards* something' better or fuller she could not name but felt must be somewhere, if only she could find it. For years, like Sarah, she continued attending church but always had the feeling that there was something 'else', something 'missing', something 'more' which she wasn't getting, and which must be due to her own lack:

> I always had this kind of feeling of searching ...
> I felt I wasn't
> sort of getting there
> and religion and faith
> was set up as a goal that you worked towards
> perfection
> and I couldn't get anywhere near it
> and umm it was always a striving
> and I felt that
> if I'd somehow tried hard enough
> and there were different routes ...
> I always had this feeling that I just couldn't
> sort of get where I wanted to...
> I've always had that sort of thirst if you like
> for something deeper
> but it's as if
> I just didn't know where it was going
> and so I always had a sense of failure
> about my spirituality
> your spiritual life actually
> yeh
> I couldn't quite get there

'Not being able to get there' is a repeated refrain in Sheila's story. For years in church 'I was still searching for/ what I felt was there and I was missing it somehow.' At the time of the interview, Sheila had largely given up going to mass, but she still found herself drawn by 'the theatre and theatricality of the mass' 'even though when I'm there I think/ Oh God! you know/ why have I come?' Not only in religious matters but also in education, she 'really wanted to go further' but her experience was one of 'not getting anything ... because I didn't know how to set about it so to speak.' Her mother fostered a desire that she would enter the convent; Sheila 'knew it wasn't what [she] wanted', 'but ... I also had the feeling I couldn't get what I wanted.' Here, the journey metaphor meshes with the language of paralysis and impasse, as women express their sense of being unable to move forward on their quest for the 'something' that eludes them.

Abdication, Absorption or Reckless Giving Up of the Self to the (Male) Other

For many, though not all, the women in my group, the experience of loss of selfhood and authentic spirituality was bound up with unauthentic relation to the other, and very often this other was the male other – father, partner, lover or God. For these women, the loss of self was a result of, or another side of, the experience of giving oneself away to, being absorbed in, becoming excessively identified with and dependent upon the male other. They spoke of 'losing' or 'throwing [themselves] away' into relationships, 'following' wherever the man leads, becoming 'wrapped up' in the other person so that their own wishes and desires were no longer even apparent to them. The struggle to find authentic selfhood and spirituality thus becomes a struggle to find authentic ways of relating to the male in which the self is not threatened or overpowered. These women exhibited a means of identity formation noted by a number of psychologists; named variously as the 'elusive self' which lacks knowledge of itself and is unable to name itself apart from its relation to the other or a particular function (Rubin, 1979), the 'tainted self' dependent upon men for self-definition (Schaef, 1982) or the 'soluble self' which is in constant danger of dissolving into the other (Keller, 1986). For women whose relationship to God was modelled on dysfunctional or collusive relationships with men (particularly the father), there was a struggle to transform the relationship to the male God such that it no longer legitimated patterns of female passivity, abdication of selfhood or victimisation. For some women, this entailed a radical rejection of male God imagery, for others, a fundamental reworking of such imagery.

For some women, the absorption in the male other was exemplified in an idealised form of relationship with the parent, or a similar father-figure, who authorised and legitimised the self, and whose loss through death or absence compelled the woman, for the first time, to separate from the paternal bond and reconfigure her own identity as a person in her own right. Ruth's story, told above (pp. 64–5), demonstrates this movement out of the paternal bond into a more owned selfhood in which she learnt to internalise the father's love, wisdom and acceptance within herself. Other women in my study seem to have resisted the need to separate from the father. Even in instances where the father had actually died, some women remained in a kind of idealised relation to his memory and described a strong, ongoing connection to the father figure through dreams or internal dialogue with him. This was particularly true for some of the women from non-western cultures, where family ties remain much stronger than in the West, and where the quest for individual identity may be less important than family loyalty. These women did not necessarily perceive the close identification with the father figure as problematic or stifling; they continued to experience a deep sense of affirmation and acceptance through the bond with the father. For these women, the father remained the great hero or exemplar of faith whose love continued to underpin their own lives.

For other women, particularly white, middle-class British women, the absorption in the male was more likely to be experienced in relation to a male partner or lover. Anne, looking back on her years as an art student, remembered quite clearly 'making a conscious effort that, if I wanted a man I had to change'; so she 'made a tremendous metamorphosis from a girl who wore big jerseys and glasses and scruffy hair and painted jeans' to a 'Chelsea swinger' with a Vidal Sassoon haircut, contact lenses and mini skirts. After the disillusionment of an early, painful sexual encounter, leaving her feeling she was 'soiled goods', Anne met someone who loved her and wanted to marry her. She remembered making a conscious choice between what she perceived at the time as 'life' and art:

I wanted terribly to be loved ...
and I made a conscious decision about
'I don't think I'm actually going to be this wonderful great artist actually'
'I don't think I can bear it
to starve in a garret'
and I remember thinking
'I I can choose art or life and I'll choose life'
and by that I meant marriage and children
and I remember thinking
'I don't want to be alone when I'm forty' ...
I needed the physical and emotional security ...
and someone who loved me was very important

Once she became committed to her husband, Anne became '*incredibly* emotionally dependent on him', following him back to his native country in another continent, though she had never left England before, didn't have a job and hadn't even met his family. Married at 23, by the time she was 25 Anne had two young children, was deeply depressed and remembered thinking to herself: 'I've got everything I always wanted and now all I have to do is grow up.'

Helen similarly described meeting and falling in love with the man she hoped to marry, and the loss of her sense of self and faith in her commitment to this relationship:

I think what I did
as so many women do
I think I just threw myself away almost
into this relationship
you know my *whole* life my *whole* identity
became wrapped up with him
... so without really thinking about it
I just let go of so many you know
of my [other] ties and commitments ...
I didn't even think about it really
they just
everything was
to be subsumed to this man and to this one relationship

Helen spoke of 'giving' herself away, 'throwing' herself 'into' her lover and the relationship, losing any sense of herself 'as a separate person':

the self that I *had* been
the self I thought I knew
just crumbled away –
partly was you know
was was brutally sort of demolished by things outside of my control
and partly *I* –
not *consciously* but but to all intents and purposes
I *gave* it away you know
to another person
so I *really* feel that whole period was a time of
losing any sense of myself

For Helen, as for a number of the women, the loss of self in the relationship to the male partner was also experienced as a crisis of faith. If the self she thought she knew had been 'demolished' and 'given away', this was mirrored by the sense of the God she thought she knew failing her or being absent. She spoke of feeling 'very confused about/ where God was in all of this':

> the God that I thought I knew
> was a God who
> uh well a God who sort of guaranteed meaning
> I suppose in my life
> and in some way rescued me saved me
> and he patently wasn't ...
> You know it was all falling to bits
> and he wasn't
> didn't seem to be doing anything about it
> em [*chuckling*]
> and I was very angry I think
> very angry with God

Sue described a 'dark' period of several years during which she abdicated all power and choice in her life to her husband:

> He got a job as a social worker in X [*name of town*]
> and I just followed him and
> I just went
> I didn't have a job
> 'I'll just go with him!' you know ...
> I just went with him
> because that was what you did wasn't it?
> you know
> the male got the job so ...

'For the sake of peace', Sue gave up a place she had on a Masters course because her husband was disapproving, she stopped going to church because he was 'anti-church', and she did 'menial jobs' even though she was a qualified social worker:

> It had all gone
> it had all gone to pieces
> I remember saying to my sister
> once when I was staying with her
> or my brother-in-law
> I can't remember which it was
> 'I've got no faith now
> it's all gone'
> it was horrible really
> [I] didn't
> didn't read anything
> didn't do anything
> churchy or religious or whatever
> it all went

Domination, Oppression, Violent Attack or Rape of the Self

A further striking set of images used by women to name their experiences of loss of self and faith is distinguished by the use of violence, force or attack to dominate, assault, break or even, at its worst, rape the self. Women spoke of being 'crippled', 'wrecked', 'punished', 'stripped', 'forced' or 'controlled', 'brutally demolished by things outside of my control', receiving a 'big blow' to the self; of 'living under siege', having one's faith and inner resources 'dragged out of you', of being 'undermined', 'pulled in five different ways', of being 'zapped' or 'dominated' by a 'very stern God'. These chilling images of domination and attack represent the 'other side' of women's experience of inauthentic relation to the male. Instead of voluntarily giving away the self to the other, the self is here experienced as being coerced, compelled, taken against its will, and, in the process, damaged, violated and abused. Where the relationship to the (male) deity is internalised in such terms, the damage wreaked on the female psyche is profound, since male violence against the female becomes legitimised theologically and takes on the power of divine sanction.

Elizabeth recognised that she had always 'had great problems with relationship with men *per se*', problems stemming from her relationships with her father, whom she described as 'a very abusive man', and her brother, also described as 'abusive'. Her experience of abusive male power had been reinforced by a male-dominated church community and reflected in the images of God she had received from evangelical teachers. An important part of her religious journey had been 'chucking out the male God' in young adulthood, and trying to rework a sense of spirituality which was not dependent upon patriarchal power. At the time of the interview, Elizabeth had reappropriated some sense of herself as a 'spiritual being' but she remained distant from formal religion and 'still [had] great problems with God'. Rejecting the male patriarch, she could not envisage what form a revised God-image might take, though she had a 'sense that God is there somewhere'. However, the 'almighty benevolent God' of her adolescence, the 'all-powerful father-figure' remained alive, if buried, in her subconscious, and, although she wanted to believe that 'God will take me as I am today', there was still a lurking fear that 'he's going to beat it [that is, her lesbian sexuality] out of me one day.' Elizabeth recognised that 'my sense of a God has got to heal ... there's a lot of healing still to take place.'

Sue had a terror of 'the male God who dominates' which was rooted in what she described (in classic understatement) as 'a formative experience' of being raped in her early twenties. This terror manifested itself, not only in feeling uncomfortable with the idea of a male God who dominates others, and in a deliberate reworking of her imagery of God in female terms, but in a deep fear of unbounded spaces and of her own potential psychic gifts, as well as a terror of 'possession' by alien powers, and a strong need to be in control:

> I need to have boundaries
> and and
> I need to have wombs/ and boundaries ...
> I need to feel I'm in control of situations
> 'cos I do get very panicky and frightened
> I do need to feel I'm in [to] control

and to almost get into deep meditation
or contemplation
kind of scares me a little bit yeh? ...

it just terrifies me
the thought of being taken over by
discarnate entities
being a channel
just just blows my mind

Meg's story of faith and calling to ordained ministry was shot through with repeated 'horrific' and 'destructive' experiences with male authority figures, in which she felt intimidated, victimised and abused, as she had been as a child by her father. Whether it was church selectors prying into her marriage and finances, clergy rejecting her applications for a post, or accountants threatening to withdraw money for training, Meg repeatedly found herself in situations where she felt 'vulnerable' to physical or psychological threat. These repeated instances of intimidation and abuse are epitomised by an incident when Meg was visited by her father shortly after she gave birth to her third child. Lying in the recovery room at the hospital, 'on a drip and pinned down', her father came into the room and 'immediately became very aggressive'. 'Something in the look' on his face, combined with 'something about ... being so vulnerable', brought to the surface a series of repressed memories of 'the stuff that had gone on between me and my father as a child', and, for the next six months, Meg was prey to 'horrific flashbacks' and 'really difficult emotional stuff', 'uncontrollable anger' and 'fears'. There were occasional echoes of the abusive father in her God-descriptions at points in the interview, as, for example, when she was speaking of her sense of calling to ordination and described it as a sense of 'being menaced by something', a 'threatening' sense of being pursued by something or someone, and wondering 'What's going on here? What sort of God is this?'

These images and stories of invasive male presence exemplify the injurious effects upon women's psyche and spirituality of living in a society marked by the rupture of male–female relationship and rooted in social structures of domination. As others have argued, abuse of any form, be it physical, sexual or psychological, is fundamentally an assault on identity, and rape represents this at its most extreme, signifying the transgression and theft of a person's very self (Fortune, 1996, p. 196). The effects of abuse are well-documented, and it is noteworthy that many of these same characteristics have emerged in the women's stories in this chapter: the erosion of self-worth, depression, anxiety, anger, self-abuse, shame and false guilt, and lack of trust in other people or in the basic security of one's world. Even for women who have not experienced overt physical or sexual abuse, the effects of living in a culture in which male violence is endemic are evident in women's descriptions of domination in its many different forms, both individual and institutionalised.

Summary and Conclusions

Whilst the women's accounts of their experiences of paralysis and alienation demonstrate great diversity, they also suggest the pervasiveness of the experience.

Although the accounts do not suggest a unitary experience, they do suggest a cluster of related experiences which are very common in women's faith lives, constellating around the themes of powerlessness, alienation, impasse and fragmentation. The women's accounts confirm the hypothesis, suggested by Rubin (1979), Belenky et al. (1986), Harris (1993), Bons-Storm (1996) and others, of a developmental crisis for women which may have its roots in adolescence or may emerge at a later stage. Whatever its origins, the experiencing of oneself and one's faith as fragmented, disconnected, unreal, paralysed, broken, alienated, abused or even dead, seems to represent a major developmental challenge for women in a patriarchal culture. Whilst some of the women had resolved the crisis during early or middle adulthood, others continued to struggle to break the deadlock of the divided self well into old age and to attempt to subvert the cultural and religious constraints under which the paralysed self takes shape. Other women seemed to be locked more or less securely into this developmental cul-de-sac and unable to make their way out of it.

Further, the women's accounts demonstrate powerfully the pain and anguish of the experience of impasse. Yet it is not the obvious suffering of an acknowledged grief such as illness or bereavement; rather, the women's accounts illuminate a suffering which is unacknowledged and frequently incapable of articulation, because it arises from tensions and conflicts within the self which have no public narrative or voice. The women's experiences of impasse are experiences of not fitting or belonging within the boundaries of sanctioned models of identity or religious belief. The intensity of their pain can be accounted for in large measure because the women nowhere find their experiences of powerlessness and struggle articulated by those to whom they look for care, guidance and understanding (Bons-Storm, 1996). The struggle to name the reality of their experiences in a cultural context where such experiences are rendered invisible exacerbates the isolation and powerlessness they feel.

Yet, alongside the reality of the women's pain and their struggle to articulate the reality of their experiences, their accounts also reveal a remarkable creativity which is suggestive of transformation and hope. One of the paradoxes unearthed by my research is the extent to which the women were able to name their experiences of immobility and disconnection in original, vivid and empowering imagery and narrative. The sheer quantity of images surveyed in this chapter alone is impressive, yet the women's inventiveness is evident, not only in the range of images *per se*, but in the novel and striking ways in which they used them. Their ability to name their experiences of impasse and powerlessness creatively testifies to their determination to wrest significance from such experiences and to move on from them. The wilderness may, indeed, be a place of sterility and death, but it can also be a place of vision, renewal and choice. The narrow place of imprisonment and constriction is experienced as a terrifying dead end, yet often it is perceived in retrospect as the place of crisis and denouement in which impasse gives way, finally, to the breaking-in of unforeseen possibilities and new life. Paradoxically, even images of deadness and lack of reality testify to an awareness of the need for a recovery of life and of feeling, and can generate a powerful longing for a more vital self. Similarly, images of fragmentation, dividedness and breakdown of the self or of faith testify to the longing for healing and harmony and witness to a basic hope for wholeness. As Ostriker (1987, p. 88) suggests:

If an empty identity and a divided self are what women see in themselves, that is not what they desire. Assertions of non-existence, invisibility, and muteness on the one hand, stony or metallic rigidity, formlessness, and deformity on the other, are signals of crisis, signs of a fragmented being unable to unify itself, unable to tolerate some part of itself that is necessary for its wholeness, yet unwilling to remain scattered.

The paradoxical journey imagery used by the women not only implicitly rejects the traditional image of the spiritual life as a lonely epic quest, but also holds out hope for a belonging and a homecoming, even if, at present, such a destination remains far off. The women who spoke of abdicating the self or becoming absorbed in the other recognised, by such language, their need to reclaim the self they had abandoned and exercise a rightful care of the self. Even the violent imagery of domination, attack and rape of the self can be read as a protest against such violation of the self and a demand for justice, freedom and right relation by the women.

In all these varied ways, the women's images suggest the potential for the experience of alienation to become a generating force for transformation. Whilst the very notion of alienation seems to contradict the affirmation of faith development, the women's accounts suggest something different. Without detracting from the severe psychological and spiritual damage done to women in and through the experience of impasse, it is possible that their marginalisation and muteness is fertile ground from which a new experience of God, and the transformation of alienating symbols, can break through. The experience of alienation which is actively appropriated, consciously owned, linguistically, symbolically and ritually encoded – expressed in anger, rage, depression and abandonment, in all their full fury – can become a kind of revolutionary force, a 'revolutionary patience', as Dorothee Sölle (1977) calls it, a ticking 'time bomb' which will 'explode in new abilities and energy in women that cannot be conquered' (FitzGerald, 1986, p. 308).

Chapter 6

The Patterns of Women's Faith Development: Awakenings

There is no place so awake and alive as the edge of becoming.

Sue Monk Kidd[1]

My hand will go through this brick.
And with it will go weakness, and hand lotion, pink dresses, and the fear of catcalls.

Gail Murray[2]

Change is coming the door stands wide.

Jean Clark[3]

Introduction

The developmental challenge posed by the experience of impasse may lead, for women, to the liberating experience of awakening, breakthrough and a reconnection to their own power of selfhood as well as to a deeper awareness of their connectedness to others and to the divine. Nevertheless, this is neither automatic nor pain-free. Analysis of my transcripts revealed the women's struggles, sometimes over many years, to break out of the paralyses which had kept them from living as fully as they wished to do, as well as highlighting the broad range of significant marker events which had acted as the trigger or gateway to such awakening. In this chapter, after considering the insights of others, I seek to identify both recurring patterns in the women's accounts as well as to draw out the differences in their stories and images. Finally, I draw together the key findings of this chapter and discuss their significance for women's faith development.

Awakenings in Women's Faith Development

The experience of breakthrough or awakening to new consciousness and spiritual vitality is described by a number of writers as a key component in women's spirituality. Having identified the experience of 'nothingness' as a common one in contemporary women's fiction, Carol Christ goes on to describe the process of

---

[1] Monk Kidd (1996), p. 12.
[2] In Spretnak (1982), p. 259.
[3] From 'Epiphany: Upon the ending of a long marriage', in Ward et al. (1995), p. 115.

awakening which may follow, 'in which the powers of being are revealed' leading to 'a new sense of self and a new orientation in the world' (1986, p. 13), issuing, in its turn, in a 'new naming'. As Christ points out, 'awakening' is a metaphor which has been frequently used by mystics 'to describe the experience of enlightenment – the movement from conventional notions of the meaning of life to a more direct experience of the "really real" or ground of being, from ordinary to extraordinary consciousness, from bondage to freedom' (p. 18). She suggests that, for women, the experience may have particular characteristics. Whereas for men, conversion often entails the giving up of worldly power, for women, 'awakening is not so much a giving up as a gaining of power ... Women often describe their awakening as a coming to self, rather than a giving up of self, as a grounding of selfhood in the powers of being, rather than a surrender of self to the powers of being' (p. 19). For women, Christ suggests, awakening often occurs through some kind of mystical experience, and this is frequently rooted in nature or in community with other women.

Maria Harris describes the moment of 'awakening' as the 'first step' in the 'dance' of women's spirituality:

> The intimations of a budding spirituality begin when people awaken to themselves: to their deepest inner selves. It begins when people awaken to their sacred selves, and to God, to Mystery, and to the presence of the awesome in the world around them. It begins as people awaken consciously to the presence of sorrow and pity in the world as well as to joy and to delight. (Harris, 1989, p. 3)

Like Christ, Harris emphasises that such awakening for women will include a claiming of the self, especially an affirmation of the body, and the awareness of the 'something greater, something more' (p. 5) within which the self is rooted, 'the echoes of a divine life within herself' (p. 13). Like Christ, too, she locates such awakening particularly in mystical experience, when women become intensely aware of the spirit-filled quality of their lives.

A number of writers highlight the importance of nature mysticism, on the one hand, and female friendship, on the other, as particularly significant contexts within which the awakening to selfhood and empowered spirituality can be birthed (Christ, 1986; Raymond, 1986; Grey, 1989; Hunt, 1991). Excluded from mainstream patriarchal culture, women seek other contexts in which they may give birth to themselves. In nature, women may find 'a sense of unlimited be-ing that she doesn't find in the world of hetero-reality'. Janice Raymond (1986) has suggested: 'In forest or meadow, on mountain or shore, there is the smell and color of life for women which has been diminished in hetero-reality. Sensation makes real. Existence here is wild and transcendent, unfettered by the constraints of hetero-relations' (p. 60).

As Simone de Beauvoir expressed it, 'among plants and animals she is a human being; she is freed at once from her family and from the males' (1970, p. 341). Similarly, female friendship creates a space within a male-defined world where women can live with integrity and 'create the world as women imagine it could be' (Raymond, 1986, p. 205). Female friendship creates a context within which women's power is reclaimed and inspiration is discovered for a new vision of selfhood, other, the natural order and even the divine (Hunt, 1991). Within such friendships, 'women affect, move, stir, and arouse each other to full power' (Raymond, 1986, p. 229). Like the call of the wild in the untamed natural world, female friendship is another 'call of the wild', 'a contagious cry from another like the Self to arise from a tamed and domesticated existence' which 'inspires a woman, again and again, to return to an original state of female existence not tamed by man' (Raymond, 1986, p. 59). As such friendship strengthens, women come to a fuller use of their powers and live life with a purposeful energy, characterised by a 'life-glad' quality (ibid., p. 238).

Such accounts of awakening can suggest a rather romantic, over-idealised vision, both of nature, envisaged as some edenic paradise untouched by human hands, and of female friendship, indeed, of female 'nature' *per se*, as if women had access to some unsullied, original 'essence' which remains untarnished by culture or patriarchy. I reject such a view. There is no original, unmediated nature, whether of landscape or of gendered human selfhood. Nature is shaped, mediated and experienced through the contingency of human culture and consciousness. This means, amongst other things, that women's friendships, as well as women's encounters with the natural world, partake of the messiness, conflicts and sin of an unredeemed humanity. Nevertheless, without denying this, it may well remain the case that female community on the one hand, and the natural world on the other, constitute environments of potential liberation and self-actualisation for women, since, whilst they are not unsullied by the shaping effects of injustice, they may be less directly controlled by patriarchal governance than other contexts.

Whilst female community and the connection with nature may provide contexts which nurture women's selfhood and therefore function as catalysts of awakening, the woman who begins to connect with her own power needs to be able to exercise that power in a wide range of arenas, not only those which feel safe and accepting – although perhaps initially she will 'try out' her new powers in environments where she knows she can depend on the understanding and support of like-minded others. However, ultimately, if the awakened self is to establish and extend its powers, the risk must be taken of asserting the new self in other, less congenial, spheres. As Hess (1997) suggests, 'Awakening requires the ability to stand apart from one's cultural prescriptions for femininity and women's place. While awakening leads women into a community of women-affirming persons rather than into isolation, it still requires the kind of cognitive strength that presupposes an independence of spirit and voice' (p. 58). Hess names this cognitive strength as 'the courage to leave the place whose language you have learned': the courage to separate oneself from extremely powerful, deeply entrenched cultural assumptions about what it means to be female, for example, or what it means to be 'Christian', even if such assumptions have provided a place of safety and affirmation for years. Hess also suggests that, for women, this journey into selfhood may require particular courage because 'while the journey into selfhood is considered heroic for men, it is considered deviant and unfeminine for women' (p. 74). There are still many powerful cultural taboos against woman's separation from her caring roles in which she is oriented chiefly to the nurturance of others; women who begin to prioritise their own needs and give attention to their own quest for actualisation and power may be experienced as a real threat to others who look to them for nurture and support. As Madonna Kolbenschlag (1979) suggests, if an awakened woman forgoes innocence and

denial, refusing to make compromises with herself or defect to patriarchy, her only
option becomes deviance.

Thus the journey towards awakening is neither an easy nor a risk-free one.
Women may have to choose between the acceptance and affirmation of significant
others and their own selfhood, paying a high price in rejection or punishment for
daring to challenge the normative patterns set down by society and for choosing to
develop their own strength and powers of selfhood. And there is another reason why
awakening, as a process, may well be painful: because it inevitably involves an
awakening to the reality of the woman's life in all its powerlessness, passivity,
oppression and conformity. If women during the experience of paralysis and
nothingness are in a kind of 'deep sleep', unconscious of and cut off from their own
pain, then, as they begin to awaken to it, they are often submerged in profound
feelings of rage, regret and mourning for what has been lost in their lives – their own
abdication of self, their alienation from their own powers, their fearfulness of taking
ownership of their lives, the many missed opportunities. In many ways, it is easier
to remain in the deep sleep of paralysis, for the alternative is pain. 'But it is only
when we are willing to see the truth about our lives as women, however painful that
truth might be, that we enter the portal of the journey' (Monk Kidd, 1996, p. 24).

How does awakening happen? FitzGerald (1986) and Osiek (1986) are agreed
that the 'breakthrough' experience arises, not through analysis, strategy or logic, but
only by embracing and assimilating the impasse. This can lead to a transformation
of the self and the entire religious symbol structure, 'a significantly new way of
seeing one's reality' (Osiek, 1986, p. 52) which will eventually accommodate the
impasse experience itself into a positive framework, such that it comes to be seen as
gain, rather than as loss. Osiek emphasises the organic dynamic within the
breakthrough experience, and the continuity between past and present: 'The change
that [conversion] brings about is not disconnected from the past, but continuous; it
builds on the strengths and purifies the weaknesses of what has been, weaving the
old threads into a new fabric in such a way that, together with the new elements,
they form a fresh and original pattern' (ibid.).

We might say, awakening is not to something new so much as something present
as potential within one but unrealised until now: 'What I sought was not outside
myself. It was within me, already there, waiting. Awakening was really the act of
remembering myself' (Monk Kidd, 1996, p. 75). Nevertheless, as in any major stage
transition, there is real and permanent change, involving disruption and dismantling
of the old structures. Monk Kidd calls this 'a sacred disintegration', in which 'the
old forms, which grew small and confining as we woke, now crumble and give way
as something new and large and mysterious rises up within us. Attachment to the
patriarchal world, which we've struggled to unname and unhinge, begins to dissolve
and die away, and we are immersed in feelings that go along with dyings' (ibid.,
p. 88). Many writers use birth imagery to speak of the process of awakening,
likening the conception and bringing to birth of a new self to the biological process
of birth:

> Conception, labor, and birthing ... offer a body parable of the process of awakening. The
> parable tells us things we need to know about the way awakening works – the slow,
> unfolding, sometimes hidden, always expanding nature of it, the inevitable queasiness, the

need to nurture and attend to what inhabits us, the uncertainty about the outcome, the fearful knowing that once we bring the new consciousness forth, our lives will never be the same. (ibid., pp. 11–12)

Rosemary Haughton (1982, pp. 58ff) suggests a sequence of stages in the process of awakening based, not on giving birth, but on the experience of passionate or romantic love. First, there is a 'remote preparation', usually a lengthy process in which the person is inclined, by circumstances and by 'education', both conscious and unconscious, to recognise and want something which they realise they do not possess. Within this context, the 'immediate preparation' can occur: something which creates a 'weak spot' and which shakes the person loose from normal expectations and settled attitudes – be it through a book, a holiday, a disaster or simply 'an intensification of the influences which have created the "remote preparation"' (p. 59). This more intense preparation then paves the way for the 'breakthrough' itself, a passionate response to something perceived as outside the self yet an experience of 'recognition so complete and profound that it is impossible to say what is recognised'. The response of the self is total, 'the thrust of the whole personality towards the strange "home" it perceives' (p. 60). Finally, the experience demands to be translated into language, and thus leads from the intensity of the personal to a communal appropriation in which the awakening of the individual 'illuminat[es] for others, as well as for the [individuals] themselves, the reality which each has encountered' (p. 61).

These writers are agreed that women's awakening is not a once-for-all experience, but something that must be entered into again and again. In terms of developmental theory, we might say that there is not simply one stage transition but many, each one recapitulating the process of deconstruction and reconstruction of the previous awakening: 'Rarely is any awareness or process on this journey a one-time event. We seem to return to it over and over, each time integrating it a bit more fully, owning it a little more deeply' (Monk Kidd, 1996, p. 98). This implies that women's struggle with nothingness, paralysis and powerlessness will never be wholly resolved. As Christ (1986) suggests, 'As long as [a woman] lives – and especially in a male-centred society – the experience of nothingness will reappear' (p. 14). Nevertheless, as women have the courage to confront each level or layer of paralysis and work through to new levels of awareness and awakening, there is a gradual and increasing growth of life and power as the new self becomes more firmly established:

> If we are patient, if we are true to ourselves, if we are willing to see ourselves through the growing seasons, an inevitable thing happens. We become hearty women who have our own ground and our own standing, sturdy as oak after the winds. We become women who let loose our strength, whose truth, creativity, and vision fly like spores into the world. (Monk Kidd, 1996, p. 98)

Narratives of Awakening

Many different kinds of awakening, both major and minor, dramatic and gradual, halting and triumphant, were described by the women in my study. In telling their stories of awakenings, they called on a wide range of images to evoke the significance of these experiences for them. They used metaphors of 'birth' of a 'new self', 'being born again', 'awakening' from death or sleep to 'new' or 'heightened awareness', a 'wide-awake opening', a resurrection or rising of the self from the ashes of death, an 'opening up', and a 'broadening of horizons' which 'widened and enriched' life. Metaphors of liberation were often used: 'a huge burden lifted off me', said one, whilst another spoke of 'release' like the snapping of an elastic band. Others compared the process to 'cutting the last tiny thread' and breaking free from that which holds one back, like a boat sailing out into the open ocean or a landmass breaking away from the land. Others used journey imagery to speak of travelling away from one place and moving to another, crossing over a boundary or threshold into some new territory, 'arriving where God wants me to be', moving on to 'a new place where I needed to be'. Others again used natural and plant imagery to speak of the growth of the self as a 'blossoming' or a 'finding of roots' or the release of sap inside an apparently dead tree. For others, awakening was a more gradual process of 'healing' and 'transforming', of 'becoming more my own person' or 'finding a centre'. Awakening was described as 'recovery of something very old', the unearthing of buried treasure, or simply, the feeling that 'it's alright to be' oneself, one's existence is ratified.

The women's stories also identified the diversity of contexts within which the experience of awakening could take form. These range from departures and journeys to the discovery of creative abilities, different sorts of relationships and limit situations such as death and illness.

Leaving Home, Making the Break, Separation[4]

For a number of the women in my study, breakthrough to a new state of faith was experienced as a result of a choice to leave what had become constraining, paralysing or death-dealing, whether this was a relationship, a community, a particular project, a religious commitment or an understanding of God. This choice was often experienced as fearful, enormously risky and against all reason, or flying in the face of authority figures, yet it was sensed to be absolutely necessary, an insistent drive towards freedom which could only be resisted at great cost.

Elizabeth, the young woman who experienced a kind of 'breakdown' at university, spoke of a turning point in her life when she decided not to return to university but to get an 'ordinary job' and buy a house. Whilst superficially, separation from home had already been accomplished when she left home to go to university, psychologically the significant exodus was the choice to go against the grain of her entire former life and quit university altogether. 'Being academic' for Elizabeth had been, from childhood, a way of forging a secure identity in opposition to her dysfunctional family. To contemplate jettisoning this identity was experienced by Elizabeth as 'the most difficult ... decision of my life at that time'. Deciding to

---

[4] See Hess (1997, pp. 156ff) for an insightful discussion about the ways in which the church can support women to leave homes where there is 'no inheritance' for them; particularly households where women are abused.

opt out of university and choosing to work instead felt 'the riskiest thing anybody could ever [do] in life' because it was both to challenge the norm for an academically able young woman like herself and, more fundamentally, it was to put at risk the self she had carefully constructed over the years. Whilst she had a sense that 'there were more important things in life than academia', she 'didn't quite know what they were' since she had never experienced them. Yet she felt that she had to leave behind the security of the known self if she were to discover the new. This was deeply frightening, leaving her with a sense 'of not knowing' or 'recognis[ing] myself'; even, at one point, thinking 'that I didn't exist'. Yet though her sense of her known, established self was breaking down, there was some other level of self, described as a 'something', a 'core', 'parts of myself that ... had laid ... bitterly neglected for all my life', which seemed to be demanding recognition and for which she needed to make a radical choice.

The decision to opt for this unknown, neglected self was not so much a rational choice as a choice to 'trust my intuition', and this, too, was a risky process because it represented giving power precisely to the neglected, unknown part of herself which she had not trusted up to this point in her life and which was telling her things both compelling and frightening. Having made the choice for intuition over against rationality, for the unknown over against the familiar, for what her own self was telling her over against the voices of other authorities, Elizabeth experienced an awakening of self and of spirituality which she described as a process of learning to live again, almost as if she had been reborn and needed to reconstruct her whole life from scratch:

> I just went through the sort of process of
> of getting used to sort of living really
> you know going to work each day and coming home
> learning to feed myself
> and learning to keep the home and ...
> I feel like you know years
> years were
> were just sort of ploughed into
> learning those very fundamental sort of skills of
> of life really

Whilst at the time, Elizabeth would not have thought of this process in terms which included God, she now felt that this rebirth of the self was a profoundly spiritual process, though she struggled with the language to express this, speaking of a 'strange overlap' between 'what is intuition' and 'what is the spiritual'. Elizabeth's description of her experience confirms Carol Christ's hypothesis that when women make a choice for their own selfhood and for claiming some neglected part of the self, they experience this as a connection to the 'powers of being' that uphold the struggling-to-be-born self.

For many women, the choice to leave home – the psychological place of security, familiarity and boundedness – entailed a long process of struggle, marked by paralysis and powerlessness, and often preceded by a whole series of lesser choices which enabled the woman to come to the point of being able to make the decisive break. Often, too, the psychologically significant turning point was not an obvious one; whilst it sometimes corresponded to an outwardly dramatic turning point, often it did not.

Rachel's departure from her religious community was a long and complex process, marked by a number of phases, each of which contained its own crisis of faith-identity and its own temporary resolution, enabling her to move on to face the next challenge, until she came finally to the point of exodus. Each of the breakthroughs was marked by a religious experience that crystallised the transition from one state into another. A major turning point came when, due to return to the country in which she had been working, Rachel became ill and recognised that she could not go back. So she asked for an extension of her leave. Although the final decision to leave actually came much later, this was the decisive moment. In language similar to that of Elizabeth, Rachel described this moment as 'the most difficult decision I have ever made in my life', emphasising the risk that is part of the process of awakening. It was so difficult because it was a public acknowledgement that there was something wrong; Rachel was, for the first time, admitting to others that she could no longer maintain the outward form of her life. More powerfully, this choice was experienced as

> taking my life in my hands ...
> taking control of my life
> and making a decision
> and following it through
> with the consequences that it would have on others
> and on me

It was 'the first time in my life really/ I had made a decision based upon/ what my body and my *need/* was telling me.' Rachel's description of her choice to listen to 'what my body and my *need* was telling me' over and against the dictates of conscience or some external authority is similar to Elizabeth's description of her choice based on 'intuition', and seems to correspond to what Belenky and her colleagues (1986) describe as the movement from 'received knowledge' to 'subjective knowledge', where intuitive and bodily knowing are prioritised over the authoritative dictates of others. This movement seems to be a particularly difficult one for women who sense themselves caught in religious paralysis to make, for it entails the rejection of the voices of patriarchal authority and a lonely stand against the combined forces of religious tradition and reason. Whilst there is a strong inner compulsion driving the woman to take this stand, she feels terribly exposed and vulnerable, her newly-sensed powers of intuition and self-knowledge fragile and untested.

Rachel's decision to ask for an extension of leave was the beginning of the end for her. Her extension was extended and extended, until finally it became clear that she would have to leave because 'there was nothing left to go back to'. All the things which had previously given religious life meaning had simply fallen away. The final phase was marked by a moment of religious experience whilst on retreat, when she came into the empty chapel one evening and, in the silence came to a realisation that it was fear alone that was holding her back from leaving. This was for her 'a terrible realisation' because it went entirely against the grain of the Gospel of freedom to which she was committed. Once she realised that she was 'living out of fear' and 'acknowledged the dark shadowy fears in me', 'they were gone':

it was like cutting the last tiny thread
and after that
everything else was just downhill
there was nothing else to hold me ...
and I felt so free
I stood up in this big wide empty chapel
put this wonderful music system on
and danced all around the room ...
and just felt
a huge burden lifted off me

Once this recognition was allowed into consciousness, it was impossible to go back to the former awareness. Although the decision still had to be acted upon, the critical point of awareness had been reached, and the carrying out of the decision was experienced as 'easy', 'simple', conflict-free.

For some women, the 'breakthrough' to a new ability to act and think for themselves came relatively late in life, and required a number of separations. Sarah was in her late sixties at the time of the interview, and recounted a number of separate, though related, 'leavings', all of which seemed in some way to be essential to her emerging sense of self and spirituality. Retirement from her demanding professional job gave her the freedom to explore other avenues, including counselling and various women's groups. These new openings eventually gave her the courage to leave the church which for years she had experienced as increasingly irrelevant to her own needs. A decision to move out from living with her long-time partner to set up house on her own was a more ambivalent choice, yet one which she recognised as crucial to developing her confidence in her own capabilities and the freedom to pursue her emerging spiritual path. Reflecting on this move, Sarah commented:

the whole experience ...
has been a very very freeing thing for me
because I've always been a person that
wanted to be a follower rather than a leader
felt very lacking in confidence
and was glad to have somebody else
to be the leader and tell me what to do
but although for some years I'd actually begun to feel
pretty disgruntled about that and
angry about it and em ...
em I still
I couldn't get away from it ...
living alone
has given me the freedom
has made it necessary for me to
do some things I've not done before
and think things out for myself
and so on

For women whose choices in the past have always been made in relation to some external authority, whether it be God, a parent, partner or the authorities of the church, the significance of making one's own choice for freedom and self-definition cannot be overemphasised. Such separation and willingness to stand alone may or may not accompany a literal leave-taking, but the significant shift is in the stance of owning and acting upon her own awareness and being willing to pay the price of separation in order to birth the new self. Conversely, a literal departure from home or relationship or faith community may or may not signal a genuine transition into new awareness, although such outward changes are often the catalysts for real stage change.

Travel to Another Country, People or Place

For a number of the women in my group, travel was a significant catalyst of developmental change. Travel has always been valued for its potential, through the experience of dehabituation, to renew and intensify self-awareness and religious faith (compare Miles, 1988, Chapter 3). Travel can provide a distance from the all-consuming demands of the everyday domestic and professional realm which enables women to see their normal life-setting and values more clearly and, in this light, to make fresh choices. The journey away from home may be necessary to loosen the connections to the normal situation and to enable one to contemplate the possibility of another life. Or, conversely, the distancing from one's ordinary situation may evoke a realisation of its real value, and send one back to it with fresh commitment. The women's experiences of travel included both of these possibilities, and others besides.

For Marion, a religious sister in her sixties, travel had always been important as a means of self-discovery, and had formed, throughout her life, a counterpart to her commitment to stability. From an early age, Marion had moved home frequently, and had spent some of her childhood in India, where she imbibed a tremendous love for the vast expanses of the countryside, associated for her ever since with the lure of solitariness, prayer and 'the wild'. Travelling, she told me, 'often sets me free', providing space and time away from everyday demands, not only to be in touch with herself, but also with the 'incredible patience of the land' and, however fleetingly, with the lives of the people who belong to and live on the land. Later on, Marion had the opportunity to live for a time in an Indian ashram. This was 'a most marvellous freeing experience', allowing her to enter much more deeply into Indian spirituality, to learn the Vedas and Upanishads and to absorb into herself some of the 'haunting and beautiful' Indian music, a process which she experienced as a kind of homecoming at the same time as an affirmation of her Christian spirituality.

Recognising the significant part that her travels had played in the 'awakenings' to fuller spiritual life and self-awareness, Marion nevertheless affirmed that the essential journey is the internal one of becoming real with herself, with others, and with God, and that this journey requires an ability to stay with the present realities of the day-to-day, whatever they are, and to discern the presence of God in the here and now:

My one prayer now is
'O God make me real
make me be the *real* me
before You and with other people' ...
And that's it really
you can't ask for anything else because
because God is *there*
in every encounter in every
everywhere you go em
and wherever you go he's been
he's there already

Sheila, like Marion, looked back on a life of travelling with a certain amount of ambivalence. She recognised a 'repeated pattern of trying to get *away* to something better', manifested in a deep psychological desire to travel. The actual experience of travel had been mixed, often failing to live up to her expectations, and merely intensifying her loneliness. Yet, in retrospect, she felt that travel had allowed her to take significant steps in freeing herself from the shackles of a restrictive upbringing and an internalised punitive God. As a child in Ireland, Sheila had longed to go away to boarding school and had pestered her parents until they allowed it. Initially, it was 'an absolute disaster' and she was 'incredibly lonely'; but after a while 'I sort of became more my own person, I seemed to be able to blossom more there'. Later, unable to take up a university place, she moved to the city to work and 'broke out a bit then', developing a passion for the theatre and going out with boys. An opportunity to go to France as an *au pair* came her way, but 'that was even a worse disaster than the convent' and she was 'really, really lonely there'. Nevertheless, 'that was the beginning of my travels', and it was followed by moving to England and living with people who weren't religious at all. She horrified her family by marrying a non-Catholic and moving to South America to live with her husband, but this allowed them a 'distance' which 'sort of softened people' and enabled a healing of the family feud. Whilst these experiences of travel formed escape-routes from painful conflicts in herself and in her family which Sheila could not fully face, they also represented a gradual 'broadening' of horizons which began to impinge on Sheila's fragile sense of self, offering her alternative choices to the ones she had found so restrictive and unsatisfying hitherto. Being away from the narrow cultural and religious environment of her family seemed to allow her to 'try on' different ideas and identities and, over time, conceive a freely-chosen self. Later trips to cultures where Christianity is not the main religion were particularly significant for Sheila. She 'found so many things in Buddhism and Hinduism/ which seemed so like Catholicism to me', thus opening up an awareness of 'the universality of this experience called religion'. Such encounters contributed to a developing sense of herself 'as a religious person but not attached to any particular church', and enabled her to leave behind what she experienced as the oppressive and limiting codes of Catholicism, and yet still to acknowledge her own deep religious roots and needs. For Sheila, as for many other women, the outer journeys both mirrored and facilitated the inner journey.

For some women who have the sense of not belonging in their own culture or environment, travel to another culture can provide a sense of homecoming and a validation of the self impossible in the 'home' setting. For Anna, the Russian academic whose experience of Communist culture was stifling, a visit to England on an academic exchange and a chance stay with a Quaker family represented the opening up of a new world and the beginning of a process of radical questioning of her society's norms. Although she was not able to leave her country again for a further 18 years, this short exchange visit as a young student took on a symbolic significance, representing the possibility of another way of life, one which included making a positive choice for moral and religious values.

For Hilary, a second-generation black British woman who had always had the sense of 'living between two cultures', visiting her parents' home in the Caribbean was a disconcerting experience. She found that she no more belonged there than she did in England, experiencing the place as 'vivid', 'like paradise' but 'foreign', and being regarded herself as 'a foreigner'. However, a later trip to Africa was 'a good experience' which provided a kind of mirror or window through which she could look and recognise herself in the people she met, especially in the women in church leadership who seemed to think like her and share her sense of faith:

> they almost gave *me* a sense of *ratifying* my existence
> of my existence of being alright ...
> em because they thought
> in the ways that I thought
> and looked at things in the way I looked at things ...
> and so that was a good experience
> and I felt it was alright to be black
> and I also saw black women in leadership ...
> which was something that I
> very rarely experienced here
> and it almost gave me a feeling 'Yes
> I can do what they are doing'
> seeing them in action

For both Anna and Hilary, these journeys out of their native environment, brief though they were, enabled a kind of 'ratification' of the models of selfhood to which they aspired yet for which they found no support in their own context. For Dala, in contrast, it was the journey 'home', to her native country, after a number of years away, which enabled her to discover that she actually belonged elsewhere. An Indian religious who had come to England to run a church-sponsored advice centre for Gujurati-speaking immigrants in a large inner-city area, Dala returned to India when her initial contract expired, with a longing to work amongst her own people. Yet in India, she was unable to find a job, even though she had qualifications. Through this experience, she felt that 'God really broke my pride':

> but God was preparing me
> I was in India jobless for one year
> and that was uh
> preparation ground for me ...
> God made me see that my place wasn't in India

The trip to India, with its humbling experience, enabled her to recognise the importance of the work in England and to return with a renewed commitment to it, coming back 'at peace' and in 'contentment', knowing that 'this is the place where God wants me to be.' Yet it needed the journey to make this discovery.

In these accounts of journeys, there is a contrast between those which are identified, perhaps in somewhat idealised fashion, as occasions of enlightenment and awakening, and those which are recognised as rather more ambivalent, failing to meet one's idealised expectations and throwing one back onto one's own resources, yet offering a new perspective upon them. For these women, travel offered both a space for discovery of new horizons and possibilities and the challenge of coming to terms with self-limitation, fallibility and the givenness of one's own context.

Coming Home, Finding One's Centre, Coming to Rest

At the polar opposite to the experience of separation lies the experience of finding one's place of belonging in intimate human or human/divine connection. For many women, knowing oneself loved and accepted by the human other was the setting for a profound homecoming and sense of awakening to self and the divine. Through the experience of intimacy, women came to a new self-acceptance, and this released energy, joy and a deep sense of connectedness to others and to the natural world. Often this was mediated through romantic and sexual love (although such relationships were also ambivalent for many of the women), but it was also experienced in the powerful bond of friendship, especially with other women, in the experience of sharing within a close-knit community, and in the love of parents and siblings (the latter emphasised especially by women from cultures where devotion to the parental home is strong), as well as in the connection to their own child or children (considered separately below).

For Helen, the experience of sexual intimacy in her early twenties was a means of overcoming a profound ambivalence about the body which she had inherited from her family, and an acceptance of sexuality as 'a fundamental part of who I am'. In contrast, Ruth had only recently found a partner with whom she felt she could allow the vulnerable, needy self to be seen, after years of being in a succession of sexual relationships which avoided genuine intimacy. Her new partner was described as her 'carer': someone who 'pours love upon me' and 'into me' 'with great generosity'. This relationship had become the locus of her self-discovery and spiritual centre. Through such experiences of sexual intimacy, these women came into a knowledge of their acceptance, affirmation and desirability by the other, an experience which was freeing and energising and which mediated to them the all-embracing love of God. Sometimes, however, the sense of intimate connection, healing and acceptance was gained at a price, especially in relationships with male partners, and women spoke of the struggle to maintain genuine self-ownership alongside intimacy with the other without collapsing the needs of the self – a theme to which we shall return in more detail in the next chapter.

For a number of my interviewees, the 'breakthrough' relationships had been with other women. For Hurdeep, an Indian Christian from a poor family who experienced a good deal of social ostracism from high-caste Hindus during her childhood, several nuns featured as important figures in her narrative as those who mediated the intimate, nurturing love of God, described as those who 'helped me', 'took care of me' and were 'like a mother ... who gave me birth'. For Sarah, whose upbringing had placed a strong taboo on all expression of emotion and sexuality, the development of a loving, physical relationship with another woman was beset with conflict and guilt. Nevertheless, it was also experienced as the means of extraordinary liberty and self-acceptance, something 'very very rich' which 'widened' and 'enriched' life and 'gave me an experience of love that I'd never had in any other way at all'. For Sue, the woman who was raped during her early twenties, 'being in relationship with a woman and being loved' had been the means of 'transforming and healing' her anger against men and God, as well as enabling her to accept her sexuality.

Sally's experience of shared intimacy with another woman provided the context for a profound turning point in her relationship to God, in which her former model of God as patriarchal father-figure finally broke down and a new vision of God as loving, tender presence was born. She described going on retreat, where her spiritual director invited her to meditate on the parable of the Prodigal Son and imagine herself in the story. Although she 'managed to change [her]self to the daughter', she experienced great difficulty in imagining the 'father-figure' welcoming her home, so much so that she was unable to finish the exercise. Later that night, she dreamt of a woman who 'came and stood over me/ and kind of *looked* at/ and then/ *came* and just *lay* with me/ and and kind of embraced me'. The following morning, when she returned to the meditation on the parable, she realised that her dream had resolved her dilemma and given her a new image of God to take the place of the father whom she had had such difficulty in conjuring. The 'return to God' was actualised for Sally through the dream image of the female lover who embraced her and lay with her. Sally recognised that this experience 'wasn't just out of the blue', but 'was part of a real relationship' with an intimate woman friend, a relationship which was 'incredibly liberating' and which 'taught me more of who God was' than any overt teaching, providing a 'way into' 'this God of incredible tenderness' and a 'Lover relationship' with that newly imaged God.

About a third of the women in my group had had experience of being in a counselling or therapeutic relationship of various kinds (reflecting the middle-class cultural milieu of many of the women), and for a number of these, this relationship had been a locus of 'awakening'. For Lolita, an Argentinean woman whose powerful sense of vocation was blocked for many years by her church's refusal to ordain women, counselling provided a context, not only for reworking many of her theological beliefs, but also for receiving the affirmation of her sense of vocation – ironically, from an atheist Jewish therapist – which was systematically undermined by her church. This therapeutic relationship enabled her to sustain the sense of calling until the time came when her church was ready to acknowledge it and her dream could be actualised.

For Anne, a therapeutic relationship provided the context in which, some years after having come to personal faith, she came to a deeper experience of the love of God. As a result of 'being loved' and 'knowing [she] was safe' within this relationship, Anne began to be able to accept herself, and accept that she was acceptable to God, and thus to experience loving relationship with God. This process involved allowing herself to feel and express powerful emotions of anger, guilt and fear which she had previously suppressed, and to allow them, not only into the safe context of her relationship with her counsellor, but also into the previously highly circumscribed space of her relationship with God, so that her prayer became transformed into something much more passionate, volatile, risky and *real*. She described this as a process of 'allowing myself to feel the pain I did feel in God's presence' and, more strikingly, 'putting the muck on the cross':

> that Christ wants our sin
> so therefore if I want to scream and yell at my mother
> and say 'I hate you, I hate you, I hate you' ...
> I can do that with the cross there
> and say 'I hate you too you great fuck-head
> O God'
> because it doesn't frighten him and ...
> all he says is 'Father forgive'

For Anne, the essential recognition in this experience of counselling was 'You are acceptable as you are, I'm still here and I'll still love you', and the concrete expression of this unconditional love by the counsellor enabled her to grasp the unconditional love of God.

Similarly for Alice, there had been a long struggle, over years, with the idea of being loved by God, and an inability to experience this love. A relationship with a spiritual director was crucial as the place of sustenance and holding, especially during the time when her child was dying painfully and slowly of an incurable disease. Within this relationship, she was able to come to a gradual acceptance of the love of God for her, but it also enabled her to hold on to her own love for her daughter whilst being able to express the anger and pain she felt about the suffering they were each experiencing. She described this as 'a piece of incarnational theology which is probably almost perfect':

> I mean here's this priest devoting
> *far* too many hours to somebody sitting at
> on his floor saying
> 'I can't believe'
> em and all the other things ...
> and he during that time
> he gave me hundreds of hours
> in a way that no spiritual director should
> but he did
> he burnt himself out in the process but
> he saw us through
> and what can we be but *hugely hugely* grateful?

The accounts so far all emphasise the significance of the one-to-one encounter as the context of healing; however, for a number of the women, the experience of acceptance and belonging within a group setting was equally powerful. Church communities, house groups or fellowship meetings, places of retreat or religious communities provided a context within which some women experienced the sense of 'coming home' to themselves, to truth and to God, suggesting that the church is not *always* a place of oppression and exclusion for women, but can also be a place of care and sustenance. For some, though not for all, of these women, a specific physical location – church building, site of pilgrimage or monastic community – had particular significance as the mediating symbol of God's love. Where the woman's home-life had been unsettled or lacking in security, there was something peculiarly powerful about an ancient historical site or a well-established religious community which could offer a grounding to the woman's developing identity. This was the case for Sue, whose childhood, adolescence and early adulthood had been marked by geographical mobility, frequent changes in her education and career, and difficulties in her marriage. She located the beginning of her emergence as a person in her own right from the time when she moved, with her husband, to a small village and got involved in the local church, school and community. 'It was like coming home'; so strong was the sense of home-coming that it felt 'like I'd been there before'. The church, in particular, was her 'family', her 'spiritual sanctuary', the place about which she still feels

> Oh I belong there
> that is home
> that is still ...
> my spiritual home is there ...
> up through that path
> and through the door ...
> um it's like a womb to me
> going in there
> it's very safe

Meg, too, spoke of the way in which physical place – particularly the church building – had been an important symbol of belonging and safety throughout her childhood, providing her with a place of calm, order and security which she did not receive from her family. One of her earliest childhood memories was of walking into a church for the first time, and thinking to herself, 'This is it, I've found it ... I've found you, it's the universe here.' That experience of 'just kind of being there' 'planted something in me', a sense 'that it was going into somewhere good somehow' which had stayed with her ever since. Very early on, then, church became for her 'my safe haven', and this feeling was identified as the source of her faith: 'Belonging to God started very much/ with that finding somewhere to belong that was safe.' Throughout her life, church buildings and groups of people had been important in providing the continuity of that sense of 'safe place'. Yet Meg was also aware of the way in which her need for safety had diminished as she had increasingly internalised the security and had learnt to accommodate greater degrees of risk and conflict in the communities to which she belonged. Thus, in speaking of a women's group which had been an important nurturing group for her more recently, she noted the way in which the group was not only a 'safe place' but also an 'open place' which was 'very challenging and very stimulating' at the same time as being 'very supportive':

> It was a different sort of safety again
> because the walls had completely [come down]
> it was that kind of safety of being in a completely open place with people

Whilst the group or the building were necessary as mediating symbols of the safety of divine love, Meg's awakening to her own internal security meant that she was no longer so dependent upon outside factors to provide the security she needed for her selfhood to flourish. She demonstrates the gradual extension of the powers of selfhood to wider and riskier contexts which we have seen is a feature of women's growth in wholeness over time. Indeed, most of these accounts of homecoming and finding a centre suggest, not one moment of awakening, but an ongoing, often gradual process of working through paralysis and dependency, usually marked by struggle and ambivalence, towards increasing confidence and security of selfhood, in which the support and affirmation of the human other is an important source of strength and encouragement.

The Experience of Motherhood

For good or for ill, giving birth to one's own child and becoming intimately involved with the work of child-rearing, is a major turning point in a woman's life, both an experience of profound biological change as well as an induction into a role and a set of expectations which are, to a large degree, socially constructed, and which may undermine, as well as strengthen, a woman's sense of self (compare Bons-Storm, 1996, pp. 98ff). For both women and men, becoming parents is one of those major life changes which may well precipitate qualitative, structural change, but for women these changes are often more profound and dramatic, both because of the significant bodily changes accompanying mothering and because of the weight of social expectation upon women to care for children. Even where a woman may challenge and reject social expectations around motherhood, she cannot but engage with these expectations in some way, shape or form. Whereas my interviews contained a range of narratives about motherhood, some of which emphasised the oppressiveness of social expectations around mothering, in what follows I focus on those narratives which highlighted mothering as a positive experience of awakening and birthing of the self for some women.

At the time of the interview with Jane, her first baby was some six months old and her experience of motherhood dominated the interview. Jane spoke of her newfound experience of herself in relation to her baby as someone capable of profound feelings of delight, joy and intimacy, with a new awareness of deep connectedness to other human beings through her baby. This self-description contrasted sharply with descriptions of herself as someone who found it difficult to be in touch with her emotions, who struggled to connect different aspects of her experience and who was working to overcome recurring patterns of getting 'stuck'. Jane's language in describing her feelings towards her baby and what he had enabled to come to birth in her could be described as religious in both content and intensity. She described him as a 'gift' with which she had been 'presented', and who had 'given so much meaning to things'. He had given her 'far more than I've ever given him', 'boosted my confidence' and 'opened up ... / all these connections with people', enabling her to be 'much more open to other people/much more connected', and experiencing a kind of solidarity with all other mothers and their children the world over, so that 'when I see injustices happening to children [I] feel enraged.' Jane's baby appeared to function for her as a kind of *alter ego*, capable both of giving and receiving affection in a way which Jane herself had been unable to do.

Meg, who had also recently given birth at the time of the interview, but to her fourth rather than her first child, was able to reflect on the experience of motherhood from a larger vantage point and express something of the paradox experienced by Jane: namely, that absorption in the demanding process of motherhood and the prioritising of the needs of the newborn infant over the needs of the self, can, in some strange way, occasion a new kind of connection to the self; that relation to the infant and the 'loss of self' demanded by the absorption in the needs of the other may nevertheless create a space within which some more immediate, bodily awareness of self can flourish; that the constantly evolving relationship with one's child provides an opportunity for reflecting upon, reworking and reforging one's own childhood and relations to one's own parents. Meg acknowledged that, in her day-to-day experience of motherhood, there was a tension between the needs of the self and the needs of the other, and that, when there was a conflict, it was often 'the me bit that gets ... chopped off the end'. Nevertheless, the being 'submerged' in motherhood also offered a path of self-understanding and integration of her past which would have been difficult to forge any other way:

> when I look at the last nine years ...
> I mean there is something about kind of
> you're almost submerged in something
> for long periods
> and *yet* I've learnt a lot about myself
> um and learnt a lot of where my reactions come from ...
> and a lot of my kind of piecing together my childhood
> has been through having children
> and I'm not sure what else would have released that
> really

Not only had the journey of motherhood provided the context of self-understanding and growth; it had also opened up for Meg dimensions of her relationship to God which could not have been mediated any other way. For Meg, 'the sheer physical closeness that you can get from children' is a way into 'the mystical experience of God'. The experience of breast-feeding in the half-light, half-dark, half-awake, half-asleep state of the middle of the night 'actually gives me a different kind of prayer life and a different kind of reflection than I would normally have', giving 'a whole kind of different slant to things'.

Whilst Meg and Jane represent different faith stances, both their accounts emphasise a bodily knowing rooted in embeddedness, physicality and interconnectedness, in which the self is not threatened by absorption in the other but freed to experience itself in a qualitatively distinct fashion. At the same time, their accounts illuminate something of women's struggle to maintain a sense of self whilst absorbed in the demands and needs of the other. Women whose sense of self is fragile or deeply wounded may find the demands of the child so overwhelming as to occlude and obliterate all sense of their own independent emotional life, with its own rhythms, needs and integrity; for such women, the experience of childbirth and mothering may contribute to the paralysis and fragmentation of self we noted in

Chapter 5. On the other hand, the very experience of having to respond to a child's or children's incessant demands *can*, over time, compel a woman to grapple with her own needs and establish a stronger self which can survive the demands of parenting. Whilst Jane struggled to articulate what the experience of motherhood might mean for her sense of spirituality, Meg articulated powerfully her awareness of intimate relationship with God mediated by motherhood, in which faith is experienced, not primarily in conceptual terms, but in the immediate bodily awareness of interrelationship with one's child, in which the self is both feeding and fed, denied and affirmed, offered and received.

Relating to the Vulnerable, Marginal or Suffering Other

For other women in my group, the experience of being in relationship to suffering, vulnerable, marginal or previously alien groups or individuals proved the means of discovering a profound connection to self and God. For Stella, an Irish Catholic sister, going to work in the Philippines in 'an extremely poor area' was 'a really freeing experience' which issued in an abiding sense of 'the amazing worth of the human person', 'the *mystery* of the person' and 'the absolute *value* of the person', and taught her how to 'allow myself to be touched by that mystery, and to be part of that'. At the time of the interview, Stella was living and working in an inner-city area overseeing the formation work of the community. Whilst outwardly a world apart from the Philippines, Stella's work with novices in her community and with the neighbours in their area entailed the same willingness to commit herself unconditionally to others, to listen and receive their stories and discern the presence of God within them. Although she sometimes railed against the demands of being such a presence to others – 'Why should I have to listen to this?' 'Why should I get involved?' – she discovered that, as she was willing to commit herself to the process of living with and 'holding parts of people's lives and stories', she was able to perceive 'the sense of how God does work in people's lives and how things unfold'. For Stella, as for other women discussed in this section, the movement towards an increasing integration of faith and freedom of selfhood was achieved, not through separation from others, but precisely through an unconditional commitment to others with whom one may share little obvious connection. Yet these women were able to sustain this kind of commitment to others because they had already established a level of selfhood which was secure enough to withstand absorption in the other.

For Hurdeep, an Indian religious who was working at an inter-faith centre, meeting and working with people of different faiths had been a major challenge to her previously conventional faith. During her upbringing in India, she was taught to perceive the practices of other faiths as 'devil worship or something' so that, initially, it was extremely difficult for Hurdeep even to contemplate attending a Sikh or Hindu temple. Yet through her work at the centre she had learnt to relate to those who hold very different religious beliefs and practices as 'person to person', 'very much in partner[ship]', so that now 'I'm not any more judgemental' [*sic*], 'there's more and more finding God in other people.' 'Today I would say "Well, there's something good in them, something good in you and something good in others"'. It was only as she had been willing to risk the loss of the previously rigid religious identity that she had discovered a larger and freer identity, reflected in a wider vision of the love of God, which was able to embrace, rather than reject, the strangeness of the other.

For Emma, a highly intelligent woman who described herself as a 'quite articulate word-based' person, working and spending time with 'people who are very different from me', especially people with severe learning disabilities, had been an essential means of encountering 'the other, the transcendent'. This had been an important ingredient in a process of moving away from a faith directed towards an external God-figure and explicit religious practices to an internalised notion of the transcendent and a faith lived out entirely in the day-to-day activities of work, meetings with others and 'ordinariness'. Emma's work at a hospital for people with severe learning difficulties had brought her into touch with 'the oppression and limits of life' and taken her into a world 'where I'm exposed to ... human otherness which is different from myself'. In the meeting with human otherness she discovered the transcendent:

> I think the point where I feel most closely um
> related to the other as transcendent
> is when I can see
> in myself the ability
> to be with the other in
> in their otherness

Spending time with one of the people in the hospital for whom she was an advocate and 'being with him' in a real meeting was, for Emma, an experience of transcendence, 'the most powerful/ sort of presence of/ of God or transcendent really', 'mediated through the one who can help us cross those boundaries'. In her emphasis on the embrace of otherness and plurality, Emma typifies Fowler's Stage 5 maturity of faith (marked by the embrace of polar opposites in some kind of synthesis, the reintegration of symbol and concrete image with conceptual thought, the recognition of mystery at the heart of things), yet she expresses this style of faith in a distinctively embedded, relational way which seems characteristic of women. Emma also recognised that this being with people who are different and 'learning different languages that people use – verbal and not verbal' was a way for her to compensate for her emotionally distant upbringing, allowing her not only to give but also to receive 'comfort and to express truth and faith' in non-verbal, non-cerebral ways.

Lesley also spoke of how the encounter with the marginalised 'other' mediated healing, acceptance and a new level of integration of faith. She told the story of attending a pilgrimage to a famous Catholic pilgrim site with a group of disabled people and their families. At the heart of her narrative, she told of an experience of inner healing and cleansing which took place when, accompanied by one of the disabled young men in the group, she went down into the grotto and they washed one another's faces and hands. In this encounter, Lesley's accustomed roles were reversed and subverted. Used to being in charge, a competent and revered authority figure in both church and work setting, she found herself in this moment the learner, the led, dependent on the young man, who, in any other situation would have been the dependent one, yet in this situation, 'was competent where I wasn't'. Holding hands, walking around the grotto with this young man, Lesley's habitual modes of thought and language became redundant and, abandoning the need for conceptualisation and control, she entered, with the young man – who, uncannily, even shared her name – into an experience of grace and healing mediated by touch, symbolic gesture and the elemental power of water. With him, she 'became simple', childlike, trusting and receptive. This experience was described in terms reminiscent of baptism, in which Lesley went down into the waters of the grotto and shed her familiar identity and status and, as she let the 'old self' go, gave birth to a new self characterised by vulnerability, simplicity, acceptance and wholeness.

As with the experience of motherhood, connection to the suffering, vulnerable other is, potentially, an ambivalent experience for women. Because women are socialised to care for others, and to put their own needs on hold in favour of the needs of others, empathy and absorption in the demands of others can put the self at danger. Hess (1997) has reminded us that female caring can go hand in hand with the loss of the self, especially during the stage of Kegan's interpersonal self or Fowler's synthetic-conventional faith stage, when the self is strongly oriented to the expectations of others and needs the approval of peers to bolster its own convictions and beliefs. The women in my study who spoke most movingly and compellingly of their experiences of connecting with the vulnerable other were all women who had moved through this stage into a more firmly established and owned selfhood and faith, and for whom therefore the danger of collapsing or evaporating the self had been overcome. They were able to offer the self to the other in genuine connection because they had a real self to share.

Discovering One's Own Creative Voice or Sphere

Awakening came for many of the women in and through the discovery of their creative gifts and abilities, the exercise of these gifts and their recognition and affirmation by others. The releasing of creative energies in painting, writing, teaching, preaching, pastoral ministry, or whatever the particular vocation may be, was experienced as both a means and a guarantee of personal power, vitality and awareness. When the woman's creative gifts were affirmed by others, whether in terms of a publicly approved role or not, the sense of power and identity was enhanced and deepened.

The discovery of her talent for painting during adolescence was an important stage of self-definition for Anne, meeting a need 'to be good at something' that marked her out from her academically gifted brother, offering her a sphere of her own not shared by her siblings. Looking back, Anne saw a 'parallel' between her painting and her spirituality, the one mirroring the other. During her adolescence and early adulthood, painting eclipsed religion as a means of discerning beauty, order and balance, but in more recent years art and prayer had come together and both were experienced by Anne as a way of seeing, a 'sort of gazingness', a way of paying attention to and being in relation to the 'Thou' who is at the heart of all existence. In a similar fashion, Lorna spoke of her rediscovery of painting in recent years as a way into a new dimension of faith. Painting was for her a costly and risky 'way of wrestling' 'with things that [are] unspeakable, wordless experience'; it was

a 'dialogue with God' in which the canvas became a 'spiritual companion'
confronting her with questions, 'What is this? What is God saying to me? What does
it mean? Why have I painted this?' Painting was a 'daily process' of 'living by faith'
in which she had to 'go back to the beginning every time'. Painting for Lorna was
a process of self-exploration and dialogue with God which converged with her
prayer so that to paint was experienced *as* 'a way of praying'. Rather like Meg's
paradoxical self-discovery through submersion in the creative activity of mothering,
Lorna's experience of being wholly absorbed in the 'lonely' work of painting
became the medium of faith and awareness of God.

For Sheila, poetry had 'put me in touch with a lot of things which I was perhaps
aware of but not/ I didn't think of them as *spiritual*'. Keeping a journal had 'become
very important to me' as 'a sort of soul journey'. The process of writing itself seemed
'to throw up all sorts of things [on] the journey', functioning as a kind of 'examination
of conscience', a means of self-exploration, and, at the same time, a 'bottomless well'
of hope and life. For Lesley, the discovery of a poetic voice alongside the development
of a preaching ministry had offered a vehicle for a 'creative and dynamic integration'
of the rational and affective dimensions of faith. She reflected on the way in which
writing for her was an experience of spirituality as gift, in which the Gospel
imperative of losing the self in order to find it is worked out:

Actually when I am least self-conscious
is when I'm sitting at my word-processor writing
and there is absolute *total* concentration
and em that is in a sense
when I totally deny myself
because I'm not
I'm not in it
and yet I am *quintessentially* in it

Here again, there is the experience of being wholly absorbed in some creative
activity and losing all sense of self, yet being most in touch with the self and its
powers.

For a number of women, the affirmation by others of a particular calling and its
realisation had been a significant turning point in the movement from a divided self
and a blocked faith to empowerment. Sue, an Anglican priest, described her journey
towards ordained ministry in imagery which reflects its significance for her own
development. The recognition of her potential for ministry and its bringing to birth
took place within the 'womb' of the parish church where she felt she had finally
'come home' after years of searching; the male priest who nurtured her vocation and
helped to realise it was the 'midwife' who 'transformed me' and 'brought to birth',
not only her vocation to ministry, but a new self, mirrored in the birth of her two
children during the same stage of her life. For Judith, ordination to priesthood had
brought 'a sense of fulfilment', 'as if I have arrived where God wants me to be', a
confirmation of her conviction that, against all the odds, 'it is possible to *achieve*, to
become whatever [you] want to be.' For Alice, the realisation of a childhood
vocation to be an academic, whilst often in tension with her vocation to prayer and
to marriage, had offered healing of the 'breakdown' she experienced as a young
undergraduate and a counterbalance to the acute suffering experienced during her

life. For Pam, a reluctant acceptance of the role of church warden was 'the biggest test of my faith' but one which had ushered in new self-confidence 'to stick up for myself', a new ability 'to be compassionate to the other person' and a deepened trust in the God who provides. For Janet, after years of putting herself in jobs where her own needs were denied, the discovery of an aptitude for adult education and allowing herself to choose jobs which she enjoyed, had been a significant landmark in a struggle to exorcise the oppressive 'voices of the fathers', the internalised judgemental attitude of her own father.

In each of these different spheres of creative work, the women came to a sense of their own capacity for meaningful activity, their own powers of being and a connection to the mysterious source of creativity which they named variously as God, Being or Spirit. For most of these women, the discovery and exercise of their creative talents or particular vocation had been a long and gradual process, frequently requiring courage to stand out against the expectations of others, to be both *visible* and accountable within the public realm, overcoming their own self-doubt and claiming a voice. Being willing to stake all on the chosen calling and taking the risks of failure, rejection and ridicule, these women's insistence on their right to a creative and public voice had enabled them to break through the impasse of voicelessness, invisibility and passivity.

Illness, Suffering, Death and Other Limit Situations

In contrast to experiences of intimate and loving relationship or of connecting to one's creative abilities, experiences of radical loss and limit were also the gateways to new awakening of self and spiritual awareness for some women. Illness, profound suffering of other kinds, the death of a partner or parent, or some other limit situation acted as a catalyst to a new stage of faith. In these situations, radical loss and grief provoked a crisis in which old assumptions, patterns of faith and identity structures were challenged at their core, discovered to be inadequate and fell apart, demanding the restructuring of new, more adequate ways of operating.

For Emma, a long and debilitating illness marked an important movement in her faith development, causing her 'to internalise God or the transcendent within me at a much deeper level' and 'to interact with the world' in a more open and receptive fashion. In terms of her spirituality and perception of God, Emma concluded that her illness 'was probably quite freeing', taking her to 'a new place where I needed to be' and enabling her to let old, inadequate faith structures drop away. For Kate, it was not her own illness but her husband's sudden heart attack, only a matter of months before my interview with her, which 'took my breath away' and 'put a lot of things into question'. The realisation that 'he could have not been there the next day ... makes you kind of think about things', she reflected, in a wry understatement. Yet for Kate, their ability to cope with the situation with 'a great sense of humour' helped her to see that her faith 'is more solid than I think it is sometimes'. The experience crystallised Kate's conviction that 'all will be well', which she discovered she held more securely than she might have anticipated.

The ultimate 'limit situation' is death, and for a significant number of my interviewees, the death of a parent, particularly the death of the father, had proved a major turning point in their lives, both inaugurating massive loss and challenging them to internalise the relationship at a deeper level. For Stella, the death of her mother shortly after she entered religious community had been painful, forcing her to confront the limitations of her chosen life, but the death of her father marked a more radical turning point. She experienced his death both as a profound loss of home and connection as she 'let go' her father and accepted her own radical aloneness, and a discovery of the 'home within my own self', as she accepted the challenge to internalise the longing for home and connection, 'finding roots again, finding a centre' within herself.

Similarly, for Mary, also a religious, the recent death of her father had compelled her to face her own vulnerability and loneliness, yet had also gifted her with a sense of her life as a 'journey to death' and shown her how to take this journey. She described this experience of death as both 'a good experience' and 'a dreadful experience', which had 'changed', 'marked' and 'affected me and my attitude to life' profoundly. As a single person without children, Mary's sense of loss at the death of her parents was acute; she contrasted her loss with that of her brothers and sisters who 'have offspring' and therefore 'a future'. 'Their life continues', 'they ha[ve] somebody to hold onto and somebody to lean onto', whereas for Mary there was a more absolute aloneness and a stripping of future hope. Yet her father's death had opened up a whole new perspective on life, at once relativising the significance of 'external things' – now seen to be 'props on the journey', 'things I can hopefully leave behind [or] just use' – and, at the same time, revealing the true value of 'the little things', none of which are 'just incidental' because 'the way I face things and the way I accept things very much determine how I move in this relationship I have of grace on this journey.'

For Lorna, the death of her father had been an important catalyst towards greater integration of her past, compelling her to recognise, not only the positive aspects of her relationship with him and the contribution these have made to her faith, but also what she described as 'the dark side' of the relationship. His death had freed her to recognise the ways in which she had spent her life 'trying to fulfil my father's expectations', driven by his perfectionism and impossibly high standards and yet constantly failing to win his approval. It had also compelled her to acknowledge the ways in which this harsh side of her relationship to her father had shaped her relationship to God, imbuing the divine Father with the never-to-be-satisfied perfectionism of her own father. Initially, the recognition of the 'dark' side of the relationship with the father had led to profound doubt and the sense that 'the *whole* of faith and spirituality is just a projection of this relationship'; but later Lorna came to realise that '*just* as before I could affirm that God was mediated to me through the *love* of my father' so now she could 'affirm the negative side of my relationship with my father and *see* it as *creative* of me'. Out of this reworking of her previously idealised relationship to her father, the need to build a more satisfactory relationship with her mother had also emerged. The recognition of the complexity and ambiguity of the relation to one parent necessarily invited reconsideration of the relation to the other. Whilst the relation to the father had been idealised, the relation to her mother had been conceived, up until now, in more negative terms. In recognising and integrating both 'dark' and 'light' in her relationship to her father, Lorna found herself challenged to recognise as 'gift' aspects of her relationship to her mother previously denied. Thus the death of the father had freed up the entire nexus of relationships within the family and invited their reconstellation in more adequate and truthful patterns.

Summary and Conclusions

The above accounts of women's descriptions of their experiences of awakening demonstrate the variety and particularity of such experiences. They may be sudden or gradual; they may be short-lived, intense experiences lasting a matter of mere hours or even minutes, or they may cover much longer periods of time during which the issues are worked with again and again until resolution is achieved; they may be perceived as a temporary or a more permanent resolution of paralysis. The accounts also reflect the middle-class privilege of the majority of the women in my study; not all women have opportunities for travel such as they describe, or have educational, vocational and artistic avenues open to them, or even have the luxury of choosing whether to mother children or not; even, we might say, the ability to relate empathically to the suffering other is born from a certain privilege which women for whom daily survival is a priority may be unable to afford.

Recognising the high degree of variety and the particularity in both the nature and the context of the experiences, a number of common and defining features can be noted. First, there is a strong emphasis on ordinary, concrete and mundane experience as the locus of spiritual awakening. Although some women spoke of visionary and mystical experience, this was more rare,[5] and the majority of the women emphasised the embeddedness of their spirituality in the world of the everyday. Even where mystical experience was important, it generally had strong roots in ordinary, mundane experience and served to crystallise or reinforce truths emerging out of the woman's everyday life. This conforms with other studies which describe the contextual and concrete forms of women's preferred ways of knowing and thinking (for example, Gilligan, 1982; Belenky et al., 1986).

Second, there is a strong emphasis on the priority of intuition, bodily knowing and instinct over rational thinking, abstract thought or the dictates of conscience or authority. This suggests that for many of the women, the process of awakening is bound up with the movement from what Belenky and her colleagues describe as the movement from 'silence' or 'received knowledge' to 'subjective knowledge', marked by 'a new conception of truth as personal, private, and subjectively known or intuited' (1986, p. 54), or, for others, with the movement to Fowler's Stage 5, when individuals reclaim and revalue image, symbol and intuition, integrating it with conceptual thought.

Third, there is often, although not always, evidence of what Rosemary Haughton (1982) describes as the period of 'preparation' leading to the critical moment of awakening or breakthrough itself. This is particularly evident in the women's

---

[5] Some of the women shared stories of mystical experience or awareness, whether mediated by dreams, the sense of a voice speaking or in sudden and acute awareness of some reality which seemed to come from outside and to be 'given'. Compare Rachel's account of departure from her religious community, which was marked by a sequence of vivid dreams, religious experience and sudden moments of revelation (pp. 116–17), and Sally's account of a dream on retreat which mediated a new image of God as female lover (p. 122).

accounts of exodus journeys and separations, as well as in their narratives concerning the discovery of creative gifts or particular vocations. Long before the women actualise the decision to break away from what they perceive to be constraining, there is an unconscious movement towards exodus, sometimes taking place over years, which is revealed in dreams or religious experience, or, less obviously, in inarticulate longings, and which is experienced in tension with conscious thought, creating the impasse described in Chapter 5. This tension builds up and finally comes to consciousness, demanding choice. As the unconscious movement towards freedom comes into consciousness, and can no longer be denied, there is a rush of psychic energy which breaks the impasse and carries the woman over the threshold of fear which had previously disabled her from making the choice she knew, at some level, she needed to make.

Fourth, the experience of awakening is marked by a sense of the coming together or coherence of different parts of the self – inner and outer, 'secular' and 'religious', emotion and thought – acting in a unity. This stands in stark contrast to the experience of the 'split self' which marked the experience of paralysis. As the woman acknowledges parts of herself previously denied, there is a liberating and dynamic sense of healing and coming to a deeper sense of reality. Again, this may suggest aspects of Fowler's Stage 5 faith, when integration of previously uncoordinated aspects of self and faith is achieved. As a result of this coming together of the self into a cohesive unity, there is a new sense of power, vitality, energy and confidence in the experience of awakening; the energies which were previously dispersed and employed in maintaining the harmful dichotomies are now released, giving rise to metaphors of liberation, transformation and rebirth.

Fifth, the experience of awakening seems to bring together the sense of actively taking responsibility for the self with the sense of a process of unfolding or bringing to birth which goes far beyond conscious choice or control. There is a new sense of being able to make choices which overcome the passivity of the paralysed self; yet the birth of a new self is also experienced as gift which is received, a grace which is given from beyond the self. This sense of gift and grace does not cancel out the initiative of the self but grounds it in the 'powers of being' which guarantee its freedom. This is a paradox which the women name in a variety of ways, calling on both language of choice, initiative and responsibility as well as language of reception, gift and mystery.

Finally, as is evident from the above, the awakening to new consciousness demands a 'new naming' of self, of reality and of God or one's core values. Things are no longer what they previously seemed; there is a sense of having crossed a threshold into new awareness, and things constellating in a new and richer pattern; this new awareness requires new language, new terms, new images for its expression. There is a developmental challenge of reconstructing not only old understandings of selfhood but also 'received' models of religion and spirituality. For some women, the former patterns of religion are so deeply embedded in passivity, powerlessness and paralysis that they seem incapable of being reworked and are rejected along with the former self-identity. For other women, there is a movement from religion experienced as an external, authoritarian system of rules, beliefs and behaviours, to spirituality experienced as a personally appropriated process of self-knowledge and awareness.

Chapter 7

The Patterns of Women's Faith Development: Relationality

Without our relation there is no God.

Carter Heyward[1]

It come to me: that feeling of being part of everything, not separate at all. I knew that if I cut a tree, my arm would bleed.

Alice Walker[2]

In supporting women's development we need to press for a deep understanding of relationship that does not perpetuate the oppressive burdens put on women to give their selves away in the name of female goodness.

Carol Lakey Hess[3]

Introduction

The third major generative theme to emerge from my findings was the theme of relationality – a theme which has been dominant in many studies of women's spirituality and identity, as we have already seen in Chapter 2. After considering how relationality is understood by some feminist theologians, this chapter maps out the ways in which the women constructed their faith-lives in strongly relational terms, as well as highlighting the exceptions to this rule and the variety of nuanced understandings of relationality present in their narratives. The chapter ends with a summary and discussion of the key findings.

Relationality in Women's Faith Development

As Christie Cozad Neuger (1999, p. 115) affirms, 'relationality has become an organizing concept for talking about women's psychology, feminist ethics, and feminist theology' in recent decades. Feminist psychologists have done much to reclaim and revalue women's nurturing and caring skills, and to demonstrate the sophisticated and nuanced epistemology of connectedness which undergirds women's moral thinking. At the same time, critical debate highlights the need to

---

[1] Heyward (1982), p. 172.
[2] Shug Avery, in Walker (1984), p. 167.
[3] Hess (1997), p. 61.

discriminate between different types of relationality. Not all relationship is good. Women, in particular, may get caught in 'compulsive and compulsory relationality' (Kaschak, 1992, p. 124). As Neuger (1999, p. 115) suggests, 'skilled relationality may be as much a gender-trained service for a patriarchal culture (with its significant costs for women and men) as it is a valuable orientation in women's lives.' There is a tight-rope to be walked between undervaluing women's distinctive relational abilities, on the one hand, and essentialising those qualities in an oppressive stereotype of woman as the 'natural' carer and nurturer of others, on the other.

A number of feminist theologians argue that women's spirituality is embedded in a profound sense of relationality, and have revisioned Christian spirituality in the light of women's distinctive relational awareness. Thus Katherine Zappone (1991) suggests: 'in its broadest sense, spirituality centers on our awareness and experience of relationality. It *is* the relational component of lived experience' (p. 12). She goes on to delineate spirituality in terms of right relation to self, to other, to the earth and to the sacred. Charlene Spretnak (1982) speaks of spirituality as a dynamic impulse towards connectedness in human relationships, social structures and the wider cosmos: 'Spirituality enables us to feel a deep connection between one another. It heals and avoids the fragmented sense that often plagues political movements, in both personal and collective terms. Our bonding is profound' (p. 397).

Carter Heyward (1982, 1984, 1989) has done much to establish a relational approach to theology, and to demonstrate its liberating effects for women. In opposition to alienating notions of deity as oppressive patriarch, Heyward develops the notion of a God who is intimately related to the world, who is source of all relational power and active justice-seeking and who calls for the voluntary participation of human beings in making right relation on the earth here and now. Such a model of God draws much from process theology (for example, Whitehead, 1926, 1929; Hartshorne, 1967, 1970) and thinks in terms of profound interdependence of all reality, including the divine–human relation. 'With us, through us, God lives, God becomes. God changes, God speaks, God acts, God suffers and God dies in the world' (Heyward, 1982, p. 9). Transcendence is not so much denied as radically reinterpreted, as

> ... that fundamental relational power which moves to cross over from people to people, race to race, gender to gender, class to class, binding us into one Body of human and created beings, healing our wounds, breaking down the assumptions and structures that keep us divided, and, through it all, empowering us, each and all, to know and love ourselves and one another as participants in this transcendence. (Heyward, 1984, p. 245)

God's transcendence is not over-and-against us but precisely the source and guarantee of our own ability to reach out and connect with all that appears 'other' and 'different' to us. Redemption is not a process conducted by a divine saviour on our behalf which overcomes our human volition and lifts us out of the pressing demands of the present, but a process of active participation in justice-making which seeks to make good the interconnectedness of all reality which is obscured and denied by sin. Sin is the denial or distortion of relationality, the unwillingness to take up our passion and power to make right relation, and, whenever this happens, God suffers, God dies, God is absent:

Without our touching there is no God.
Without our relation there is no God.
Without our crying, our raging, our yearning, there is no God.
For in the beginning is the relation, and in the relation is the power that creates the world
through us, and with us, and by us, you and I, you and we, and none of us alone.
(Heyward, 1982, p. 172)

Mary Grey (1989, 1993) has built on the work of Heyward to rework Christian
notions of redemption, atonement and revelation in terms of relationality, or what
she now prefers to name 'connectedness'. She sees a certain convergence, not only
in feminist theology, but also in current ecological thinking, creation theology,
organic philosophy, pastoral counselling and women's fiction, all of which point
towards the cosmic significance of connectedness. Together they confirm the basic
feminist conviction that 'interdependence and relating are the very threads of the
complicated tapestry of the world – its warp and woof, to use an old weaving
metaphor' (Grey, 1989, p. 31). Grey understands the basic task of redemption as that
of re-connecting the severed connections, the tangled threads of the creation,
whether that be redeeming broken personal relations, distorted social structures or
the damaged web of creation itself. Such 're-connecting' or 'redeeming the
connections' 'claims to be *divine*, because it is re-rooting in the basic relational
energy of the universe' (Grey, 1993, p. 62).

Grey sees two fundamental movements or 'poles' to the process of redemption or
re-connecting: *self-affirmation* on the one hand, and *right relation* on the other.
Women in particular need to come to a sense of self before they can establish right
relation with others. Grey traces this process in a number of contemporary works of
fiction, and detects certain recurring patterns, in particular, the awakening to a *lack* of
self which then leads to a process of struggle, vision, passionate longing, remembering
past intimations of wholeness and gradually, the emergence, not of the lonely,
autonomous hero of traditional mythology, but a connected, flexible and relational self
who knows herself to be interdependent with others. Thus the second pole of *right
relation* is not so much in opposition to the process of self-affirmation as the context
within which it occurs. This is the process of coming into right relation with others,
with the earth, with the cosmos, and with God as source of all relationality, in
relationships which are marked by mutuality, responsiveness and coinherence.
Relationship here ranges from intimate sexual relationships or friendships through
political activism and working in tandem with the rhythms of the earth.

The notion of relationality, as it is employed by feminist thinkers, is a rich one,
and seems to include a number of different components. Zappone (1991) identifies
what she sees to be central characteristics of a relational spirituality, which might be
posited to be distinctive of women's faith. Most fundamentally, there is a rejection
of dualism which separates supernature and nature, spirit and matter, humanity and
nature, mind and body, spirituality and sexuality; and an affirmation of the essential
interdependence of all things. This leads to a strong emphasis on holism and
inclusivity in feminist spirituality; for example, King (1989) asserts that 'the
spiritual dimension within contemporary feminism has much to do with the
determined quest for wholeness and integration, the attempt to heal deep divisions
and overcome all dualisms' (p. 88).

The stress on relationality includes a strong sense of connectedness to the earth and to matter, and is thus explicitly incarnational, with a positive regard for the physicality and bodiliness of human experience. Feminist analysis demonstrates how both the demise of nature and the oppression of women have gone hand in hand, reinforcing and supporting each other within the dualistic framework of patriarchy (for example, Merchant, 1980; Ruether, 1979, 1992; Griffin, 1982; Halkes, 1991). Conversely, the liberation of women logically entails the liberation of the earth, and the spiritual praxis of feminists includes a strong commitment to recreating a renewed relation to the earth (see Zappone, 1991, ch. 5), reflected in understandings of the universe as the 'body of God' (McFague, 1993; Jantzen, 1984) and a stress on the immanence of the divine presence within the world rather than beyond it.

Closely connected to this sense of the sacramentality of the universe is an emphasis on spirituality as life-affirming, rooted in women's experience of giving birth to, and nurturing life, in contrast to a religious orientation dominated by a fear of death, as patriarchal religion has been seen by some to be (for example, Daly, 1986). Another aspect of a relational spirituality which follows closely from the insistence on an incarnational, this-worldly commitment to life in all its physicality is a strong commitment to justice and the redemption of political and structural relationships, so that spirituality is not confined to the interpersonal sphere but extends to the larger web of social structures which undergird and shape personal relationships. This commitment to justice is stressed particularly by Carter Heyward who insists that the power of love can never be confined to the personal realm because the passion for right relation which characterises the love of God must extend to every area of life, and will not be satisfied until all enjoy the fullness of life which being in right relation entails.

Finally, a fully developed relational spirituality also incorporates due attention to diversity and difference within an epistemology of connectedness. The notion of interdependence itself implies the inherent value of every living being, issuing in a reverence for all life, and the freedom of each living thing to be its distinctive self, thus necessitating the embrace of otherness within an essential connectedness. As Audre Lorde has reflected, 'Without community, there is no liberation ... But community must not mean a shedding of our differences, nor the pathetic pretence that these differences do not exist' (1984, p. 12). Zappone distinguishes between a 'differentiated connectedness' which 'becomes stronger the more we know that we are not identical to another human being' and the experience of 'fusion' in which the self merges with the other and loses the sense of its own separateness (1991, p. 26). Difference and connectedness do not need to be conceived in competition with each other; it is precisely the ability to maintain the connectedness to the other in the face of difference, without threatening the selfhood of either party, which characterises mature interdependence and distinguishes it from symbiotic fusion on the one hand, and alienated isolation on the other. The otherness of the other challenges one to stretch and grow to accommodate both the inalienable difference of the other *and* the point of connection between oneself and the stranger, whose difference paradoxically reveals what is unique and valuable about oneself which would have remained unknown outside this relation.

The stress on connectedness and relationality in women's ways of knowing, thinking and constructing spirituality, has been critiqued strongly by some feminists. In the theological realm, for example, the work of Susan Thistlethwaite (1990) and others (for example, Hogan, 1995; Graham, 1995) has drawn attention to the limitations of feminist theologies of relationality to account for the experience of black and working class women. An over-emphasis on relationality, Thistlethwaite suggests, may simply mirror white middle-class women's preoccupation with personal relationships and obscure the very different interests of women struggling against racism or poverty.[4] At the same time, womanist pastoral theologians such as Marsha Foster Boyd (1991), Carolyn McCrary (1991, 1998), Christine Wiley (1991), Clevone Turner (1997) and Beverly Daniel Tatum (1997) highlight and delineate black women's different experiences and understandings of relationality, suggesting not so much an absence of strong connectedness in black women's experience as a broader, more communally-oriented sense of interdependence rooted in kinship networks and solidarity against racism. Turner, for example, suggests that black women's experience of intracultural connection through family, kinship and womanist networks, enables black women to develop the strength of self to be able to counter the strong negative messages of racism and function biculturally. Intercultural mutual connection only becomes possible within the context of strong empathic relationships within one's own racial group. Thus, whilst recognising the potential dangers of the notion of connectedness, I agree with Grey and others that a theology of relationality can account for, and attend to, difference between women. As Neuger (1999, p. 128) proposes, 'relationality as a construct seems to be open enough to allow for diverse ways of describing its function in varieties of constructs.' Without an insistence upon our interconnectedness, albeit in ways which attend to and celebrate difference (or, in the case of unjust structures of inequality, overcome such difference), we risk reinforcing the structures of injustice which alienate and isolate groups one from the other, and perpetuate the divisions which engender suspicion and fear. I affirm, with Kathleen Fischer (1989, pp. 40, 42):

> At the heart of reality is a mutual rhythm of giving and receiving, the receiving of others for the enrichment of self and the giving of self for the enrichment of others ... Within an organic worldview we are not first isolated individuals who later choose to enter into relationships. Rather, the self emerges from relationships, existence is a gift from a previously existing world. Connectedness is prior to freedom and independence ... In such a world, interdependence is not an ideal; we cannot escape it. We do not become related when we love one another. We are already related. Every act of love strengthens the cosmos; each act of hate weakens it.

Patterns of Relationality

The women in my study expressed a relational construction of faith and selfhood in a number of diverse but interconnected ways. The majority offered explicitly relational models of faith, either understanding faith as being in relation with God and/or the Other, or offering other relational metaphors and models of faith.

---

[4] Mary Grey (1999) discusses and responds to some of these criticisms.

Relationality was also expressed in terms of a strong empathic connection to others, an incarnational sense of the sacredness of the ordinary and through the prizing of integration as the ideal of faith. In some ways, given the nature of Christianity as a theistic religion in which personal relationship to God is central, the emphasis on relationality may not seem surprising in and of itself; nevertheless, the range, depth and extent of the women's understandings of connectedness, both to self, other and to God, are significant.

Faith as Being in Relation with God and/or the Other

The majority of the women in my study expressed an understanding of faith as being in relationship to God and/or the Other, and for most of them, the concept of relationality included the horizontal dimension of human relationships as an expression or locus of the divine–human relation, as well as broader notions of relation to the earth and creation.

The women called upon different metaphors drawn from the human sphere to describe the relationship between the believer and God. God was imaged in hierarchical relational terms as parent, sovereign or lord, but more frequently in relationships of mutuality as lover, partner or friend; and in both male and female imagery. In some of the accounts, God was known as the benevolent Father who has never forsaken his child and who will meet all her needs; as the 'ever grateful, giving' 'father figure', 'always lavishing lots of things on us'; as the Husband and Lover whose commitment and mutuality forms and shapes a 'partnership' of love; and as the 'best friend' who 'suffers along with me' and 'dies every time a bit of me dies'. For other women, female imagery dominated and God was named as nurturing Mother suckling the infant, the one who had brought faith and vocation to birth, or as the 'God of incredible tenderness' imaged as a woman embracing the subject and inviting her into a 'Lover relationship'.

Despite the variety of relational metaphors, what was crucial for these women was the constancy and dependability of divine presence in their lives; a reality which was regarded as the source and ground of their own shifting identity and the guarantee of ultimate truth and meaning even when experience appeared constantly to contradict both. This conviction was expressed by a number of the women through metaphors of faith as the 'core', 'centre' or most abiding reality of their lives. Thus, Meg spoke of the 'core' of her spirituality as the ongoing sense 'of ... God just being there', a sense of presence/that has never deserted me', a sense which 'doesn't always make it alright at all – it can actually be very negative':

> and yet somehow even in
> in the most negative and dry
> and kind of absent
> there is *still* a presence ...
> And sometimes that's absolutely all there has been
> just that sense of presence
> with very little filling
> very little articulation
> very little way of sharing it with anybody

This sense of the presence of God at the core of life, holding things in being and nurturing one's life, was shared by Alice, whose relationship with God had been, until recently, always 'flawed' by her inability to believe herself personally loved and accepted, yet was nevertheless *there*:

> there *was* a relationship
> I mean it *was* deeply flawed because I
> always thought I was unacceptable
> but I'd gone on crawling to his feet ever since I was eighteen
> I'd never missed Sunday communion if I could help it

Marion articulated a sense of the 'all-pervading patient waiting presence' of the Lord, symbolised by 'the blessed sacrament'. She expressed the conviction that 'he is *much* more keen to get in touch with me than I with him', that 'he's always there available ... even in darkness and desolation.' For Marion, it was this utterly dependable love of God which provided the arena for her own struggle 'to be real' before God and others. Anne spoke in terms of being in relation with God as 'Thou' or 'You' and discovering herself loved, accepted and healed in and through this relationship. Anne's experience had taught her that it is relationship with God *per se* which is redemptive, rather than adherence to a particular doctrine, religious experience or church tradition: 'The real healing is being in a relationship [with God]'; 'it's about being with God, there aren't any short cuts.'

In other interviews, the continuity and dependability of the relationship with God was expressed through metaphors of dialogue and conversation. For Hurdeep, faith was articulated as an intimate personal relationship of 'going to Jesus', 'turning to God' in every situation, characterised by a dialogue which had remained largely unbroken since childhood. She told God what she couldn't share with anyone else, unburdening the secrets which others had confided in her. She questioned God about his inscrutable ways: 'Why did you do that? Why is [this person] suffering? Why can't you [do] this and that?' She begged him to respond to her: 'Oh, what am I doing wrong?' or 'What do you think I should do?' The dialogue also included listening, 'sitting quietly', 'silenc[ing] myself' in order to be receptive to the presence of God. Alongside her need for God, she affirmed a degree of mutuality in the relationship when she said, 'there's also a God who needs you, you know?'

Kerry also described relationship with God in terms of ongoing dialogue, albeit of a more conflictual nature, characterised by struggle, anger and argument:

> my my daily living is one long prayer
> umm and living on my own I tend to say things
> and when I do have a prayer time
> I don't actually
> you know have to get on my hands and knees and pray
> I just sit there and I and I I talk
> whether verbally or silently
> and challenge God a heck of a lot
> throw it back
> and uh don't don't get verbal responses
> [*laughs*]

'When the desert is a bit long', she challenges God:

> 'How long?
> how long do you expect me
> to just do what I've been doing
> plodding along ummm
> doing doing your so-called work
> umm and yet I I don't feel any rewards coming my way'
> [*laughs*]

Despite her frustration at what this relationship of fidelity seemed to demand of her, relationship with God was seen as the place where she could be most authentically herself, in all her anger, need and dividedness, knowing that God would both accept her as she was and draw her into deeper integrity.

Whilst in these various ways, the women testified to the constancy of the relationship to God, this constancy was not seen as a guarantee against change in the nature of the relationship itself. Indeed, it is precisely the capacity of the relationship with God to evolve and reconstruct over time which is the measure of its durability in the women's lives. A number of the interviewees emphasised the changing nature of the relationship with God, and the transformation of particular forms of relationship to the divine which had become, at a certain point, inadequate and untenable. In particular, several spoke of the loss of an exclusive love-relationship to the divinity, usually imaged as male lover or father, which had characterised their early faith lives, and the discovery of a more diffused and internalised relation to the divinity which was more integrated with their other human relationships. Thus Rachel described the loss of a deeply personal relationship with Jesus which sustained her throughout a rather isolated childhood and adolescence, and through her early years in religious life, and its metamorphosis into a much more diffused awareness of God in and through relationships with others and the exercise of her own capacity for choice. A major turning point came for Rachel when she recognised that her relationship with God must be 'dynamic, everchanging, evolving, moving', 'not a static given', and that, just as *she* was 'evolving and changing' so 'God is evolving and changing', and this changing relationship would require new forms of expression.

Similarly, for Judith, whilst the relationship to God still remained 'extremely close' in adulthood, there had been a movement away from a childhood dependence to a more secure and a broader vision of God. Having felt abandoned by her mother when the parental relationship broke down, she recognised her 'desperate need for a God of love' in childhood, and the focus of this relationship during much of her early life upon her own need. Now as 'a mature adult' she had 'moved away/ from this desperate need for a God of love'. Feeling much more secure in the knowledge that 'God is around me [and] God is interested in me', she no longer had to cling so tightly:

> so I can let him go [*laughing*]
> I don't need to hold him so tightly ...
> I'm not going to lose him
> he's still going to be there

In this freedom to 'let go' the old relation, a new awareness of God had emerged, 'no longer limited to my [own] need ... / and that need being fulfilled', but characterised instead by a 'broader vision' of the 'God of justice' who is not only committed to the personal salvation of those he loves, but also to worldwide justice:

> Now I I have moved on and ...
> it's the God of justice that is
> significantly there in my life ...
> and it's justice for all
> you know
> 'What does God require but
> you know to walk humbly and to do justly' etcetera
> umm so it's the God of justice that I'm aware of
> close around me ...
> it's a much broader God
> who is interested
> in a number of areas in my life
> a God who's interested in his environment and his creation
> a God who is interested in what is happening in Bosnia
> in err South Africa
> Ireland and
> Enniskillen
> a God who is interested in what is happening within the two political parties
> and the impending election

This description of a faith characterised by a strong emphasis on justice and on the needs of the other in balance with the needs of the self, is reminiscent of Fowler's Stage 5 faith, in which the balance of different needs is held alongside a new quality of openness to the other and a recognition of paradox and mystery.

The changing nature of the relation with God included an increasing awareness of the interdependence of relationship with God and relationships with others – a key feature of Fowler's Stage 5 and Kegan's inter-individual self. As the exclusive and idealised love-relation to the divine was 'lost' and diffused in a more risky relation to others, the reality of the presence of God was discovered in a new way in the presence of the human other. Marion, a religious sister, described her journey from an understanding of faith as 'all between God and me' to a realisation 'that it's you and the community and God in community'. Her struggle to 'be real' with herself and before God was paralleled by a process in which 'the interaction between people in the community has become more and more real.' She now saw 'this dimension of loving God through each other' as 'the crux' of faith, 'both the cross' and 'the great joy'. There was a sense in which 'in no other life could I be saved, 'cos I needed ... the encouragement and the rebuke and the honesty and so on and the struggle of sisters.' The love of God was mediated not only through the relationships with her sisters, but also in the people with whom her work had brought her into contact – 'school [children], mentally handicapped, alcoholics, students or nursing the elderly or guests' – these were all accepted as 'a way of revealing God'. Relationship with the other, be it sister or stranger, *was* for Marion the theophany of God.

Undergirding Dala's work of 'bridge-building' between people of different faiths and cultures in an inner-city community centre was a similar sense of the presence of Christ in the human other. Her newfound conviction of the 'international oneness' of all people in Christ 'who really holds us together', had evolved in recent years as she had been willing to risk the loss of her previously defended relation to God, from which people of other faiths had been excluded. For a long time after she first came into contact with Muslims and Hindus, Dala had struggled to reconcile her deep Christian convictions with the evident faith of these other believers. She 'kept thinking about it' and asking 'How can it be possible [for these people to be saved]?' For a long time she had puzzled over this and 'nobody could help me'. But gradually, as she prayed to God about it, 'one word' kept coming to her, the 'one word' of 'Love': 'What is Christ? Christ is love.' If that is so, then Christ is present wherever people are in relationships of love and mutual care: 'so *Christ* is with his people probably/ who *don't* know him in the name of Christ.' Out of the love of Christ for all people, and her experience of this love, Dala was able to offer her home as a place 'for people to meet as friends', 'where everybody's welcome' and where, together, they could 'build a bridge between communities'. As people met together in the 'bridge' place, they discovered that

> learning brings a kind of understanding
> when we understand people then we *accept* them
> and when we *accept* them then we *respect* them
> the respect for people comes from accepting
> and when you respect them then
> then that wall which is created
> it's fallen down
> the barrier is gone

Whilst it was Dala's experience of the love of Christ for her which enabled her to reach out in friendship to the strangers, her own deepening relationships with others who are very different from her had, in turn, become the arena where she experienced the love of God anew. A single woman living far from her native home, Dala expressed her sense that God had 'blessed' her 'more than he needed to', 'more than he should have', repaying her 'tenfold' for the sacrifice of her own family by 'giv[ing] me *tremendous* love in my heart' for others and, in return, providing her with 'the love and care of family' through her neighbours and friends. Although she still missed her own family,

> my neighbours they are my brothers like to me [*sic*]
> and their wives are my sisters to me
> the children are like my own children...
> So I think God has blessed me by
> when they say 'how many children?'
> I say 'I have *so* many children I can't count them' ...
> on my fingers
> so they are my family

The generous love of God which surpassed all her expectations was incarnated in the love of her neighbours for her, whilst her own capacity for love which, in her culture would typically have been channelled into relationship with a husband and children, had spilled over 'for a wider range of people' than she would ever have conceived possible, for all people 'regardless of age' or creed.

This sense of the interconnectedness of relationship with God and relationship with others was shared by Stella. Faith, for Stella, arose out of 'very deep involvement with other people' and was conceived as faithful presence with and to others, a 'cherishing' of the 'absolute value' and 'mystery' of the person rooted in the conviction that 'we're stewards of one another'. The 'greatest mystery ... is another human person', 'whether that person is a small farmer in [the Philippines] whom nobody would ever hear of again if he disappears/ or whether it's somebody who comes in here [that is, to the community where she now lived] and shares their life story'. What is important is 'allowing myself ... to be touched by that mystery and to be part of that'. Faithfulness to God means being where Jesus is 'most vulnerable' in the 'most poor and most needy' and responding to those needs. Such faith demands a dialectic between commitment to others and withdrawal to 'sit at my own fire'. On the one hand, one's 'growth in faith' takes place 'in the context of relationships' and 'reflecting on these and struggling with them'. On the other hand, it's essential to be true 'to your own self' and to keep in touch with your own centre in order to maintain the commitment to others. When alone she still experienced being '*with* other people's stories and what's going on for them', and 'in a sense that's part of my story now; it brings up things for me that I have to work with.' Conversely, 'being *with* what I hear from them is being with me ... There's the sense that their story mirrors my story or that it's almost the same one.' There is a profound sense of interdependence here, rooted in a strong sense of self, which does not ignore or downplay difference but, in the interchange with the otherness of the other, finds new aspects of the self revealed and strengthened.

For some of the black women in my study, there was less of an emphasis upon the interconnectedness of relationship with God and relationship with others, and a strong sense of the relationship with God as the source of oppositional power, sustaining the self in *opposition* to the forces of racism and oppression which they experienced in society and in the church, and which soured and skewed human relationships. The British black women, in particular, seemed to see themselves as standing *apart* from others, including to some extent even their own families, friends and black sisters. Lay and clergy both saw themselves as called out from the community to become 'pioneers', 'leaders' and 'models' of what faith can achieve in the midst of adversity. The relationship with God was the core reality which affirmed the value of the self over and against the values of the wider society, including the church, which constantly undermined the worth of black people and set limits on their selfhood. Thus, for Hilary, faith was seen as the means to survive a hostile and alien worldly reality, and present life was regarded as 'a journey' 'we're walking through' on the way to the 'home' of 'heaven'. There was a conviction that 'one day/ God's going to bring deliverance', 'one day/ everything will be all right', 'if not here/ then in heaven'; but there was no expectation of being 'at home' in the present structures of world or church, and there was a strong sense of human relationships being a locus of struggle, disappointment and pain.

Similarly, Judith's faith was the source of her survival in a hostile world, although this manifested itself somewhat differently from Hilary's eschatological orientation to heaven. Judith was driven by a 'passion' and 'mission', not merely to 'survive' but to 'thrive' in this world, and to demonstrate to her children and the wider black community that there is 'no limit' to what they can do and be. Her favourite biblical motto was: 'I can do all things through God who strengthens me' (Philippians 4:13). Fuelled by faith she declared, 'I can become/ I can achieve', and her message to other black people was: 'God is interested/ and God wants you to be successful.' Whilst Judith had a strong sense of connectedness to other black people, especially to black women, it was of a different nature to that described by the white women, marked by a sense of suffering solidarity against oppression, and a passion to succeed and achieve on behalf of those who had not had the chances she had had or the confidence she had been given. Speaking of the black community of which she was a part, and her own role as their leader, she articulated the conviction that:

> I *belong* to them
> you know I listen to them
> and they talk so *proudly* about me
> you know I'm *theirs*
> I'm their daughter
> it's *wonderful*
> they own me

The emphasis was less on interpersonal intimacy such as the white women often articulated, and there was a stronger sense of the collective identity of black women and the symbolic role which black women leaders can play in inspiring and encouraging other black women to live life to the full. This coheres with the emphasis in womanist pastoral theology (for example, Boyd, 1991; McCrary, 1991, 1998; Wiley, 1991) on black women's sense of interdependence and communal solidarity, and the need for black women to be nurtured by intraculutral connections in order to have the strength to function biculturally.

Other Relational Images and Metaphors of Faith

Closely connected to the central image of faith as personal relationship to the other, but distinct from it, was a broader theme of faith as connectedness, relationality, interdependence. What distinguishes this theme from the first one is that, whilst it includes reference to human and human–divine relationship, it goes wider. Faith is the perception, experience or intuition of the essential interconnectedness of things and a commitment to work in cooperation with that essential reality to help realise it in the conditions of this world.

This implicit epistemology of connectedness was expressed in a variety of ways, in metaphors of meeting, touching, bridge-building and weaving; seeing or perceiving beauty, order and pattern; and connecting with the depths or dimensions. Faith was conceived as 'relating across difference', 'building a bridge between communities' and 'provid[ing] an opportunity for people to meet as friends', so that they can experience their essential connectedness across the barriers that frequently divide, including cultural, ethnic and religious barriers. For Stella, faith was about 'touching into the deeper level' of things, 'touching into the meaning of all that's going on' which requires a 'staying with' and a 'holding' of 'other people's stories' so that one can 'touch into it from another dimension'. For Ruth 'the gospel is about the fact that the life of Jesus can touch the way you go about life', offering a source of relational power and energy for one's human relationships and work commitments. Such language of touch suggests the intimacy and bodiliness of connecting with the meaning of things, which does not happen apart from, but only in and through the flesh-and-blood commitments of human encounter.

Metaphors of the web or tapestry, on the other hand, suggest the hidden strength and durability of the connections that relate all things, as well as the intricacy of the work of relationality. Helen saw the task of faith as 'weaving into the one pattern' or 'tapestry' the many 'strands' and 'threads' of her past, 'both positive and negative', 'reworking' the 'givens' of 'the experience I have been born with'. In this work, she saw herself as 'spinning the web together' with God, working in cooperation with God to forge a 'pattern' out of the disparate threads of her life. Similarly, Lorna regarded the task of spirituality as making 'a sort of woven day of prayer' out of all the disparate activities of work, silence, creative activity, domestic chores and relationships. For both women, it was important that nothing was left outside the web of faith; everything that happened, no matter how apparently insignificant or difficult, must be received as part of the pattern to be woven.

Metaphors of depth and dimension suggest both the mystery and the pervasiveness of the reality of interconnectedness. Hannah spoke of the 'dimension of profundity' and 'depth' in which all life and relationship is rooted, requiring both a language of 'transcendence' and 'immanence' to express its mystery. Kate talked of the 'rootedness of all that is' in the 'God who is good'. For Mary, faith was 'gift' and 'mystery' 'to be tapped into', a 'bigger dimension' or 'deep waters' which draw one out beyond the limits of the self or one's own understanding into a larger reality. There is a sense here that, however much one may perceive the underlying connections between things, the larger pattern always eludes grasp. Yet, for these women, this did not threaten or undermine the sense of meaning so much as ground it in a larger mystery, whose depths both sustain and enlarge the horizons of the self.

Metaphors of balance, order and pattern suggest the essential coherence of the reality of interconnectedness. Elizabeth referred to a sense of 'order' and 'pattern' as part of her awareness of spirituality: 'there is a way things happen you know ... there is an order to it', which she encountered in 'resonances' between her own and others' experiences. Stella spoke of the importance of 'be[ing] open to what new patterns might emerge' in her own life. Kate described this intuition of pattern as 'a whole system of beingness that's eternal'. For Lesley, the insistence on the 'rationality' of faith, 'that Christianity can be a truth recognised by intelligent, intellectual people' was important because it witnesses to the essential coherence of reality and acknowledges 'the human mind ... as part of God's creation'. Similarly, Hannah spoke of the 'wisdom', 'power', 'purpose' and 'design' of God which provides an 'underlying compass' by which to steer human decisions. For Helen, God was the one who guaranteed that there *is* a pattern to existence, as well as the one who worked alongside her to *make* that pattern:

God *is* the pattern emerging
as I am
but but perhaps God is is is the love that guarantees that there *is* a pattern

there *is* a meaning
at the end of the day
which
not that God creates that apart from me
I mean it's my responsibility as well
to make the pattern of it

Mary developed a striking analogy between God and the weather, emphasising the
all-pervasiveness of God's presence in the world and suggesting the underlying
dependability of God's purposes, even though they can be experienced as variably
as the many different moods of the weather:

whether it was winter or summer
or windy or not
God was there in all of that
in the storm or in thunder
God was there eh
God was there in the sunshine
you didn't think of life without G' –
when you thought of life and creation and anything
God is all of that
so yeh hailstones or anything
God was all of that
whatever it was
and that's the same with life as well
in good times and in bad times
God was was there *really* ...
Somehow
and even when God isn't
when things aren't good
God is still good!
[*chuckling*]

Visual metaphors of perception and insight suggest both the hiddenness of the
underlying reality of relationality and the discipline or 'art' required to discern this
reality. Anne talked of prayer being like painting: both are concerned with
disciplined looking, with paying attention to the reality of things, with 'really
gazing', a 'sort of gazingness'. Likewise for Lorna, prayer and painting were deeply
connected, and she regarded her painting as a *way* of praying, a way of wrestling
with experience and attending to what God might be saying through it. For Anna,
faith was understood as 'the capacity and the desire to *see* this beauty and life of
spirit in every tiny little thing and share it'. Hannah described faith as a 'basic optic'
or 'outlook' on life, which 'communicate[s] itself in the choices you make', and
which perceives the connections between the realm of God and the realm of human
life. For Alice, prayer was a means of paying attention to the reality of God and
adoring God in his mystery and beauty; she described 'trying to look at God and be
aware of the presence of God and look away from myself'. Marion spoke of the
other side of this relationship when she drew on the Gospel story of Jesus looking
on the young man and loving him (Mark 10:21) to express her sense of the love of

God beholding the creation and each person within it. Implicit in all these visual metaphors is the core conviction of the underlying order, pattern, even beauty of the universe, a reality which manifests itself to those who will commit themselves to be present to the complexity of experience with the measure of faithfulness and patience which all genuine prayer and art demand.

Fittingly, many of these diverse metaphors were used in close proximity and rich interplay with each another, so that the women's very use of language suggests the interconnectedness of apparently unrelated experience. Thus Stella brought together metaphors of human intimacy and spatial awareness when she spoke of 'touching into the depths' of experience; Anna wove together metaphors of the web and depth and dimension when she spoke of faith as both 'part of me' and herself 'part of it'; Hannah used an unusual mixture of spatial and journey imagery when she spoke of faith as a 'dimension of profundity' which provides the 'underlying compass' by which to guide and steer life decisions; Mary held together images of gift, mystery, depths, pattern and weather in her description of faith. In these and other examples, the mixing of metaphors is indicative of a dynamic linguistic creativity which mirrors the interconnectedness these women experienced as central to faith. There is also evident here a holding together of apparent opposites within paradoxical language suggestive of Fowler's Stage 5 faith; these women exhibit a maturity of faith which excludes nothing from its compass but seeks to hold all in a balance and interconnectedness not fully graspable by the intellect but intuited by faith.

The Connectedness of Empathy

One of the most powerful ways in which the women in my study expressed a relational faith was through their profound empathic connection to others in pain, suffering and need. The openness to the other which was at the core of their spirituality inevitably opened them to the pain of the other and demanded a response to it. The emphasis on empathy is not surprising, given that women in most cultures are socialised for empathic caring – what Carol Lakey Hess describes as compassionate caring that is focused on the other, involving a kind of self-emptying and an openness to vulnerability and change in the light of the other's needs (Hess, 1997, pp. 96ff). The danger in such empathic caring, if it is not balanced by what Hess describes as 'conversational caring' (dialogic engagement, reciprocal mutuality) and 'prophetic caring' (caring about another enough to confront and challenge them), is that it reinforces women's tendency to give the self away in an over-identification with the needs of the other. For many of the women in my study, a central struggle in their faith development was how to hold together the needs of the self and the demands of the other; and this was focused with particular intensity in the struggle to respond to others' suffering without putting the self at jeopardy.

For a number of the interviewees the consciousness of others' suffering went back to childhood and was rooted in family situations of loss, broken relationships or physical deprivation. Helen acknowledged that 'at some very deep level I think I was always conscious of the struggle of my family, particularly of my mother's struggle'; 'I internalised' 'my mother's pain' 'and I used to try and make it better.' Rachel told how her childhood faith had been imbued with an intense awareness of the suffering of others and a conviction that her own pain could be 'offered up' for the needy and could, in some mysterious way she could not explain, have a redemptive effect. Explaining that her childhood relationship with God had been closely 'bound up with' 'something to do with sacrifice', she gave several examples of this 'offering up' of her own pain for others: 'walk[ing] along the street with my coat open' in the *'freezing* cold on the North East coast/ and bitter *bitter* North winds', 'feel[ing] the pain of the cold and the wind/ and offer[ing] it up/ for missionaries and the world's suffering/ through heat in Africa'; and 'stick[ing] my feet out/ of the covers' at night *'on purpose'* in a *'freezing* cold bedroom' with 'no heating' with the intention 'This is for missionaries/ suffering from the heat in Africa.'

For Mary, the childhood consciousness of others' suffering was expressed in a belief that mundane, concrete actions such as not finishing one's meal or picking up pins would have a direct effect on others elsewhere whose lives might be very remote from hers, but were nevertheless 'all of God as well':

> And stupid things like em
> not wasting things
> not wasting food because
> people starve em
> O somehow 'If you don't waste this
> somehow God will will know
> and somebody else might have food' ...
> You know 'cos God is also
> in other places as well ...
> It was
> it's part of the mystery I don't know
> but it's just an awareness
> of other people

Pauline's experience of connecting with the suffering of others is a particularly interesting one because it demonstrates in a striking fashion the danger for women of losing their own sense of self in over-identification with others' pain. Following the death of her father, Pauline began to have what she described as 'off-the-wall' experiences or 'out-of-the-body experiences' in which she 'connect[ed] with people' and could 'actually know how they're feeling and sometimes can even tell ... what they're saying' as well as 'feel[ing] people's pain and anguish'. In Pauline's connection with the other, she seemed frequently to lose the sense of her own separateness almost totally, becoming wholly identified with the other person's thoughts and feelings for the duration of the experience. The awareness of the other's pain was often 'so strong' that 'it actually quite literally knock[s] me off my feet.' She lost touch with her own sense of self so that she felt herself lifted out of the situation, describing herself looking down at the congregation in her church as if she wasn't present, feeling 'detached', 'not part of it at all', 'out of the body'. She spoke of a need to 'have a sense of my own/ of who I am', a need 'to make sure that Pauline is there and is protected and is a wholesome person', of needing to know 'where I can be and where I can't be'. Such language conveys the fragility of Pauline's sense of self, the potential loss of her sense of boundaries, and her sense of losing herself completely in the identification with the other's suffering.

Whilst experienced by some as problematic, their capacity for empathy nevertheless remained a key component of faith for a majority of the women in my study. Lorna, for example, described her sense of her life as one 'of giving and serving and holding' others in their vulnerability and need. Both her prayer and her painting provided the means of 'wrestling with' those in difficult circumstances and 'bearing that pain'. Her choice to paint the passion of Jesus as experienced by prisoners of conscience during her final year of a degree course exemplifies this work of vicarious identification with the other in their suffering. Paradoxically, though the experience of painting is 'such a lonely furrow', 'something very inner that I couldn't share with other people', Lorna was able to use it to connect with the other and to 'hold' and express in some kind of meaningful patterning their 'terrible agony'. Hurdeep regarded her present work in interfaith dialogue as a work of vicarious presence, visiting and listening to people's problems and absorbing the things they are not able to tell anyone else. She believed that 'all the experiences' of her life had prepared her for this work, including her humiliating rejection by high-caste Hindus in her childhood, her alienation when she first joined religious life, and her intense loneliness when she first came to Europe. Her own suffering enabled her to identify with the aloneness and marginality of immigrant groups in England and to win their trust and respect.

In contrast to those like Pauline who struggled to resist fusing with the pain of the other, these women exemplify a mature capacity to care for the suffering other in ways which do not put the self at risk but strengthen its rootedness in the love and compassion of God. As they risked vulnerability to the anguish of others, they came to experience a profound solidarity with the suffering other which empowered them, fuelling further their identification with the pain of others. Their capacity to bear the suffering of others without being overwhelmed by the enormity of pain seemed to depend on a number of factors: first, the stability of their own sense of selfhood, rooted in a strong measure of self-acceptance and self-knowledge;[5] second, their ability to receive from others, as well as care for them (what Hess refers to as 'conversational caring', 'a to-and-fro movement between two others who respect difference while also finding commonality' [1997, p. 104]); third, their conviction of the redemptive presence of God, or at least some kind of transcendent presence, in all human suffering, such that they were not required to carry the suffering of others alone, but believed that God inhabits this suffering with them; and fourth, their capacity to appropriate creatively their own pain and that of others in some kind of meaningful work, whether this be the work of prayer, painting, preaching or pastoral ministry. In such work, the women demonstrated their conviction that suffering is not the final word, but may be transformed so as to become creative; in such work, too, they received sustenance and nurture from beyond the self which strengthened them for the work of empathy.

---

[5] Cf. Hess: 'In order to empathize with another, one must have a well-differentiated sense of self and the capacity to allow for the space and differentness of the other in addition to a capacity for connection with and response to another. Otherwise, the boundary between self and other becomes so blurred that one cannot be fully present to another' (1997, p. 99).

The Sacredness of the Ordinary

A concrete expression of the women's sense of the interconnectedness of all things was their commitment to the sacredness of the ordinary, what might be called the sacrament of the everyday. Rather than being seen in opposition to the transcendent, the mundane sphere was regarded as the locus of encounter with mystery, otherness and the presence of the divine for many of the women, who articulated the sense of a spirituality rooted in, taking shape from and committed to the routine chores of home-making and hospitality. These women affirmed that 'religion and spirituality [is] an everyday part of life', faith is 'natural', 'very much integrated into everyday life'; 'very *ordinary*' resulting in a 'simple sense of God ... present in life', so that one can say 'God is very much part of my daily living.' This was a theme emphasised especially, but not exclusively, by women working from the home, or whose primary work was that of childcare and homekeeping.

Elizabeth spoke of spirituality as 'very much in the everyday' and 'part of the domestic experience'. It was strongly connected with her experience of homemaking, conceived of as 'coming home to yourself, being able to sort of sit in yourself' and having a sense that 'God is there somewhere in that experience.' Having lived so much of her life 'out of touch with myself' where religion was experienced as something 'very external', it had been a significant shift for Elizabeth to internalise the sense of the spiritual in her self and in her house as an extension of herself. Spirituality for Elizabeth was experienced in the ordinary, everyday routines of caring for herself and her home:

> to be in my home
> to walk round and water my plants and
> you know do things like that
> and then sit down and think
> 'well I'm going to read a book' and I will
> em that's where it is it's
> it's in my house ...
> perhaps it's not in a
> em it's not in a building
> or it's not in a body of people or it's
> it's not in a church
> it's um
> it's very much in the everyday

Lorna articulated a similar sense of the importance of 'valu[ing] the small things' and 'invest[ing] them with meaning'. She spoke of her vocation as one of making a 'woven day of prayer' out of the ordinary, 'small things' of each day:

> And because my life has
> has not been a *career*
> um in the normal sense of the word
> and because it's important for me to *value* the small things
> it is possible for me to invest them with meaning
> so to pray and make some soup
> and to paint a picture

and to hang out the washing
all these things become a
a sort of woven day of prayer

For Emma, too, it was essential that faith is rooted in the concrete and everyday. Whereas for a long time in her life, she had maintained a set of religious practices as a way of nourishing her commitment to the everyday, she no longer felt this need. Her commitment to 'openness to the whole world' and relating to others in a way that 'risks the self' had now 'become the practice', had 'become the spirituality'. She felt 'very centred in the intrinsic worth of the activities' she was committed to, and didn't feel the 'need ... to find another arena where I centre down or focus up'. There was almost a sense in which the practice of faith as a 'separate department' of life would be a distraction from and a dilution of the power and immediacy of the everyday. She still recognised a 'place for penitence and refocusing and so on' but now 'that happens in the course of events really', in an 'organic' way. Emma spoke several times of the 'organic' quality of her spirituality – a word she used to refer to a spontaneous, naturally evolving pattern of things, without need of an 'agenda' or 'outcome'. Thus, she might use the washing up as a 'transition point' from one activity to another or weeding in the garden as a way of 'feeding' spirituality: these are 'things that I *use* for centring and being still and reflecting/ that I didn't use in that way before and which aren't specifically religious'.

A number of women elaborated metaphors of hospitality and feeding to speak of the incarnational quality of their spirituality. Hospitality was a central image of faith for Meg, with strong roots in her family life and relationship to her children. Coming from a dysfunctional family where she felt she was never understood, Meg was conscious that the hospitality of others had been life-giving for her. During a difficult time in her marriage, those who 'offered us a bowl of soup occasionally, just giving us kind of space' were crucial 'survival points', as was their own developing practice of offering hospitality to others. The bodily experience of breast-feeding her own children had deepened the significance of this metaphor of hospitality:

the first time that you're somebody's sole source of nourishment
is quite extraordinary ...
when it first happens
and kind of dawns on you
and the kind of metaphors that opens up really
in terms of giving and feeding and
and hospitality again

Lorna had the vision of creating a 'house of prayer' which would offer hospitality to others around the life of prayer, and in which prayer would not simply be 'the beginning and the end of the day' but 'somehow ... the *reason* for the day, the food of the day'. For Mary, whilst the pattern of living in community had changed enormously since she first entered religious life, belonging to a eucharistic community nevertheless remained crucial for her, with its opportunities for 'table-fellowship', 'being honest with other people and finding a space where you can be honest'. She described the experience of community life, centred on regular celebration of the eucharist, as 'something that feeds me and the people I work with', 'nourishment for the journey', 'the bread of life', the very 'source of life'.

Whilst the theme of the sacredness of the ordinary was a strong one in my study, there were exceptions. For a number of the women, the home was not so much the site of integrated spirituality as one of conflict or loneliness. For women with families, the home frequently represented the place of inexorable demand, the place where the needs of partner and children are in conflict with one's own needs for rest and sustenance. For some, though not all, of the single women, the home was seen as the place where they were responsible for the multiple tasks of homemaking without support from others, and where they were confronted with their essential aloneness in an acute form. It is important to recognise, too, the middle-class cultural milieu of the majority of the women in my study; a cultural milieu in which women enjoy the luxury of a materially comfortable homelife. The reality of poverty and deprivation in other women's home lives does not necessarily rule out the possibility of a strongly incarnational, sacramental spirituality, but my research does not permit such a generalisation to be made. I do not wish to romanticise women's relation to domestic labour nor eliminate questions of justice in the distribution of domestic labour, so much as highlight the strongly concrete, this-worldly, incarnational quality of the women's faith which, for many of them, was expressed particularly in this focus on home and family life.

Integration as Experience and Ideal of Faith

Perhaps the most pervasively relational theme to emerge in the interviews was the ideal of integration, holism and inclusivity which, for almost all of the women, represented the goal of their spirituality. Such integration was sometimes glimpsed in moments of grace or illumination, or, for the older women, recognised as increasingly true of their experience; more often, it was spoken of with longing as the ideal towards which the present reality aspired. The emphasis on the integration of all experience within a holistic faith is implicit in much that has already been discussed in the earlier sections of this chapter. It is a direct outflowing of the conviction that all things, are, at heart, interconnected, and, for many of the women, represented a deliberate choice to move away from dualistic ways of thinking and acting which operate on the basis of separation and hierarchy.

The women in my study spoke about their experience of and longing for integration in a variety of images, metaphors and stories, as well as in more explicitly conceptual terms. Hannah spoke of the importance of different areas of experience 'hanging together', whilst Alice used the image of 'trying to balance up' and 'prioritise' 'the different things' in her life and 'keeping the really important in the middle'. Pauline saw her life as a 'jigsaw' and faith as the process of 'trying to put the pieces together', whilst Stella spoke of the inner and outer worlds 'mirror[ing]' and 'support[ing]' each other. Ruth used a novel image of two gardens – a 'secret garden' and a 'vegetable garden' – which were currently quite separate and which she knew needed to be brought together in order to achieve a greater wholeness. Kerry used similar landscape imagery when she envisaged her spirituality as the tension and relationship between the desert and the oasis. Mary spoke of taking 'the journey' 'towards death' with integrity whilst Marion imaged the integration process as a continual struggle 'to be real' before God and with others and to accept the 'givenness' of each day as 'enough'.

Many of the women explicitly named integration as a characteristic of mature faith. Thus, Hannah recognised in her own faith journey an increasing 'understanding that embraced more and more of life', and commented:

> one way I would like to see maturity of faith is
> um in terms of the extent of integration of experience
> So that um faith I think only matures when our um ...
> the more spiritual experience if you like
> actually makes sense of
> the domestic the social the political
> and *vice versa*
> that the thing begins to hang together

For Hannah, those people who were most important in teaching her about life were those 'who communicate this integrity', whose 'spiritual life and working life/ and domestic life ... all have a oneness'. Judith spoke of her ministry in terms of a vision of holism:

> So I hope in my ministry
> both in terms of church and society
> that is what I try and do
> um to bring wholeness
> fullness to people
> where they no longer compartmentalise their life
> so that that bit is a religious bit for Sunday
> that bit is the bit for bingo
> that bit is for work
> but that we would break down the compartments
> and see themselves as fully
> in a holistic manner
> fully whole ...
> allowing God into all the various bits of their lives

For a number of the women, integration remained the far side of their present experiences of disconnection, fragmentation and impasse. These women knew themselves to be divided, preventing the emergence of a holistic spirituality. Yet to the extent that they recognised their dividedness and believed passionately in the possibility of a faith which could reconcile their present conflictual state of being, they were already moving some way towards an inclusive spirituality. Kerry's narrative was strongly conflictual, reflecting her ongoing struggle to integrate oasis and desert, solitude and intimacy, private person and public role, and the twin defining cultures of her native Antipodean upbringing and European influences which often appeared to pull in opposite directions. What was important to Kerry was the refusal to hide her divided self or to play games with God by 'polishing my wings for Sunday' and 'running away from God' during the rest of the week. Only by allowing her faith to inhabit every aspect of her life did Kerry see any prospect of arriving at the integration of experience for which she longed:

in the past I used to feel I could run away
you know I could run away from God and do all the things I wanted to do ...
And then and then polish my wings for Sunday
you know
but now it's like uh
'I'm going to go to the pub' you know ...
I'm gonna you know
all the things that that
people in my own culture would *frown* on
you know I say 'Let's go'
'This ... this is my life
and uh if you want me to
to be faithful and continue to be faithful
then ... you have to tack along with me
to the places that that I think its OK
I think they're OK to be in'
and if I think that all these places that my society frowns on as sinful
if I think they're OK
then yeh they must be OK
especially if we are in a relationship

Kerry here roots her struggle for integration within the relational setting of her commitment to God and God's commitment to her. If the relationship is one of genuine mutuality, then God must be prepared to inhabit all the spaces of her life, not only the 'nice' or 'religious' ones. The struggle for integration cuts two ways, and makes demands of God as well as her!

Ruth explicitly acknowledged that she was living a 'double life' represented by the 'two gardens' which were images for two sides of her life currently in tension. On the one hand, there was a 'secret garden' 'behind the gate with the ivy' which was 'a beautiful place to go in and out of', which represented the inner world of her spirituality, emotional life and sexuality. On the other hand, there was 'another garden', a 'formal garden' with 'its own structures and necessity', a 'vegetable garden' which was the ordinary, everyday life she shared with her family. These two gardens were kept quite separate – 'they don't meet, oh no they don't meet' – and Ruth recognised that they needed to be brought together 'either by making one garden into *the* garden or making the other garden into *the* garden', yet 'I can't see my way to that at the minute, because I'm very entrenched in that double life.' So the issue for Ruth was 'how do I live in the minute' 'with integrity', knowing that she could not yet integrate these divided parts of herself. What authenticity means whilst one remains in a state of dividedness is, on the one hand doing all that one can to achieve a greater wholeness in one's life and, on the other, refusing to be anything but absolutely honest before God about one's lack of wholeness:

I say to God
'O shit! I'm very sorry but
[*laughing*]
I can do no other' kind of stuff
'This is it
this is actually me and

you know and uh
I am not an ascetic
I am not a disciplinarian
I am not actually gonna give up some of these things
I'm not' [*laughs*]

There is a paradox here: whilst remaining a long way from the integrity of wholeness towards which she aspired, Ruth nevertheless practised an integrity of truthfulness about her lack of wholeness which, she believed, might bring her nearer to the 'ultimate goal' of 'growing into the image of Christ'.

Where these women struggled to bring together presently divided parts of their lives, other women spoke of integration, not only as an ideal towards which they aspired, but as a characteristic of their present spirituality. These were women who, often through intense struggle, had learnt to incorporate previously warring aspects of themselves into a more unified whole. They had arrived at a spirituality which is able to affirm paradox, mystery and the grace of being in and through apparent contradiction in ways reminiscent of Fowler's Stage 5. Yet this deeper level of integration had been achieved, characteristically, not by separating out from the relationships in which their lives were embedded, but by entering into them more deeply, surrendering themselves to the demands of relational ties yet without surrendering the self.

For Emma, as we saw above, the practice of faith had been wholly incorporated into the daily living out of life, with its openness to the other. Life and faith were so integrated that there was no longer a need for a 'separate compartment' of religious practices; such 'practices' as there were arose spontaneously and 'organically' from the unfolding of the everyday. This sense of the unity of faith and life was reflected, too, in the balance which Emma had managed to achieve between her own needs for solitude and the demands of relationship with her husband and children. Having children, she reflected, 'just toughens you up really' and 'teach[es] you how to be available to other people' as well as how to 'develop strategies for finding your own time'. Although in the early days of parenthood, it was hard – 'and still is sometimes' – Emma felt that, as time had gone by, she had learnt to 'balance my inner and my outer needs' so that 'by and large, I would say that I don't feel that there's many areas of my life which keep cutting across other ones.' She had achieved a 'hard won knowledge of who I am and what I need', learnt 'through living it and trying it'.

The sense of the labour of integration was shared by Mary, who emphasised the importance of a constantly renewed commitment to faith as the basis for unifying all the diverse experiences of life. Although so much changes, what won't change is the 'journey' itself and death as the end point of the journey; even if the direction changes, 'my journey started this way and I'm keeping on the journey'. In this journey, everything is important, 'nothing is just incidental', and 'the way I face things and the way I accept things very much determine how I move in this relationship I have of grace on this journey.' But the commitment has constantly to be renewed and rethought, so that it grows with one and is able to be an integrating force. 'I've made a commitment', Mary affirmed, 'and at the moment/ I want to stick with that commitment', 'but that doesn't mean that the commitment mightn't change.' With any vocation, there is the need to 'rethink' and 'recommit' 'if the journey is going to be/ a thought through [journey]/ with your whole life in it'. The commitment 'has to be evaluated' and 'weighed up' in the light of 'the changes that happen' and allowed to 'mature' so that 'it's something that grows with [you] as you grow.'

For Marion, though there was still an ongoing struggle with 'a hinterland of stuff in my life' and a sense of a 'breakthrough' still to come, there was also an increasing sense of the interconnectedness of all things in the love of God, which 'is unimaginably more real than I often think it is', and an acceptance of all that has been in her life, both good and bad, light and shadow, as part of who and what she is, all of which is able to be offered to God:

> at the end of the day ...
> I belong to God um
> and somehow that he's going to accept what I
> what I offer to him of my life
> however long or short its going to be
> as valid
> and as worth something
> eh even though I go through
> stages thinking that it's not worth it

This sense of acceptance of all that has been in one's life, and the work of forging it into a unity, was echoed by a number of the women. Sarah recognised the way in which many of the key influences in her life – 'like family and church and work and that relationship' – 'have all been things that have hampered me as well as being things that have enriched me'. In recognising 'both sides' of these shaping experiences, she saw the work of integration as 'the ability to integrate all those different parts and become a more whole person by including those very things'. Nothing was to be rejected, however painful or apparently fruitless. Sheila spoke of a recent 'revelation' when she realised that 'the shadow [side of experience] wasn't all blackness, it was also gift.' Helen envisaged 'the task of adulthood and of spirituality' as that of integrating 'all the bits and pieces of one's life' into a whole, and spoke of 'coming to accept the woundedness ... along with the many blessings' as part of 'the one pattern'.

The ability to accept all the outward events of one's life was a reflection of a deeper acceptance of the self one is, including all one's woundedness and limitations, as 'valid' and 'worth something' in the eyes of God, if not in the eyes of others; and this itself led to a profound sense of joy, peace and gratitude in the acceptance of all that has been and will be. This sense of self-acceptance in and through the love of God was expressed vividly by Judith in an incident in which, seeing herself naked before God, she suddenly realised that it was 'alright' for God to see her as she was, since he had made her to be this way:

> I remember one day praying in the bathroom
> and thinking 'Oooh I'm naked God can see me'
> [*both laughing*]
> 'but that's alright

he made you
it's OK'

Whether integration remained an ideal towards which they moved or a reality which they had begun to grasp, there was a strong commitment amongst the women to relationship to God as the arena within which to draw together the disparate and contradictory elements within their lives. Integrity before self, God and others, in the sense of an intentional transparency about the reality of one's life in all its incompleteness, and the willingness to be changed by and within the primary relationships of their lives, were essential components of these women's spirituality.

Summary and Conclusions

This chapter has demonstrated the centrality of a relational consciousness to the women's faith lives, largely confirming the hypothesis that women's identity, development and spirituality are embedded in a strong sense of connectedness to the other. Whilst I have sought to recognise the dangers of a simplistic appeal to relationality in women's faith development – the tendency to idealise certain conventional or essentialist notions of women as those primarily responsible for the nurture and care of others, as well as the tendency to downplay differences between women's experiences of relationality – I propose that a more nuanced and sophisticated account of relationality can overcome such limitations. In attempting to offer a more rounded account of women's relational constructions of faith, we may note the following summary conclusions.

First, the range of relational conceptualisation is striking. The women employ personal and impersonal metaphors, gendered and non-gendered understandings of God; they draw on classical Christian metaphors of God as Father, Redeemer and Lord, as well as contemporary metaphors of the web and tapestry of life; they mix and connect different metaphors and models in novel and imaginative ways. As with their images of paralysis, there is an enormous creativity in the language they employ to speak of their relational understandings of self, other and God. This suggests the significance and breadth of their experiences of relationality and the profound degree to which such experiences have informed their understanding of faith.

Second, the women's accounts demonstrate the dynamism and flexibility of their relational consciousness. Whilst their sense of enduring connection to God or Being and others remains constant, the way in which this is construed changes over time, often quite dramatically. This supports Fowler's key contention of substantive qualitative change in the construction of faith across the life cycle. In their different ways, they demonstrate the paradox that it is only as they risk the loss of the sustaining relation which holds their lives in place that they come to rediscover it in new and unexpected ways. However, in contrast to Fowler's developmental descriptions, these women's accounts suggest the achievement of a more flexible and grounded self-in-relation via embeddedness in the demands of relationship rather than via separation and autonomy. This is not to deny the struggles that women experience as they attempt to balance the needs of the self with the needs of the other, nor that, in some cases, women *do* separate themselves from the suffocating relation (as we saw in Chapter 6) in order to achieve greater autonomy and freedom. Nevertheless, in most cases it appears that women work through this struggle within the context of enduring relational ties. They may break off from particular relationships or communal commitments which are perceived as stultifying and paralysing of the self, but in doing so, they are sustained by other connectional ties. In line with earlier studies (for example, White, 1985; Leary, 1988; Devor, 1989), my findings suggest that a faith development theory which is able to account for the developmental needs and experiences of women will need to incorporate such insights into a reworked model of faith in which relationality achieves a greater prominence.

Third, the women's accounts demonstrate the generativity of a relational consciousness. Particularly in their understanding of the interdependence of the divine–human relationship and relationships with others, they testify to a conviction of the fecundity of relational energy, which is not depleted as it is expended, but expands to include more and more as it is exercised in the labour of love. This conviction offsets the tension which many of the women experience as they struggle to integrate the needs of self with the demands of the other, and to resist the pressure to fuse so completely with the other that their own identity is submerged. Whilst this tension was a real one for the women, many of them had come to discover an affirmation of selfhood and an increase in ability to attend to the other as they found their lives sustained by the loving relationship to the Other present in every human encounter.

Fourth, the women's accounts demonstrate that a relational faith expresses itself differently in different settings. In particular, there seem to be important differences between the ways in which white middle-class women and black women construe the relationship to God and others. Relational connection to God appears to function as the source of an oppositional consciousness for some black women, in which connection to God fuels the struggle for justice against social structures and relationships which seek to deny the full personhood of black people; this stands in contrast to white middle-class women's sense of the coherence between relationship to God and relationship to others in which connection to God and connection to others reflect and mirror each other rather than stand in opposition. Other differences highlighted include the different attitudes to the mundane and domestic sphere held by single women, women with children, and women from different class backgrounds.

Finally, in contrast to the themes of paralysis and awakenings within women's spirituality, relationality appears to represent not so much a moment or phase within a developmental sequence of faith as a more fundamental epistemology which underlies and undergirds the whole of a woman's spiritual journey. In paralysis, the reality of relationality seems to be most at threat, contradicted by the woman's sense of alienation and impasse, yet even here there is a sense, sometimes dim, sometimes strong, that the self is held in place by a deeper reality of love and grace, a reality which holds out the promise of redemption. The various moments of awakening are often experienced as a renewed awareness of the relatedness of the self to its own powers of being, to the powers of nature, and to others – both those with whom one has obvious affinity and those who are alien or strange yet known in new ways to be affiliated to the self – and to the source of all connectedness, however that source may be named. Such awakening to a renewed sense of connectedness issues in a new naming of the self and spirituality, characterised by strongly relational language and imagery. Whilst the *awareness* of relationality may be eclipsed during the crisis of paralysis and may come to renewed expression after the various experiences of awakening, the women's descriptions of their deep, underlying sense of connectedness testify to the enduring reality of relationship which undergirds the self through all its various crises and breakthroughs.

Chapter 8

Conclusions and Implications for Christian Education and Pastoral Practice

If a pedagogy which takes women students seriously is to have a chance, and if such a pedagogy is also appropriate for all people, then the conditions which enable justice to occur must be created and enabled in the broader social, political, and economic contexts where teaching happens. And although the first birth is of the person, any pedagogy which stops at the Birthing of oneself is simply too narrow for our time. Birthing must spill over to the Birthing of just environments in society itself, for Birth and Breakthrough ... are 'resurrections into justice'.

Maria Harris[1]

Introduction

In this closing chapter, I reflect on the general significance and the practical implications of my research findings. In the first part of the chapter, I turn back to the theoretical discussion about faith development and consider what light my findings might shed on Fowler's theory in particular, and what theoretical revisions would be required of his theory in order to better account for women's faith. I then go on to consider the educational and pastoral implications of my findings for the learning and care of women and girls.

Implications of My Findings for Faith Development Theory

One of the subsidiary aims of this study was to discern whether current models and theories of faith development are able adequately to account for women's experience. In the discussion which follows I seek to evaluate how my findings relate to Fowler's theory, confirming it in certain respects and challenging it in others, and to discuss their relevance for the development of new models of faith development.

My findings do not invalidate Fowler's faith development theory; nor, indeed, could they, since I did not set out to test the validity of his faith stages as such. I have drawn extensively upon Fowler's theory at a number of levels and am indebted to it, even if I also remain critical of central aspects. My study shares Fowler's understanding of faith as a lifelong, dynamic process of meaning-making and patterning whose structures can become transparent in the self-narratives offered by

---

[1] Harris (1988), p. 88.

persons in the interview setting. My findings confirm the basic hypothesis of faith as an orderly and patterned deep structure in women's lives which integrates and gives coherence to all the disparate events of their lives.

Beyond this basic coherence of my findings with Fowler's underlying understanding of faith, there are other ways in which Fowler's theory can illuminate my findings. For example, Fowler's description of the process of change from one faith stage to another, with its characteristics of disrupted equilibrium, cognitive dissonance and the period of the 'neutral zone' after the deconstruction of one faith stage and before the emergence of another, provides some useful tools for analysing women's experiences of paralysis, paradox, dividedness and apophatic faithing. It may be that some of the dissonance, discomfort and anomie described by the women can be accounted for in terms of faith stage transition, perhaps in particular by the transition from Fowler's Stage 3 to Stage 4, in which the confidence and certainty of synthetic-conventional faith is deconstructed in order to pave the way to a more discriminating and consciously owned individuative-reflective faith. In addition, the women's accounts of faith 'awakenings' can be illuminated to a certain extent by Fowler's faith stage descriptions. Many of these accounts cohere, at significant points, with Fowler's description of Stage 4 faith, with its characteristics of self-chosen, self-conscious and critically owned faith which is capable of internalising authority and taking a more explicit responsibility for one's own values and commitments than previously. Fowler's recognition of the traumatic nature of the transition to Stage 4 faith, and its frequent correlation with an emotional home-leaving, also coheres with the women's accounts of home-leaving, travel and separation in Chapter 5.

Other accounts of the women's experiences of awakening seem to match Fowler's descriptions of Stage 5 conjunctive faith more closely, as do some of their accounts of relational faith in Chapter 7. The ability to hold in tension paradox and polarity, to live self-consciously and creatively with ambiguity and to be open to multiple perspectives on reality, which are hallmarks of Fowler's Stage 5, are strongly evident in many of the women's narratives: in the paradoxical relation to the vulnerable, needy other, in which the women discovered deeper dimensions of the self and the relation to God through openness to the stranger; in their accounts of illness, death and loss which necessitated the reworking of previous understandings of relationship and the move towards a paradoxical embrace of the fallibility and woundedness of human love at the same time as receiving it as divine grace and encounter; in the accounts in Chapter 7 of the changing relation to the divine and the transformation of a Stage 3-type idealised parent–child relation or Stage 4-type lover–lover relation into a much more diffused awareness of God in and through the relation to the human other and the work of justice; in their use of multiple images of connectedness which hold together apparent paradox, tension and contradiction; in their affirmation of transcendence in immanence and the sacred in the mundane in their accounts of a sacramental and incarnational spirituality; in their ability to empathise deeply with the other in their suffering whilst still holding to the conviction of the redemptive love of God; and perhaps above all in their accounts of integrated faith in which they evoked the powerful sense of a faith capable of holding together all the disparate contradictions, conflicts, ambiguities and pluralities of experience in a full-hearted acceptance of all that is within the mystery of the love of God.

Nevertheless, whilst Fowler's theory can offer helpful insights into some aspects of the women's accounts of their faith lives, there are other aspects of my findings which seem to demand different interpretation, which push against the grain of Fowler's theory, or for which Fowler does not seem to offer an appropriate or adequate account, and which are more adequately understood from alternative theoretical perspectives. I shall highlight four key findings which seem to challenge Fowler's account at important points, or at least call attention to aspects of women's faith which are not given prominence in Fowler's account.

First, the dominance of concrete, visual, narrative and embodied forms of thinking over propositional, abstract or analytical thought in the women's faith accounts, as well as the evidence of what I have called 'apophatic' forms of faithing, challenge the strong emphasis on the cognitive component of faith in Fowler's theory. Whilst Fowler's stage account does offer some significant role for narrative and metaphor in the development of faith, it tends to be sidelined by the strong emphasis on critical reasoning and analytical thinking, especially in the movement to Stage 4, owned faith. A preference for the language of concretion and narrative, in Fowler's stage account, would tend to suggest either the mythic-literal faith style of Stage 2, or the reworking of concretion the other side of critical reasoning, the 'second naivete', of Stage 5. What Fowler's account seems to miss is an adequate account of the role of intuitive knowing, imaginative, metaphoric and concrete forms of thinking, in the movement to owned, responsible and self-consciously chosen faith. For many of the women in my study, it seems that such styles of thinking and awareness were at least as important in the achievement of a more owned faith as critical thinking and analysis. Because of its strong reliance on Piaget, Fowler's account, I suggest, overemphasises the significance of abstract thinking and formal logical thought in the development of adult faith. This needs to be balanced by greater attention to the roles of affect, imagination, symbol and narrative, not only in the earlier, pre-logical stages and the later, post-logical ones, but throughout the whole stage sequence.[2] Relational and psychodynamic theories could offer something important here, providing interpretative frameworks for analysing the function of the symbolic and affective realm.

If the significance of narrative, symbol and the language of concretion is underplayed in Fowler's account, even more so is the possibility of giving recognition to the kind of faithing I have described as 'apophatic', since it seems to represent the antithesis of Fowler's model of articulate, conceptually clear and consciously owned faith. I do not wish to say that apophatic faith is anti-intellectual, irrational or nonvolitional; but that it is an agnostic, paradoxical and elusive kind of knowing which operates at the edges of rational and critical thinking, rooted in denunciation and negative naming, which often does not even know that it knows, because it is most aware of what it does *not* know. Fowler's account does not seem to allow for such kinds of faithing as legitimate and viable forms of mature faith; they stand outside his map of faith. Even Stage 5 faith, with its emphasis on paradox and mystery, is articulate and self-conscious about its embrace of polarity and ambiguity, *knows* that it has chosen paradox and knows *why* it has chosen it; whereas the majority of the women in my study who exhibited

---

[2] See Fowler (1996) for a more nuanced account of the emotions in each of the stages.

apophatic styles of faithing could not have articulated this sense of faithing for themselves. Within the terms of a cognitive developmental model, such lack of consciousness would argue for regarding the faith stance as pre-critical and nonvolitional. Nevertheless, I want to argue that such forms of faithing, along with the preference for narrative and concrete forms of faithing, represent crucial means of faithing for women, and perhaps others, who feel themselves to be marginal to mainstream religious traditions and academic culture. They represent part of what we might term the 'underside' of Fowler's faith descriptions, and alert attention to aspects of his account which, whilst not entirely absent, nevertheless require fuller explication and more detailed attention. A more dialectical type of faith development theory might better be able to account for such features, since it would recognise the ways in which socio-political context frame and shape the kinds of faith that are available to women in a patriarchal culture.

Secondly, my research has highlighted the dominance of personalised and relational forms of appropriating faith over abstract and impersonal means, and Chapter 7 demonstrated the centrality of a relational consciousness to the women's faith lives, confirming the hypothesis that women's identity, development and spirituality are embedded in a strong sense of connectedness to the other. Whilst Chapter 6 also demonstrated that, for some women, the pattern which Fowler has described of separation out from the demands of relationship into a more autonomous faith (as integral to the movement from Stage 3 to Stage 4 faith) seems to hold good, this does not represent the pattern for all the women in my study, by any means. Many of the women's stories suggest the movement towards a more flexible and self-consciously owned faith, not in separation or critical distance from the relationships and commitments in which their lives are embedded, but precisely in and through these relational ties. Thus, my findings lend support to those of other studies that, for women, the passage from 'conforming' to 'owned' faith may well be rather different from that described by Fowler, and, therefore, that Fowler's account of the middle stages needs to be redrawn in order to account more adequately for women's relational faith consciousness. Again, it is not that Fowler's theory pays no attention to the demands of relationship; indeed, relationality is a key component in his description of faith and is stressed in the early stages, particularly in Stage 3's concern with the maintenance of interpersonal relationships and mutual perspective taking. Yet in the process of development to critically owned faith (Stage 4) and beyond to the embrace of paradox and mystery in Stage 5, the significance of relationality seems to get lost, as if, in the later stages, it is transcended. My findings, along with those of other studies already quoted, suggests that, in future accounts of faith development, women's experience of relationality should find a more central place – and perhaps, too, this will illuminate in significant ways men's struggles towards a faith in which connectedness to the other and the preservation of one's own selfhood are not in competition, but in harmony.

The third feature of my research which I suggest offers an interesting challenge to Fowler's approach to faith development concerns not only the content of my findings but the process of the research methodology itself. My choice of an open-ended interview methodology allowed the distinctive shape of each woman's interview to emerge and become a feature of analysis, and I have argued that the pattern of the interview itself reflected, in significant ways, the larger shape of the woman's faith development. This methodological approach allowed for the distinctive shape and texture of each woman's faith narrative to come into view, in contrast with Fowler's methodology which, whilst allowing for distinctiveness, imposes a prior order and shaping upon the individual's narrative through the use of a semi-structured format. I suggest that both methodological approaches – that is, semi-structured and open-ended – are useful, and can complement each other. In faith development research, the use of open-ended interviews, along the lines of my own study, might bring into greater prominence the distinctive shaping power of individuals in giving expression to their faith, which would complement Fowler's emphasis upon the structuring power of the faith stages. A more profound sense of the unique shape and structure of each person's faith journey would not necessarily contradict Fowler's affirmation of broader structural features, but it would correct an overemphasis which tends to limit the perception of difference.

The fourth feature I want to mention here concerns one of the major generative themes to emerge from my study, that of paralysis. Developmental models *per se*, and cognitive developmental theories in particular, focus upon progress and movement, highlighting the impetus within the stages towards the next, 'higher', level of consciousness or pattern of behaviour. As such, they sideline or ignore the reality of paralysis, impasse, lack of movement, even regression, which the women in my study testified to so powerfully. I suggest that we need other kinds of models, and language drawn from other spheres, to interpret the women's experiences of paralysis and impasse. For example, FitzGerald (1986) demonstrates how models drawn from mystical tradition, such as John of the Cross's 'dark night of the soul', can illuminate helpfully women's experiences of paralysis and impasse in ways which developmental language cannot. Or again, the more earthed, narrative and metaphorical language of women's contemporary fiction and poetry can offer helpful ways of speaking about such experiences in ways which do justice both to the painfulness of women's experiences of paralysis and to their potential for creativity. If developmental paradigms have something to say to such experiences, it is likely to be lifespan, relational and dialectical developmental theories rather than cognitive ones which are most useful, since they are more sensitive to the relational, socio-political and cultural contexts of women's lives.

Stage developmental theories such as Fowler's can be useful heuristic tools for organising and interpreting the complex phenomena of human faith. Yet, theories and models are precisely that: not the 'whole truth', but more or less adequate ways of organising, relating and interpreting observed behaviour and experience. No one model or theory can account for every aspect of human behaviour. By highlighting certain features, it will inevitably screen out or marginalise others. The very strengths of stage development theory – the suggestion of order and coherence in apparently random behaviour; its intuition of pattern across great diversity; its description of movement towards increasing flexibility, integration and complexity; its amenability to educational and pastoral application through the description of a normative pattern of development – are also its weaknesses. The imposition of a universal pattern of development tends to screen out the unique and irreducible particularity of lived faith experience and the contextual variations of culture, gender and class; the highlighting of progression and movement detracts awareness from paralysis, impasse and the experience of being stuck; the prioritising of rational, cognitive and linguistic expressions of truth marginalise other, more intuitive, bodily and relational forms of knowing.

Thus, whilst recognising the heuristic value of developmental models, I affirm the need for other kinds of models to set alongside them in order to relativise and correct their imbalances, and to call attention to aspects of human experience which they marginalise. The kinds of models of women's spirituality which I have outlined in earlier chapters of this study, such as those by Christ (1986), Osiek (1986) and Harris (1989) – and indeed, such as the rudimentary model of alienation, awakenings and relationality I have put forward in this study – provide important correctives and alternatives to Fowler's model, highlighting aspects of women's experiences not accorded centrality in his account, and offering a different language with which to analyse and interpret such experiences. Such models do not *replace* Fowler's theoretical account of faith development so much as correct and relativise it, offering another means of interpretation, another kind of language, another heuristic model to set alongside that of Fowler (as well as others) and thus enrich our understanding of faith.

In other words, I am arguing that it is not a question of 'either/or' but of 'both/and'. We need different kinds of models and theories to account for the richness and specificity of human experience. This is not to say that 'anything goes' and that there are not 'better' and 'worse' theoretical accounts. Certainly it is important to analyse the different interpretative approaches offered by different theories and models, and to discriminate between apparently conflicting understandings. There needs to be rigorous dialogue between different accounts of faith, in order to tease out the strengths and weaknesses of each, and to see where fresh enquiry is needed. But dialogue depends upon the integrity and mutual respect of each partner, rather than the replacement of one, inevitably limited, understanding by another. Thus, I am not calling for a rejection of Fowler so much as an ongoing conversation between his model and others, and the revision and restatement of his theory in the light of new research findings, at the same time as other approaches are developed and strengthened.

Research into the distinctive features and patterns of women's faith and spirituality is, itself, at an early stage of development. It is too soon to expect a fully elaborated model or theory of women's faith to emerge. At this point within the development of the field, there are a number of rudimentary models of women's faith which can critique and expose the limitations of existing, androcentric theories. The very rudimentariness of these models is an incentive to further exploration and research and to ongoing dialogue with existing, more fully developed models such as Fowler's. I hope that my own study may encourage others to continue that exploration in new and creative ways.

Implications of My Findings for Educational and Pastoral Practice

My research findings, and the rudimentary models of the processes and patterns of women's faith development which I have proposed, do not admit of prescriptive educational and pastoral application. Nevertheless, they do, I believe, suggest broad principles which can shape the pastoral care and Christian education of women and girls.[3] There is nothing essentially new about the principles outlined below: the emphases they represent are quite familiar in feminist theological and educational discourse, though they are hardly prominent in the educational and pastoral practices of the church. As principles, they admit of translation to a wide range of settings and sites, including formal and informal learning situations, secular and religious settings, large-scale and small-scale contexts. I would hope that they bear translation to a variety of social and cultural settings, but I am aware that their translation into diverse settings requires sensitivity to particular cultural and social constraints, customs and mores. It cannot be assumed that they are universally valid or appropriate.

Without wishing to limit the range of settings in which these principles can be applied, I have in mind three particular contexts within which the educational and pastoral needs and interests of women and girls require prioritising, and to which I address my recommendations. First, I am thinking of the formal learning and training environment of theological education in the adult school setting: in other words, university and higher education theology departments, theological college, seminary and course settings. This is not so much one setting as many, including full- and part-time options, residential, part-residential and non-residential settings, distance learning, local group and centre-based learning, and a combination of these modes in mixed-mode format. Within these different settings, a diverse range of learning methods, both formal and informal, didactic and experiential, group-focused and individual-focused, are employed. In many such settings, there are large numbers of women students, although such institutions are usually staffed by more men than women educators. The particular educational and pastoral needs of women in these settings therefore remains a crucial concern.

The second main setting, or cluster of settings, I have in mind is the wider educational and pastoral life of the churches beyond specific and formal institutions of schooling. This includes a broad range of activities and sites: formal liturgy and preaching conducted in the church building; informal acts of worship in home, hospital, school or prison settings; large group gatherings, and small group meetings, in a variety of locations; informal gatherings of friends and fellow-Christians meeting over meals or around the kitchen table; cross-denominational as well as intra-denominational and interfaith settings and groupings, and one-to-one encounters of pastoral visiting, counselling and spiritual direction. Again, within these settings, women often form the majority of the laity, and are increasingly present in leadership roles, both lay and ordained. Yet patterns of learning and pastoral care are still embedded in androcentric ways of thinking and functioning. Thus, in this setting, too, the needs of women and girls require prioritising.

The third setting I seek to address is the context of women's networks, communities and groupings in which women-only learning and mutual care takes place. This might include formal and informal gatherings within and across women's religious communities, as well as gatherings under the umbrella of women's organisations, both inside and outside the church, and local or regional groups. Paradoxically, whilst the opportunities for formal learning for women in the theological sphere have probably increased in the past ten or fifteen years, certainly

---

[3] See also Slee (1989, 2000).

in terms of the ready availability of courses in feminist theology, women's studies and gender studies, at the same time, opportunities for more informal, experiential and grass-roots learning have diminished. National networks such as Women in Theology, which flourished in the 1980s, have been, in many ways, the victims of their own success. Having achieved many of their original objectives, such as the promotion of publishing and academic courses of study in feminist theology and related fields, they have disbanded or lost their original energy and creativity. Yet many women both within the churches and outside formal church allegiance express the need for women-only settings where there is space and opportunity for a range of learning, sharing and exploration.

The principles enunciated below offer fruitful suggestions for creating forms of learning and pastoral care for women in these three settings, as well as others. In each case, I seek to demonstrate how the particular principle enunciated emerges from my research findings before going on to discuss its practical implications for key areas of pastoral practice and Christian education.

The Grounding of Practice in Women's Experience

My research findings confirm the strongly experiential bias in women's spirituality. Whilst some of the women did speak of mystical or numinous religious experience, for most, spirituality was rooted firmly in the everyday, mundane world of work, relationships, home life and contact with others. Chapter 6 demonstrated how the women's experiences of awakening were mostly triggered by common experiences such as travel, motherhood, relationships of different sorts and meaningful work or artistic activity. Chapter 4 also demonstrated the women's preference for embedded, concrete, narrative and metaphorical modes of thinking and talking about faith over abstract, conceptual forms of thought. This finding matches that of Belenky and her colleagues who noted the preference of the women in their study for a pragmatic kind of knowledge rooted in action and observation, rather than in words, and 'tuned to the concrete and particular', in contrast to the kind of theoretical knowledge prized by academic institutions (Belenky et al., 1986, p. 201).

My research also highlights the hiddenness and invisibility of women's faith experience, both in their painful struggles with paralysis and alienation, in their spiritual awakenings, and in their commitment to relational connections with others. The alienation which the women expressed in their experiences of paralysis was exacerbated, if not partly formed, by the sense the women had of their experiences not being named, recognised or acknowledged publicly within the life of the churches and communities to which they belonged. Their experiences of awakenings through relationships with others, embodied forms of knowing and embedded commitments frequently failed to conform to the stereotypes of the spiritual life which they had received, which prized the flight from the mundane, the denial of the body and the passions and the prioritising of religious ideals over the demands of connection.

Thus a key principle undergirding the pastoral care and religious education of women must be the grounding of practice in women's experience, and, in particular, a commitment to the naming and disclosing of women's hidden experiences. This principle suggests, on the one hand, the need to prioritise an inductive and experiential approach to women's religious education and pastoral care and, on the other hand, the need to bring into greater visibility the unacknowledged realities of women's lives and affirm them as authoritative and creative.

Both of these emphases are prominent in much feminist theology, pedagogy and pastoral practice. Thus, in considering the feminist practice of theological education, the Mud Flower Collective insist that it must 'begin with our own lives-in-relation': 'We believe that this is where all research, teaching, and learning should begin ... In order to have responsible and creative dialogue, in such a way that each participant actually learns, we must begin with the study of our lives' (Mud Flower Collective, 1985, p. 24).

Similarly, Belenky and her co-writers advocate an approach to the teaching of women which is strongly contextual, begins with women's personal experience and is geared towards a pragmatic, lived knowledge which relates theoretical and abstract understanding to the demands of women's real lives (Belenky et al., 1986, pp. 198ff). Maria Harris, in her commitment to an aesthetic approach to religious education, emphasises the engagement with feeling and experience via the arts as a counter to the predominantly conceptual and verbal approach to most university education. Harris' definition of teaching as 'the incarnation of subject matter in ways that lead to the revelation of subject matter' (1987, p. xv) puts embodied engagement with reality at the heart of education and makes the primary 'subject matter' of all learning the life of the learner herself:

> Teaching, when seen as an activity of religious imagination, is the incarnation of subject matter in ways that lead to the revelation of subject matter. At the heart of this revelation is the discovery that human beings are the primary subjects of all teaching, subjects who discover themselves as possessing the grace of power, especially the power of re-creation, not only of themselves, but of the world in which they live. (Harris, 1987, p. xv)

Subject matter can be incarnated through verbal forms, especially through metaphor, through earth forms which teach via materiality, and through embodied forms, primarily the human body itself but, however it is done, the aim of such embodiment is to empower the learner to come into self-possession, to discover truths about themselves and about the world in such a way that they can act meaningfully in it. Harris' model of teaching has much to offer the whole church, but has particular resonance for women learners, who have been deeply alienated from learning in the academy which has denied the embodiment of ideas in concrete experience and the primary context of learning in students' own lives.[4]

Not only in feminist approaches to learning, but in women's preaching, liturgy and spiritual direction, there is a strong emphasis on beginning with women's experience. Elaine Graham notes the strongly personal and particular nature of much women's preaching, which not only affirms the concrete realities of women's lives but also implicitly critiques the tendency of conventional preaching to universalise and totalise limited, male experience: 'The dogmatism engendered by

---

[4] Such an experiential emphasis in education does not deny the importance of theoretical or abstract knowledge, nor the need to engage with tradition, but it does require that such material is always brought into dialogue with learners' lives and the wider social context in which learning takes place.

abstraction is undermined by the immediacy and concretion of hearing, and sharing, another's situation' (Graham, 1996, p. 176). Kathleen Fischer asserts women's experience as the authoritative source for a feminist approach to spiritual direction, and names as a first principle of such practice 'respect for women's experience' (1989, p. 12). Through story-telling, work on dreams and images, and the creation of ritual, the spiritual director seeks to unearth the revelatory content of women's experiences. The whole movement of feminist-inspired liturgical creation (for example, Ruether, 1985; St Hilda Community, 1991; Ward et al., 1995; Ward and Wild, 1995b) can be seen as a celebration and affirmation of women's experiences as a source for knowledge of the divine.

Taking seriously women's experience as the starting point for learning, for pastoral care and spiritual growth necessarily entails a commitment to the naming and disclosing of women's hidden experiences, for, under patriarchy, much of women's experience has remained invisible, unnamed and underground. This is another strong theme in feminist preaching, liturgy, education and spiritual direction. Heather Walton and Susan Durber, in their collection of women's preaching, speak of the significance of making women visible in the text over against the majority of preached sermons which make no reference to women at all, and the naming of issues which are specific to women against 'the profound silence from our pulpits on vital subjects like rape, abuse and violence against women' as well as 'the joy women experience, for example in sexuality and procreation' (Walton and Durber, 1994, p. xiii). Much feminist liturgy has been devoted to precisely such a naming of the hidden realities of women's lives. In their collection of *Human Rites*, for example, Ward and Wild bring together rituals, not only for the birth of a child, but also for still-births, abortions or miscarriages; not only for marriage but also for lesbian and gay partnerships, friendships of various kinds, and for divorce and separations; not only for rites within the 'temple', but also for ceremonies in the home, workplace and outdoors; not only to mark recognised rites of passage but also to celebrate menarche, menopause and other forms of female self-affirmation; not only to name female bodiliness and sexuality, but also to protest against the sexual and physical abuse of women and all forms of female oppression. In such ways, women's experiences are explicitly ritualised as potentially sacred, salvific and revelatory of the divine.[5]

As I have stressed throughout this study, the appeal to women's experience as a primary source of feminist theology, spirituality and pedagogy, must not be read as a device for enforcing a false consensus amongst women who, in reality, experience many differences, conflicts and tensions. An experiential and inductive feminist pastoral and educational practice must wrestle seriously with issues of race, class and other forms of diversity. Noting the 'danger of turning inward, even when the inwardness is toward our people and not only into our individual selves', the Mud Flower Collective insist:

> Beginning with our lives, we must do so in as diverse a cultural situation as we can find – if not face to face with people of different cultures, then at least through engagement with

---

[5] Ward and Wild's (1995b) collection is not exclusively focused on women's rituals, but its breadth and range do exemplify key characteristics in feminist liturgy.

their books, art, music, and rituals. Educationally, this pluralism requires that we learn to listen more astutely; that we suspend the urge to idolatrize our own perceptions and beliefs; and that we challenge one another, rather than acting like passive receptors. (1985, pp. 25–6)

Taking diversity seriously in educational and pastoral practice has implications at many levels of both content and process. It requires that we draw fully on the writings, artistry, autobiographies and analyses of women of colour, lesbian women, working-class women, and all those women who tend to be sidelined by white, middle-class culture. It requires attending to the processes we practise in education and pastoral care to ensure that they are genuinely inclusive, and not simply based on white middle-class women's preferences. By translation in such ways, the principle of giving educational and pastoral priority to women's experiences will ensure that women are enabled to support one another in the radical particularity of their lives, rather than reinforcing false uniformity.

Creating Relational and Conversational Settings

Another significant finding of my study concerns the relational nature of women's faith. Chapter 7 demonstrated how the women's spirituality was profoundly relational in nature, rooted in a strong sense of connection to others, to the wider world and to God as the source of relational power. The women's preference for relational modes of faithing was demonstrated, not only in the content of their faith stories, but in the manner and style of their narratives in the conversational context of the interviews.

The second principle thus concerns the need to create settings and practices which reflect and endorse women's relational and conversational ways of knowing. A number of writers call attention to this need. With reference to women's education, Belenky and her colleagues affirm women's need for what they describe as 'connected teaching', characterised by affirmation of the student as knower, the collaborative pursuit of knowledge in a setting marked by genuine dialogue, and the commitment to the integration of subjective and objective ways of knowing (Belenky et al., 1986, pp. 214ff). Chopp similarly highlights dialogue as a key characteristic of feminist theological education, insisting that dialogue is not simply an abstract debate about ideas, but 'real interaction among embodied persons, with openness and respect for mutual critique' (1995, p. 107). Hess describes a form of 'conversational education' in the community of the church which can meet women's needs by holding together 'hard dialogue and deep connections' with others, with scripture and tradition, and with God (Hess, 1997, pp. 182ff).

Such connected ways of teaching contrast with the traditions of academia, which have inculcated knowledge through separation, scepticism and doubt, and modelled the 'banking' concept of teaching (Freire, 1972) in which learners are regarded as empty vessels to be filled with the knowledge transmitted by the experts. Belenky and her co-writers offer the model of the 'midwife teacher' who affirms the student as knower, draws out her knowledge and assists her in giving birth to her own ideas, in contrast to the 'banker teacher' who deposits knowledge in the learner's head (Belenky et al., 1986, pp. 217ff). Whereas banking education anaesthetises, midwife teaching assists in the emergence of consciousness, enabling the student to more truly feel, and know what they feel. Midwife teachers focus on the student's knowledge, not their own, placing their own expertise at the disposal of the student's growth. Midwife teachers provide a culture for growth by encouraging genuine dialogue, marked by the collaborative pursuit of understanding, permission for uncertainty and tentativeness, the embrace of diversity and the connection of the student's subjective experience with the objective knowledge provided by scholars (ibid.).

The model of the 'midwife teacher' can be applied to other contexts of pastoral care. Thus, Margaret Guenther writes of the spiritual director as midwife who is present at the threshold of spiritual life, assists at the birth, encourages and interprets the birth-giver's experience, knows when to confront and when to wait patiently, and finally celebrates the new life when it emerges (Guenther, 1992, pp. 84ff). Similarly, Jill Marsh has applied the model of midwife to the ordained minister (Marsh, 1996), suggesting that the chief function of the minister is to accompany people at different stages of their lives, and to 'use the relationship between her/himself and others to decide about how best to support God's activity in the process that is taking place' (p. 11). Within such a relationship of trust and support, women can begin to articulate their own needs, name their own experience, gain a sense of voice and agency, and awaken to critical consciousness.

Bons-Storm calls attention to women's need for an affirming other who will take seriously her stories and 'encourage her weak sense of subject quality to grow', an ally who will 'explore her situation and her self-narrative together with her, trying to find out where her strengths and weaknesses lie' (1996, p. 141). Bons-Storm insists that 'women first have to tell their stories among themselves, get used to their own voices, and listen to one another' before they have the courage and strength 'to endure the scorn of the dominant discourse' (ibid., p. 147). This points to the need for women-only groups and settings so that women may tell their own stories in their own words, and communicate with one another in the conversational practices which are distinctive to women and which are not generally characteristic of mixed-group settings.[6] Opportunities for girls and women to meet and talk together without men present are vital as spaces where they can determine the agenda for themselves and explore issues in their own conversational practices. Such settings are also important for enabling women to express the anger, rage and pain which are attendant upon their exploration of their experience, as they mourn the loss of both personal and communal freedoms and name the realities of injustice (see Harris, 1988, pp. 46ff).

At the same time, alongside the creation of single-sex groupings, there is also the need to develop new conversational practices in which women and men can listen and talk to each other in more mutual and cooperative ways. What such conversation might look like is captured beautifully by Marge Piercy in her poem 'Councils'.[7] Piercy suggests that such conversation needs to take place in small groups, sitting on the floor, 'on stones and mats and blankets'. There must be no front to the speaking, and no platforms, stages or tables. Conversations might take place in the

---

6 See note 8, Chapter 3, pp. 55–6.
7 In Piercy (1982).

dark, for 'in the dark we could utter our feelings', 'we could propose/ and describe and suggest.' No speaker would utter more than twice or less than once. In this kind of earthy, respectful, collaborative conversation, women and men have different but complementary responsibilities. As women dare to speak and assert what they know to be so, as men learn to listen and 'stop dancing solos on the ceiling', each can find a new way of connecting.

Other writers emphasise the relational qualities of feminist preaching and liturgy which, in different ways, can nurture and strengthen women's sense of self. Thus, Carol Norén asserts that, for feminists, 'the sermon cannot be a monologue reinforcing dominance and submission by virtue of an elevated pulpit and/or the preacher as one set apart for special and sacred work' (1992, p. 155). Rather, 'preaching must become relational and dialogical'; it must be 'understood as belonging to the community, in particular the community of women' (ibid.). Similarly, Elaine Graham understands the tendency of women preachers to tell others' stories as an example of 'conversational practice' which 'match[es] the personal with the collective', and 'invit[es] the hearers to place their stories alongside those of others' (1996, p. 177). A core value in feminist liturgy is the creation of ritual which is genuinely collaborative, rooted in shared leadership and mutually empowering forms of relating. Thus, writing of the liturgical practice of the St Hilda's experimental community based in London, Suzanne Fageol reflects:

> Being feminist meant it was important to us to establish intimacy and relationship with each other. By coming together initially in non-eucharistic worship, we could develop friendship. We would have opportunities to get to know one another as human beings through dialogue about our common purpose and through sharing our views on faith and God. As different members took responsibility for providing liturgical material for worship, we established a pattern of equality between women and men, clergy and laity. Everyone was included and encouraged to exercise whatever gifts of ministry they brought. (St Hilda Community, 1991, p. 17)

Again, such practices cannot sidestep conflict, divisions and the struggles amongst women for power, as the story of the St Hilda community itself makes abundantly clear (see Furlong, in St Hilda Community, 1991). But they represent ways of embodying feminist models of community as the 'discipleship of equals' gathered round a 'roundtable' seeking new ways of relating and living out freedom (see Kanyoro, 1997). It is only within such communities where there is a fundamental commitment to mutual care and connection that there is the safety for the kind of 'hard dialogue' Hess names as an essential quality of authentic conversation. 'Real talk', marked by the qualities of collaboration, empathy and receptivity, is not afraid to confront difference, conflict and difficult conceptual work, but it does so within the context of care (Hess, 1997, pp. 184ff).

The Foregrounding of Imagination

One of the hopeful findings of my research is its demonstration of the remarkable linguistic and metaphoric creativity of women as they seek to give expression to their struggles to achieve authentic selfhood, relationships with others, and connectedness to ultimate reality. The range and originality of the women's images of God, their metaphors of the divine–human relationship and their understanding of spirituality are impressive. The vitality even of their metaphors of powerlessness and impasse is striking. These findings suggest women's capacity for linguistic and symbolic imagination, and highlight the potential creativity of the symbolic realm for them.

A number of writers have drawn attention to the critical significance of imagination in women's religious education and pastoral care.[8] Kathleen Fischer (1989) names the transformation of religious imagination as one of the key components of feminist spiritual direction (pp. 65ff), whilst Rebecca Chopp (1995) highlights it as one of the essential characteristics of feminist educational process, alongside justice and dialogue. Maria Harris has done much to illuminate the special function of imagination in adult religious education (1987), and, in her study of women and teaching (1988), shows how imagination is essential to the work of remembering, ritual mourning and artistry, which she identifies as three of the key movements in women's religious education. For Harris, the unique function of the imagination is to give form, shape and embodiment to that which is to be taught so that it leads to the revelation of subject matter, the encounter with the divine.

Marjorie Proctor-Smith (1990) emphasises the role of the imagination in feminist liturgical practice. She argues that women's imaginations have been 'colonized' by patriarchal culture, a process whereby the 'arts of survival' are 'turned to rituals of self-hatred': 'Anamnesis for women requires the creation of feminist imagination, which permits women to appropriate our past and to envision our future in ways that reject self-hatred and make survival possible' (p. 37). Imagination has both a constructive purpose and a reconstructive one for women, enabling a critical deconstruction of patriarchal ways of seeing and the creation of new ways of seeing. It enables women to reconnect with a past which has been lost to them, to critique and reject inadequate and oppressive forms of understanding, grasp hold of the opportunities of the present, and live in hope towards an unrealised yet beckoning future.

In the practices of Christian education and pastoral care, there are many ways in which women's imagination can be engaged. As Chopp (1995, p. 109) suggests, there is a need to widen the resources of theological education to include literature and poetry, and, one might add, the visual and plastic arts, drama, movement, music and film. The teaching of faith is still too much dominated by the rational and cerebral mode, which prizes the dogmatic tradition of systematic theology but tends to underplay the symbolic realm within scripture and spirituality. Yet women's traditions of spirituality are often enshrined in such symbolic forms; lacking opportunities for public leadership or teaching roles, women in the past codified and transmitted their experience through poetry, hymnody, craft forms and popular piety, including much that is now anonymous. There is a need to reclaim such traditions, and to make full use of the work of women writers, artists, poets and musicians, both past and present, as a way of handing on women's spiritual traditions to future generations. The engagement with the creative work of other women is an empowering act for female learners, because it testifies implicitly to the creative

---

[8] For a more sustained discussion of the role of the imagination and the arts in religious education, see Slee (1992).

potential in each and every woman. Hearing the distinctive and authoritative voice of the woman poet or novelist, for example, who has often had to forge her speech out of great struggle, acts as a prophetic summons to other women to dare to speak out their truth, to try out their own voice and language, and to know they are not alone in doing so. Viewing women's art similarly communicates at a profound level the legitimacy of women's efforts to embody their truth, and challenges the notion enshrined in so much art of woman as the object of the male gaze, rather than those who actively scrutinise, behold and portray what they see. Working with women's art, then, whatever the subject matter or the medium, enables female learners to internalise at a deep level their right to take up a subject position in the world, to be those who proactively shape their experience into meaningful forms, forms which themselves communicate a distinctive view of the world to others. This is so, whether the subject matter is explicitly religious or not. When the subject matter *is* explicitly religious, a further message is conveyed to women about their right to take up a subject position in the sacred realm itself, right at the heart of the temple, in the place which has been for centuries reserved for male actors. Thus, creative work by female poets, liturgists and artists that explicitly addresses religious themes is extremely important in affirming and supporting women's spiritual quest. Female images of God and Christ, for example, which draw on women's experience to re-image God in female form, can speak powerfully to women about the presence of the divine in their own bodies and struggles in ways which male images can never do.

Yet educators need to go beyond the *use* of such artistic resources to the active encouragement of learners to engage in artistry as a way of exploring and discerning truth. Teachers can learn much about the educative and revelatory potential of the imagination from those engaged in spiritual direction, preaching and feminist liturgy. Much of the work of spiritual direction concerns the imaginative exploration of story, imagery and symbol. Directors from the Ignatian tradition, in particular, have developed skills and techniques for employing the imagination to deepen the relationship with God and the understanding of self and others. Painting or drawing familiar images of God, exploring new ones in scripture, or using the imagination to enter into scriptural stories are common methods employed in spiritual direction. Fischer (1989) discusses how these methods can be problematic for women, and need to be reworked in the light of feminist critique. Thus in spiritual direction with women, there is a need to both heal and expand dominant male God-language, by transforming the religious imagination and integrating new images of God into women's spiritual lives. Similarly, praying with scripture can be problematic for women, since in so many texts women are missing altogether, and, when present, are frequently marginal or stereotypical figures who merely reinforce oppressive patterns of self-understanding and relating. Fischer and Hess both offer a number of strategies for spiritual directors and educators to enable women to work creatively with scripture. These include working positively with stories of biblical women; finding hope in liberating passages which, whilst not addressed in their original context to women, may be reappropriated for women; remembering and mourning women's pain via stories of abuse and 'texts of terror' (Trible, 1984); and, listening to the silences in scripture, and employing imagination to recreate the lives of women who exist only between the lines of patriarchal texts (Fischer, 1989, pp. 93ff; Hess, 1997, pp. 195ff).

Where the work of spiritual direction is generally conducted within a one-to-one setting, liturgy and preaching take place within a gathered community where the realities of women's lives can be evoked and their potential for transformation can be proclaimed publicly. Much contemporary feminist preaching and liturgy demonstrates the transformative power of imagination to heal, liberate and disclose fresh revelation in women's experience. The great outpouring of feminist liturgies in recent decades is testimony both to the felt need for such alternative liturgical expression by women across the world, and to the creativity released within women when they claim the right to make their own ritual expressing their own lives' concerns and struggles. The liturgical innovation of this movement encompasses radical experimentation with language, gesture, movement, silence and the use of space, and offers hope of transformation to the church's worship, as well as providing a space where women can exercise freedom and imagination in their quest for a more holistic spirituality.

The Accompaniment of Women in Silence, Paradox and Apophatic Faithing

Whilst the foregoing principles emphasise the importance of bringing into expression the realities of women's spiritual lives, whether through speech, symbol or embodied forms of knowing, this principle concerns the underside of naming and form-giving, namely the importance of being a presence to and with women in the places of silence and not knowing. My research has highlighted the significance of what I have described as 'apophatic' faithing, in which women express their sense of truth in negative, denunciatory or paradoxical, contradictory terms. Such a faith stance may be called upon in transitional times or may mark a more enduring commitment on the part of some women. In addition, during times of paralysis and impasse, a majority of the women experienced the inadequacy of language to express the reality of their struggles and the insufficiency of existing spiritual models or theological terms to capture their experience.

These common experiences of being caught in a place where language, concepts and models do not 'fit' reality require a different pastoral and educational response. They require a willingness and ability on the part of pastors and educators to desist from the effort to name or give form to experience, and to inhabit the place of silence and apophatic faithing alongside women who find themselves there. They require the creation of spaces for waiting, for silence, for apparent nothingness. They require the affirmation of not-knowing, of darkness, and of contradiction as essential components of mature faith, rather than its negation. As Margaret Atwood's poem, 'Journey to the interior' suggests, the standard guides and maps no longer serve:

> A compass is useless; also
> trying to take directions
> from the movements of the sun,
> which are erratic;
> and words here are as pointless
> as calling in a vacant
> Wilderness.[9]

---

[9] In Atwood (1998), p. 16.

Yet faith traditions do have resources which can speak to apophatic faith, and these need to be made available to women. Fischer suggests making use of the writings of *The Cloud of Unknowing*, Meister Eckhart, St John of the Cross, Simone Weil and Thomas Merton, for example (Fischer, 1989, p. 62). Such an accompaniment of women whilst they are unable to give meaningful or adequate shape to their experience is an essential means of legitimating their experiences of silence and invisibility, and of affirming their potential creativity. It requires both insight and sensitivity on the part of pastors and educators to discern when is the appropriate moment for silence, waiting and desisting from the active pursuit of meaning, and when the moment has come for moving out of unknowing into form-giving. There is no magic formula or technique to determine this moment; it is only as pastors and educators are willing to inhabit the empty space of not knowing, without attempting to control what happens in that space, that they will learn, by experience, how to respond to the grace of new insight and faith as and when it is given.

Some examples of what such a work might mean can be given. In spiritual direction, there is a need to work with the silences, pauses and emptinesses of the encounter, as well as with the stories, metaphors and images that arise through speech. The spiritual director or soul friend needs to be able to inhabit the place of not knowing alongside the woman, enabling her to befriend it and discover that it need not overwhelm or negate her but can be the gateway to truth. This requires on the part of the spiritual director an ability to be present to her own silences and unknowings, and some experience of the potential creativity of such phenomena. The spiritual director can encourage women to explore contemplative ways of praying, in which images and words are abandoned, and the pray-er remains in silence and darkness waiting upon God who is mystery and beyond. The director may suggest reading and reflection upon key texts from the contemplative tradition as a way of encouraging women to recognise that their experiences of darkness and unknowing are validated by saints throughout the centuries. Exploring through prayer, poetry or painting images such as the dark night of the soul, the cloud of unknowing and the desert may provide fruitful ways into the potential creativity of such experiences.

In preaching and teaching, the traditions of desert spirituality, contemplative prayer and apophatic faith can be plumbed more deeply and explored as a means of interpreting women's experiences of silence and contradiction. Preachers have a key role in naming and validating such experiences. As well as calling upon traditional resources such as those mentioned, preachers and teachers can also employ women's contemporary art, fiction, drama and music to explore themes of silence, contradiction, invisibility, alienation and paralysis. Such themes are fully present in much modern and post-modern work.[10] In her writings, Brenda Lealman offers many examples of how the work of contemporary artists and poets, male as well as female, can provide a starting point for exploring unknowing and apophatic ways of faith. She draws particular attention to the exploration of paradox through parable, koan and riddle, through surrealist visual art, and through the use of a particular kind

---

[10] For sources on women's experiences of nothingness, paralysis and unknowing in fiction see, for example, Christ (1986) and Grey (1989); in poetry, cf. Ostriker (1987); in autobiography, cf. Heilbrun (1989).

of question 'which cannot find satisfaction in simple solutions and certainties' (Lealman, 1982, p. 77). She suggests that religious education has an important role in exploring themes such as those of waiting, listening, breath, wind and wilderness (Lealman, 1993, p. 63), all of which connect powerfully with women's experiences of paralysis and unknowing. Such themes also admit of broader, socio-political exegesis, encouraging attention to structural issues of justice in the church and the world at the same time as addressing personal needs.

In teaching, attention to apophatic ways of faithing suggests not only material content to be explored but also the need to affirm the gaps and pauses in the *process* of learning: moments which receive little attention and yet are as essential to learning as the moments of concentrated attention and active participation. The spaces and gaps in between thinking may be moments when truth is able to steal up on one, unawares. The times when one leaves off writing or painting are the times when the imagination is freed to go down deep, into the subconscious, and re-emerge with something new. As Maria Harris suggests, just as 'all music has places of rest' so 'a spirituality of pedagogy must have room for prayerful silence' (1988, p. 30). Unknowing needs to be prized as the essential precondition of enquiry, discovery and new knowing.

Similarly, denunciation as a form of learning needs to be accorded great honour, as it is that form of knowing practised by prophets and poets and those who refuse to put up with reality as it is. The deconstruction of familiar, socially endorsed models and patterns of understanding can be frightening and disorienting, yet, for women, the 'unlearning' of such roles is an essential precondition to authentic knowledge. Bons-Storm (1996) speaks of the need for women to become 'rebels', to develop the 'rebellious voice' which 'contradict[s] and disobey[s] the dominant sociocultural narrative and its proper roles for women' (p. 84). Similarly, bell hooks (1994, p. 12) speaks of teaching as 'transgression': 'a movement against and beyond boundaries' which enables education to be the practice of freedom. Teaching and preaching can support women to become such rebel selves by telling the stories of women rebels and iconoclasts from the past, by denouncing the stereotypes and false role-models enshrined in so much religious tradition, and by exploring what feminist practices of prophecy can mean in our own time. Women need to know that they can be amongst the company of prophets, protestors and rebels who have denounced injustice in its many forms; and that prophecy can begin in the inchoate sense of nameless discomfort which many women feel and can find no words to express.

Summary and Conclusions

Whilst the pastoral and educational principles sketched out in this chapter may not be new, they bear and, I believe, require, reiteration. From my knowledge of British institutions of theological education and the churches they represent, there is a long way to go before such principles are taken seriously in the pastoral care and education of women and are permitted to shape and critique the life of the whole church. If taken seriously and applied creatively, such principles can, I believe, radicalise and renew the practices of theological education and pastoral care in the churches, as well as beyond. They represent ways of enacting justice for women and the creation of educational and pastoral practices which are genuinely inclusive, because they are attuned to the marginalised ways of knowing and faithing which have been repressed and denied, both in academia and in the churches. As such, I believe these principles are potentially empowering for all, for men as well as women, for children as well as adults, for clergy as well as laity, for white people as well as black. For the releasing of repressed knowledge is a gift to all, not only those whose knowledge has been repressed; and where one is awakened, all may share in the greater release of life and hope. It is my desire that this study, in its attempts to attend to and broadcast the repressed voices of women's spirituality, can contribute to this larger work of empowerment and justice-making.

Bibliography

Acker, J., Barry, K. and Esseveld, J. (1983), 'Objectivity and truth: problems in doing feminist research', *Women's Studies International Forum* 6, pp. 423–35.

Ackerman, D.M. and Bons-Storm, R. (eds) (1998), *Liberating Faith Practices: Feminist Practical Theologies in Context*, Leuven: Peeters.

Ahern, G. and Davie, G. (1987), *Inner City God,* London: Hodder & Stoughton.

Amirtham, S. and Pobee, J. (eds) (1986), *Theology By the People: Reflections on Doing Theology in Community*, Geneva: WCC.

Anderson, K. and Jack, D.C. (1991), 'Learning to listen: interview techniques and analyses', in Gluck, S.B. and Patai, D. (eds), *Women's Words: The Feminist Practice of Oral History*, London: Routledge, pp. 11–26.

Anderson, S.R. and Hopkins, P. (1992), *The Feminine Face of God: The Unfolding of the Sacred in Women*, New York: Bantam.

Astley, J. and Francis, L. (eds) (1992), *Christian Perspectives on Faith Development*, Leominster: Gracewing/Eerdmans.

Astley, J. et al. (1991), *How Faith Grows: Faith Development and Christian Education*, London: National Society/Church House Publishing.

Atwood, M. (1998), *Eating Fire: Selected Poetry 1965–1995*, London: Virago.

Austin, J.L. (1975, 2nd edn), *How To Do Things With Words*, Oxford: Oxford University Press.

Ballard, P. and Pritchard, J. (1996), *Practical Theology in Action: Christian Thinking in the Service of Church and Society*, London: SPCK.

Bassett, P.E. (1985), 'Faith Development and Mid-Life Transition: Fowler's Paradigm as it relates to Personality Profile', unpublished Ph.D. thesis, Baylor University.

Belenky, M.F., Clincy, B.M., Goldberger, N.R. and Tarule, J.M. (1986), *Women's Ways of Knowing: The Development of Self, Voice, and Mind*, New York: Basic Books.

Bell, C. and Roberts, H. (eds) (1984), *Social Researching: Politics, Problems, Practice*, London: Routledge & Kegan Paul.

Bennett Moore, Z. (2001), 'Pastoral theology as hermeneutics', *British Journal of Theological Education* 12.1, pp. 7–18.

Blassingame, J.S. (1972), *The Slave Community*, New York: Oxford University Press.

Boff, C. (1987), *Theology and Praxis: Epistemological Foundations*, London: SCM.

Bonino, J.M. (1975), *Doing Theology in a Revolutionary Situation,* Philadelphia: Fortress Press.

Bons-Storm, R. (1996), *The Incredible Woman: Listening to Women's Silences in Pastoral Care and Counselling,* Nashville: Abingdon.

Bowlby, J. (1988), *A Secure Base: Parent–Child Attachment and Healthy Human Development*, New York: Basic Books.

Bowles, G. and Duelli Klein, R. (eds) (1983), *Theories of Women's Studies*, London: Routledge & Kegan Paul.

Boyd, D. (1982), 'Careful justice or just caring: a response to Gilligan', *Proceedings of the Philosophy of Education Society* 38, pp. 63–9.

Boyd, M.F. (1991), 'The African American church as a healing community: theological and psychological dimensions of pastoral care', *Journal of Theology* 95.

Brabeck, M.M. (1983), 'Moral judgment: theory and research on differences between men and women', *Developmental Review* 3, pp. 274–91.

Bradley, R.B. (1983), 'An Exploration of the Relationship between Fowler's Theory of Faith Development and Myer-Briggs Personality Type', unpublished Ph.D. thesis, Ohio State University.

Brainerd, C.L.J. et al. (1978), 'The stage question in cognitive developmental theory', *The Behavioural and Brain Sciences* 2, pp. 173–213.

Bridges, W. (1980), *Transitions: Making Sense of Life's Changes,* Reading, MA: Addison-Wesley.

Broughton, J.M. (1983), 'Women's rationality and men's virtues: a critique of gender dualism in Gilligan's theory of moral development', *Social Research* 50, pp. 597–642.

Brown, G. and Desforges, C. (1979), *Piaget's Theory: A Psychological Critique,* London: Routledge & Kegan Paul.

Brown, L. (1989), 'Narratives of Relationship: The Development of a Care Voice in Girls Ages 7 to 16', unpublished Ph.D. thesis, Harvard University.

Brown, L.M. and Gilligan, C. (1992), *Meeting at the Crossroads: Women's Psychology and Girls' Development*, New York: Ballantine Books.

Cameron, D. (1992, 2nd edn), *Feminism and Linguistic Theory*, Basingstoke: Macmillan.

Canham, E. (1983), *Pilgrimage to Priesthood,* London: SPCK.

Cannon, L.W., Higginbothan, E. and Leung, M.L.A. (1991), 'Race and class bias in qualitative research on women', in Fonow, M.M. and Cook, J.A. (eds), *Beyond Methodology: Feminist Scholarship as Lived Research*, Bloomington: Indiana University Press, pp. 107–11.

Chafe, W.L. (1980), 'The deployment of consciousness in the production of a narrative' in *The Pear Stories: Cognitive, Cultural and Linguistic Aspects of Narrative Production*, Norwood, NJ: Ablex, pp. 9–50.

Chase, S.E. (1995), 'Taking narrative seriously: consequences for method and theory in interview studies', in Josselson, R. and Lieblich, A. (eds), *Interpreting Experience: The Narrative Study of Lives, Volume 3*, London: Sage, pp. 1–26.

Chodorow, N. (1978), *The Reproduction of Mothering: Psychoanalysis and the Sociology of Gender*, Berkeley, CA: University of California Press.

Chopp, R.S. (1995), *Saving Work: Feminist Practices of Theological Education*, Louisville: Westminster John Knox Press.

Christ, C.P. (1986, 2nd edn), *Diving Deep and Surfacing: Women Writers on Spiritual Quest*, Boston: Beacon Press.

Coates, J. and Cameron, D. (eds) (1988), *Women in Their Speech Communities*, London: Longman.

Cone, J.H. (1974), *God of the Oppressed*, New York: Seabury Press.

Conn, J.W. (ed.) (1986), *Women's Spirituality: Resources for Christian Development*, New York: Paulist Press.

Coon, L.L. et al. (1990), *That Gentle Strength: Historical Perspectives on Women in Christianity*, New York: Paulist Press.

Cooney, J.A.M. (1985), 'Holistic Relationality: Themes of Transition in Women's Faith Development', unpublished Ed.D. thesis, Boston University.

Cooper-White, P. (2000), 'Opening the eyes: understanding the impact of trauma on development', in Stevenson-Moessner, J. (ed.), *In Her Own Time: Women and Developmental Issues in Pastoral Care*, Minneapolis: Fortress, pp. 87–101.

Cornwall Collective (1980), *Your Daughters Shall Prophesy: Feminist Alternatives in Theological Education*, New York: Pilgrim Press.

Cotterill, Pamela (1992), 'Interviewing women: issues of friendship, vulnerability, and power', *Women's Studies International Forum* 15, pp. 593–606.

Couture, P. D. (1999), 'Pastoral theology as art', in Miller-McLemore, B.J. and Gill-Austern, B.L. (eds), *Feminist and Womanist Pastoral Theology*, Nashville: Abingdon Press, pp. 169–87.

Cowden, M.A. (1992), 'Faith Development in Women: A Comparison of the Moral Development Theories of Carol Gilligan and Laurence Kohlberg and the Faith Development Theory of James Fowler', unpublished Ph.D. thesis, Temple University.

Cupitt, D. (1991), *What is a Story?* London: SCM.

Daly, M. (1986, 2nd edn), *Beyond God the Father: Toward a Philosophy of Women's Liberation*, London: Women's Press.

Davis, P.H. (2000), 'Horror and the development of girls' spiritual voices', in Stevenson-Moessner, J. (ed.), *In Her Own Time: Women and Developmental Issues in Pastoral Care*, Minneapolis: Fortress, pp. 103–13.

Demarinis, V.M. (1993), *Critical Caring: A Feminist Model for Pastoral Psychology*, Louisville, KY: Westminster/John Knox Press.

Devault, M. (1990), 'Talking and listening from women's standpoint: feminist strategies for interviewing and analysis', *Social Problems* 37, pp. 96–116.

Devor, N.G. (1989), 'Toward a Relational Voice of Faith: Contributions of James Fowler's Faith Development Theory, Psychological Research on Women's Development, Relational Feminist Theology, and a Qualitative Analysis of Women Ministers' Faith Descriptions', unpublished Ph.D. thesis, Boston University.

De Beauvoir, S. (1970), *The Second Sex*, Harmondsworth: Penguin.

Donaldson, M. (1978), *Children's Mind*, Glasgow: Fontana.

Donovan, V.J. (1982, 2nd edn), *Christianity Rediscovered: An Epistle from the Masai*, London: SCM.

Du Bois, B. (1983), 'Passionate scholarship: notes on values, knowing and method in social science', in Bowles, G. and Duelli Klein, R. (eds), *Theories of Women's Studies*, London: Routledge & Kegan Paul, pp. 105–16.

Duelli Klein, R. (1983), 'How to do what we want to do: thoughts about feminist methodology', in Bowles, G. and Duelli Klein, R. (eds), *Theories of Women's Studies*, London: Routledge & Kegan Paul, pp. 88–104.

Dykstra, C. and Parks, S. (eds) (1986), *Faith Development and Fowler*, Birmingham, AL: Religious Education Press.

Edelsky, C. (1981), 'Who's got the floor?' *Language in Society* 10, pp. 380–95.

Egan, H. (1978), 'Christian apophatic and kataphatic mysticisms', *Theological Studies* 39, pp. 399–426.

Erikson, E. (1980), *Identity and the Life Cycle*, New York: W.W. Norton.

Estés, C.P. (1992), *Women Who Run With the Wolves: Contacting the Power of the Wild Woman*, London: Rider.

Etter-Lewis, G. (1991), 'Black women's life stories: reclaiming self in narrative texts', in Gluck, S.B. and Patai, D. (eds), *Women's Words: The Feminist Practice of Oral History*, London: Routledge, pp. 43–58.

Finch, J. (1984), '"Its great to have someone to talk to": the ethics and politics of interviewing women', in Bell, C. and Roberts, H. (eds), *Social Researching: Politics, Problems, Practice*, London: Routledge & Kegan Paul, pp. 166–80.

Fiorenza, E.S. (1983), *In Memory of Her: A Feminist Theological Reconstruction of Christian Origins*, London: SCM.

Fiorenza, E.S. (1995), *Jesus: Miriam's Child, Sophia's Prophet*, London: SCM.

Fischer, K. (1989), *Women at the Well: Feminist Perspectives on Spiritual Direction*, London: SPCK.

Fishman, P. (1983), 'Interaction: the work women do', in Thorne, B., Kramarae, C. and Henley, N. (eds), *Language, Gender and Society*, Rowley, MA: Newbury, pp. 89–101.

Fiske, M. (1980), 'Changing hierarchies of commitment in adulthood', in Smesler, N.J. and Erikson, E.H. (eds), *Themes of Love and Work in Adulthood*, Cambridge, MA: Harvard University Press, pp. 241–2.

FitzGerald, C. (1986), 'Impasse and dark night', in Conn, J.W. (ed.), *Women's Spirituality: Resources for Christian Development*, New York: Paulist Press, pp. 287–311.

Fonow, M.M. and Cook, J.A. (eds) (1991), *Beyond Methodology: Feminist Scholarship as Lived Research*, Bloomington: Indiana University Press.

Fortune, M.M. (1996), 'Rape', in Isherwood, L. and McEwan, D. (eds) *An A to Z of Feminist Theology*, Sheffield: Sheffield Academic Press, pp. 195–7.

Fowler, J.W. (1980), 'Faith and the structuring of meaning', in Brusselmans, C. and O'Donohoe, J.A. (eds), *Toward Moral and Religious Maturity*, Morristown, NJ: Silver Burdett, pp. 51–85.

Fowler, J.W. (1981), *Stages of Faith: The Pyschology of Human Development and the Quest for Meaning*, London: Harper & Row.

Fowler, J.W. (1984), *Becoming Adult, Becoming Christian*, New York: Harper & Row.

Fowler, J.W. (1986), 'Faith and the structuring of meaning', in Dykstra, C. and Parks, S. (eds), *Faith Development and Fowler*, Birmingham, AL: Religious Education Press, pp. 15–42.

Fowler, J.W. (1987), *Faith Development and Pastoral Care*, Philadelphia: Fortress Press.

Fowler, J.W. (1991a), *Weaving the New Creation: Stages of Faith and the Public Church*, San Francisco: HarperCollins.

Fowler, J.W. (1991b), 'Stages in faith consciousness', in Oser, F.Z. and Scarlett, W.G. (eds), *Religious Development in Childhood and Adolescence*, San Francisco: Jossey-Bass Inc., pp. 27–45.

Fowler, J.W. (1992), 'Foreword', in Astley, J. and Francis, L. (eds), *Christian Perspectives on Faith Development*, Leominster: Gracewing/Eerdmans, pp. ix–xv.

Fowler, J.W. (1996), *Faithful Change: The Personal and Public Challenges of Postmodern Life*, Nashville: Abingdon.

Fowler, J.W. (2000), *Stufen des Glaubens: Die Psychologie der menschlichen Entwicklung und die Suche nach Sinn*, Gütersloh: Kaiser.

Fowler, J.W., Nipkow, K.E. and Schweitzer, F. (eds) (1991), *Stages of Faith and Religious Development: Implications for Church, Education and Society*, London: SCM.

Freire, P. (1972), *Pedagogy of the Oppressed*, Harmondsworth: Penguin.

Freud, A. (1963), 'The concept of developmental lines', *Psychoanalytic Study of the Child* 18, pp. 245–65.

Freud, S. (1973), *Introductory Lectures on Psychoanalysis*, Harmondsworth: Penguin.

Garcia, J. and Maitland, S. (eds) (1983), *Walking on the Water: Women Talk about Spirituality*, London: Virago.

Gardner, H. and Winner, E. (1982), 'The child is father to the metaphor', in Gardner, H. (ed.), *Art, Mind and Brain*, New York: Basic Books.

Gardner, H., Winner, E., Bechhofer, R. and Wolf, D. (1978), 'The development of figurative language', in Nelson, K.E. (ed.), *Children's Language*, Hillsdale, NJ: Erlbaum.

Genter, D. (1977), 'On the development of metaphoric processing', *Child Development* 48, pp. 1034–9.

Gilligan, C. (1982), *In A Different Voice: Psychological Theory and Women's Development*, Cambridge, MA: Harvard University Press.

Gilligan, C. (1983), 'Do the social sciences have an adequate theory of moral development?', in Haan, N., Bellah, R.N., Rabinow, P. and Sullivan, W.M. (eds), *Social Science as Moral Enquiry*, New York: Columbia University Press, pp. 35–51.

Gilligan, C. (1986), 'Remapping the moral domain: new images of the self in relationship', in Helleter, T.C., Sosna, M. and Wellbery, D.E. (eds), *Reconstructing Individualism*, Stanford, CA: Stanford University Press, pp. 241–56.

Gilligan, C. (1987), 'Remapping development: the power of divergent data', in Cirillo, L. and Wapner, S. (eds), *Value Presuppositions in Theories of Human Development*, Hillsdale, NJ: Laurence Earlbaum, pp. 37–53.

Gilligan, C., Lyons, N.P. and Hammer, T.J. (eds) (1990), *Making Connections: The Relational Worlds of Adolescent Girls at Emma Willard School*, Cambridge, MA: Harvard University Press.

Gilligan, C., Ward, J.V. and McLean Taylor, J., with Bardige, B. (eds) (1988), *Mapping the Moral Domain*, Cambridge, MA: Harvard University Press.

Giltner, F.M. (ed.) (1985), *Women's Issues in Religious Education*, Birmingham, AL: Religious Education Press.

Glaser, B.G. and Strauss, A.L. (1967), *The Discovery of Grounded Theory: Strategies for Qualitative Research*, Chicago: Aldine.

Glaz, M. and Stevenson-Moessner, J. (eds) (1991), *Women in Travail and Transition: A New Pastoral Care*, Minneapolis: Fortress Press.

Gluck, S. (1979), 'What's so special about women? Women's oral history', *Frontiers* 2, pp. 3–11.

Gluck, S.B. and Patai, D. (eds) (1991), *Women's Words: The Feminist Practice of Oral History*, London: Routledge.

Goldberger, N., Tarule, J., Clinchy, B. and Belenky, M. (eds) (1996), *Knowledge, Difference and Power: Essays Inspired by Women's Ways of Knowing*, New York: Basic Books.

Goldman, R. (1964), *Religious Thinking in Childhood and Adolescence*, London: Routledge and Kegan Paul.

Gould, K.H. (1988), 'Old wine in new bottles: a feminist perspective on Gilligan's theory', *Social Work* 33, pp. 411–15.

Graham, E.L. (1995), *Making the Difference: Gender, Personhood and Theology*, London: Mowbray/Cassell.

Graham, E.L. (1996), *Transforming Practice: Pastoral Theology in an Age of Uncertainty*, London: Mowbray/Cassell.

Graham, E. (1997), *Transforming Practice: Pastoral Theology in an Age of Uncertainty*, London: Mowbray.

Graham, E. and Halsey, M. (eds) (1993), *Life Cycles: Women and Pastoral Care*, London: SPCK.

Graham, H. (1984), 'Surveying through stories', in Bell, C. and Roberts, H. (eds), *Social Researching: Politics, Problems, Practice*, London: Routledge & Kegan Paul, pp. 104–24.

Grant, J.G. (1989), *White Women's Christ and Black Women's Jesus: Feminist Christology and Womanist Response*, Atlanta: Scholars Press.

Green, L. (1990), *Let's Do Theology: A Pastoral Cycle Resource Book*, London: Mowbray/Cassell.

Gregg, R. (1991), 'Pregnancy in a High-Tech Age: Paradoxes of Choice', unpublished Ph.D. thesis, Brandeis University.

Grey, M. (1989), *Redeeming the Dream: Feminism, Redemption and Christian Tradition*, London: SPCK.

Grey, M. (1993), *The Wisdom of Fools*, London: SPCK.

Grey, M. (1999), '"Expelled again from Eden": Facing difference through connection', *Feminist Theology* 21, pp. 8–20.

Griffin, S. (1982), *Made From This Earth: An Anthology of Writings*, London: Women's Press.

Griffiths, M. (1995), *Feminisms and the Self: The Web of Identity*, London: Routledge.

Guenther, M. (1992), *Holy Listening: The Art of Spiritual Direction*, London: DLT.

Gutierrez, G. (1988, 2nd edn), *A Theology of Liberation*, London: SCM.

Halkes, J.M. (1991), *New Creation: Christian Feminism and the Renewal of the Earth*, London: SPCK.

Hampson, D. (1990), *Theology and Feminism*, Oxford: Blackwell.

Harding, S. (1986), *The Science Question in Feminism*, Milton Keynes: Open University Press.

Harding, S. (1987), 'Introduction: Is there a feminist method?', in *Feminism and Methodology*, Bloomington: Indiana University Press, pp. 1–14.

Harris, M. (1986), 'Completion and faith development', in Dykstra, C. and Parks, S. (eds), *Faith Development and Fowler*, Birmingham, AL: Religious Education Press, pp. 115–33.

Harris, M. (1987), *Teaching and Religious Imagination*, San Francisco: Harper & Row.

Harris, M. (1988), *Women and Teaching*, New York: Paulist Press.

Harris, M. (1989), *Dance of the Spirit: The Seven Steps of Women's Spirituality*, New York: Bantam.

Harris, M. (1993), 'Women teaching girls: the power and the danger', *Religious Education* 88, pp. 52–66.

Hartshorne, C. (1967), *A Natural Theology for Our Time*, La Salle, IL: Open Court.

Hartshorne, C. (1970), *Creative Synthesis and Philosophical Method*, London: SCM.

Haughton, R. (1982), *The Passionate God*, London: DLT.

Havighurst, R. (1980), 'Social and developmental psychology: trends influencing the future of counselling', *The Personnel and Guidance Journal* 58, pp. 325–40.

Heilbrun, Carol (1989), *Writing a Woman's Life*, London: Women's Press.

Herzel, S. (1981), *A Voice for Women*, Geneva: WCC.

Hess, C.L. (1997), *Caretakers of Our Common House: Women's Development in Communities of Faith*, Nashville: Abingdon Press.

Heyward, I.C. (1982), *The Redemption of God: A Theology of Mutual Relation*, Washington, DC: University Press of America.

Heyward, I.C. (1984), *Our Passion for Justice*, New York: Pilgrim Press.

Heyward, I.C. (1989), *Touching Our Strength: The Erotic as Power and the Love of God*, San Francisco: Harper & Row.

Hogan, L. (1995), *From Women's Experience to Feminist Theology*, Sheffield: Sheffield Academic Press.

Holland, J. and Henriot, P. (1983, revised edn), *Social Analysis: Linking Faith and Justice*, Maryknoll: Orbis Books, in collaboration with the Center of Concern, Washington, DC.

hooks, b. (1984), *Feminist theory: From margin to center*, Boston: South End Press.

hooks, b. (1994), *Teaching to Transgress: Education as the Practice of Freedom*, London: Routledge

Hunt, M. (1991), *Fierce Tenderness: A Feminist Theology of Friendship*, New York: Crossroads.

Jacob, E. (1987), 'Qualitative research traditions: a review', *Review of Educational Research* 57, pp. 1–50.

Jantzen, G. (1984), *God's World, God's Body*, London: DLT.

Jayaratne, T.E. (1983), 'The value of quantitative methodology for feminist research', in Bowles, G. and Duelli Klein, R. (eds), *Theories of Women's Studies*, Boston: Routledge & Kegan Paul, pp. 141–61.

Jayaratne, T.E. and Stewart, A.J. (1991), 'Quantitative and qualitative methods in the social sciences: current feminist issues and practical strategies', in Fonow, M.M. and Cook, J.A. (eds), *Beyond Methodology: Feminist Scholarship as Lived Research*, Bloomington: Indiana University Press, pp. 85–106.

Jick, T.D. (1979), 'Mixing qualitative and quantitative methods: triangulation in action', *Administrative Science Quarterly* 24, pp. 602–10.

Jones, A. (1985), *Soul Making: The Desert Way of Spirituality*, London: SCM.

Jordan, J.V. (ed.) (1991), *Women's Growth in Connection: Writings from the Stone Center*, New York: Guilford Press.

Jordan, J.V. (ed.) (1997), *Women's Growth in Diversity: Writings from the Stone Center*, New York: Guilford Press.

Josselson, R. (1995), 'Imagining the real: empathy, narrative, and the dialogic self', in Josselson, R. and Lieblich, A. (eds), *Interpreting Experience: The Narrative Study of Lives, Volume 3*, London: Sage, pp. 27–44.

Josselson, R. and Lieblich, A. (eds) (1993), *The Narrative Study of Lives, Volume 1*, London: Sage.

Josselson, R. and Lieblich, A. (eds) (1995), *Interpreting Experience: The Narrative Study of Lives, Volume 3*, London: Sage.

Kanyoro, M.R.A. (ed.) (1997), *In Search of a Round Table: Gender, Theology and Church Leadership*, Geneva: WCC.

Kaschak, E. (1992), *Engendered Lives: A New Psychology of Women's Lives*, New York: HarperCollins.

Kegan, R. (1982), *The Evolving Self: Problem and Process in Human Development*, Cambridge, MA: Harvard University Press.

Kegan, R. (1994), *In Over Our Heads: The Mental Demands of Modern Life*, Cambridge, MA: Harvard University Press.

Keller, C. (1986), *From a Broken Web: Separation, Sexism, and Self*, Boston: Beacon Press.

Keller, E.F. (1978), 'Gender and science', *Psychoanalysis and Contemporary Thought* 1, pp. 409–33.

Kelly, L. (1988), *Surviving Sexual Violence*, Minneapolis, MN: University of Minnesota Press.

Kerber, L.K. et al. (1986), 'On "In a Different Voice": An interdisciplinary forum', *Signs* 11, pp. 304–33.

Kierkegaard, S. (1980), *The Sickness Unto Death*, Princeton: Princeton University Press.

King, U. (1989), *Women and Spirituality: Voices of Protest and Promise*, Basingstoke: Macmillan Education.

Kohlberg, L. (1981), *Essays on Moral Development, Vol. 1: The Philosophy of Moral Development*, San Francisco: Harper & Row.

Kohlberg, L. (1984), *Essays on Moral Development, Vol. 2: The Psychology of Moral Development*, San Francisco: Harper & Row.

Kohut, H. (1977), *The Restoration of the Self*, New York: International Universities Press.

Kolbenschlag, M. (1979), *Kiss Sleeping Beauty Goodbye*, San Francisco: Harper & Row.

Kramarae, C. (1981), *Women and Men Speaking: Frameworks for Analysis*, Rowley, MA: Newbury.

Laird, J. (1991), 'Women and stories: restorying women's self-constructions', in McGoldrick, M. (ed.), *Women and Families: A Framework for Family Therapy*, New York: Norton.

Lartey, E.Y. (1997), *In Living Colour: An Intercultural Approach to Pastoral Care and Counselling*, London: Mowbray/Cassell.

Bibliography

191

Lealman, B. (1982), 'Blue wind and broken image', in Tickner, F.M. and Webster, D.H. (eds), *Religious Education and the Imagination* (Aspects of Education 28), Hull: University of Hull, pp. 74–84.

Lealman, B. (1993), 'Drum, whalebone and dominant X: a model for creativity', in Starkings, D. (ed.), *Religion and the Arts in Education*, Sevenoaks: Hodder & Stoughton, pp. 55–66.

Leary, J.P. (1988), 'The Relationship of Coping with Chronic Stress and Faith Development in Women: Mothers of Multihandicapped Children', unpublished Ph.D. thesis, Boston College.

Levinson, D. (1978), *The Season's of a Man's Life*, New York: Knopf.

Le Guin, U. (1989), *Dancing at the Edge of the World*, New York: Harper & Row.

Leibert, E. (2000), 'Seasons and stages: models and metaphors of human development', in Stevenson-Moessner, J. (ed.), *In Her Own Time: Women and Developmental Issues in Pastoral Care*, Minneapolis: Fortress, pp. 19–44.

Lieblich, A. and Josselson, R. (eds) (1994), *Exploring Identity and Gender: The Narrative Study of Lives, Volume 2*, London: Sage.

Loades, A. (ed.) (1990), *Feminist Theology: A Reader*, London: SPCK.

Loevinger, J. (1976), *Ego Development: Conceptions and Theories*, San Francisco: Jossey-Bass.

Lorber, J. (1988), 'From the editor', *Gender and Society* 2, pp. 5–8.

Lorde, A. (1984), *Sister Outsider: Essays and Speeches*, Freedom, CA: Crossing Press.

MacHaffie, B.J. (1986), *Her Story: Women in Christian Tradition*, Philadelphia: Fortress.

Mader, S.T. (1986), 'Depression as Loneliness in Post-Generative Women: A Crisis of Faith Development', unpublished Ph.D. thesis, University of Boston.

Maltz, D. and Borker, R. (1982), 'A cultural approach to male–female miscommunication', in Gumperz, J.J. (ed.), *Language and Social Identity: Studies in International Sociolinguistics*, Cambridge: Cambridge University Press.

Marsh, J. (1996), 'Minister as midwife', *Epworth Review* 23, 1, pp. 10–14.

Marshall, J. (1986), 'Exploring the experiences of women managers: towards rigour in qualitative methods', in Wilkinson, S. (ed.), *Feminist Social Psychology: Developing Theory and Practice*, Milton Keynes: Open University Press, pp. 193–209.

Mason, M.G. (1980), 'The other voice: autobiographies of woman writers', in Olney, J. (ed.), *Autobiography: Essays Theoretical and Critical*, Princeton, NJ: Princeton University Press, pp. 207–35.

McCormack, T. (1975), 'Towards a nonsexist perspective on social and political change', in Millman, M. and Kanter, R.M. (eds), *Another Voice: Feminist Perspectives of Social Life and Social Sciences*, Garden City, NY: Anchor.

McCrary, C. (1991), 'Interdependence as a normative value in pastoral counselling with African Americans', *Journal of the Interdenominational Theological Center* 18.

McCrary, C. (1998), 'Wholeness of women', *Journal of the Interdenominational Theological Center* 25.

McFague, S. (1993), *The Body of God: An Ecological Theology*, London: SCM.

Merchant, C. (1980), *The Death of Nature: Women, Ecology and the Scientific Revolution*, San Francisco: Harper & Row.

Mies, M. (1983), 'Towards a methodology for feminist research', in Bowles, G. and Duelli Klein, R. (eds), *Theories of Women's Studies*, London: Routledge & Kegan Paul, pp. 117–39.

Miles, M.R. (1988), *The Image and Practice of Holiness: A Critique of the Classic Manuals of Devotion*, London: SCM.

Miles, R. (1994), *Not In Our Name: Voices of women who have left the church*, Nottingham: Southwell Diocesan Social Responsibility Group.

Miles, M.B. and Huberman, A.M. (1994, 2nd edn), *Qualitative Data Analysis: An Expanded Sourcebook*, London: Sage.

Miller, J.B. (1976), *Toward a New Psychology of Women*, Boston: Beacon Press.

Miller-McLemore, B. (1999), 'Feminist theory in pastoral theology', in Miller-McLemore, B.J. and Gill-Austern, B.L. (eds), *Feminist and Womanist Pastoral Theology*, Nashville: Abingdon Press, pp. 77–111.

Miller-McLemore, B.J. and Gill-Austern, B.L. (eds) (1999), *Feminist and Womanist Pastoral Theology*, Nashville: Abingdon Press.

Minster, K. (1991), 'A feminist frame for the oral history interview', in Gluck, S.B. and Patai, D. (eds), *Women's Words: The Feminist Practice of Oral History*, London: Routledge, pp. 27–41.

Mitchell, C. (1985), 'Some differences in male and female joke-telling', in Jordan, R.A. and Kalik, S.J. (eds), *Women's Folklore, Women's Culture*, Philadelphia: University of Pennsylvania Press.

Monk Kidd, S. (1996), *The Dance of the Dissident Daughter*, New York: HarperSanFrancisco.

Morgan, P.A. (1990), 'The Faith Development of Women in Crisis: A Constructivist Window to Intervention', unpublished Ed.D. thesis, University of Houston.

Morton, N. (1985), *The Journey is Home*, Boston: Beacon Press.

Mud Flower Collective (1985), *God's Fierce Whimsy: Christian Feminism and Theological Education*, New York: Pilgrim Press.

Navone, J. (1977), *Towards a Theology of Story*, Slough: St Paul's.

Nairne, K. and Smith, G. (1984), *Dealing with Depression*, London: Women's Press.

Neuger, C.C. (ed.) (1996), *The Arts of Ministry: Feminist-Womanist Approaches*, Louisville, KY: Westminster John Knox Press.

Neuger, C.C. (1999), 'Women and relationality', in Miller-McLemore, B.J. and Gill-Austern, B.L. (eds), *Feminist and Womanist Pastoral Theology*, Nashville: Abingdon Press, pp. 113–32.

Neuger, C.C. (2000), 'Narratives of harm: setting the developmental context for intimate violence', in Stevenson-Moessner, J. (ed.), *In Her Own Time: Women and Developmental Issues in Pastoral Care*, Minneapolis: Fortress, pp. 65–86.

Niebuhr, H.R. (1960), *Radical Monotheism and Western Culture*, New York: Harper & Row.

Norén, C.M. (1992), *The Woman in the Pulpit*, Nashville: Abingdon Press.

Oakley, A. (1974), *The Sociology of Housework*, Oxford: Martin Robertson.

Oakley, A. (1976), *Housewife*, Harmondsworth: Penguin.

Oakley, A. (1981), 'Interviewing women: a contradiction in terms', in Roberts, H. (ed.), *Doing Feminist Research*, London: Routledge & Kegan Paul, pp. 30–61.

Opie, A. (1992), 'Qualitative research, appropriation of the "other" and empowerment', *Feminist Review* 40, pp. 52–69.

Orr, J. (2000), 'Socioeconomic class and the life span development of women', in Stevenson-Moessner, J. (ed.), *In Her Own Time: Women and Developmental Issues in Pastoral Care*, Minneapolis: Fortress, pp. 45–63.

Ortner, S. (1984), 'Theory in anthropology since the sixties', *Comparative Studies in Society and History* 26, pp. 126–66.

Oser, F. (1980), 'Stages of religious judgment', in Brusselmans, C. and O'Donohoe, J.A. (eds), *Toward Moral and Religious Maturity*, Morristown, NJ: Silver Burdett, pp. 277–315.

Oser, F. (1991), 'The development of religious judgment', in Oser, F.Z. and Scarlett, W.G. (eds), *Religious Development in Childhood and Adolescence*, San Francisco: Jossey-Bass, pp. 5–25.

Oser, F. and Gmünder, P. (1991), *Religious Judgement: A Developmental Approach*, Birmingham, AL: Religious Education Press.

Osiek, C. (1986), *Beyond Anger: On Being a Feminist in the Church*, Dublin: Gill & Macmillan.

Ostriker, A.S. (1987), *Stealing the Language: The Emergence of Women's Poetry in America*, London: Women's Press.

Parks, S. (1990/1991), 'Faith development in a changing world', *The Drew Gateway* 60, 1, pp. 4–21. Reprinted as 'The North American critique of James Fowler's theory of faith development', in Fowler, J.W., Nipkow, K.E. and Schweitzer, F. (eds), *Stages of Faith and Religious Development: Implications for Church, Education and Society*, London: SCM, pp. 101–15.

Perry, W.H. (1968), *Forms of Intellectual and Ethical Development in the College Years*, New York: Holt, Rinehart & Winston.

Philbert, P.J. (1982), 'Symposium review: *Stages of Faith*', *Horizons* 9, 1, pp. 104–26.

Piaget, J. (1929), *The Child's Conception of the World*, London: Routledge & Kegan Paul.

Piaget, J. (1962), *The Moral Judgement of the Child*, New York: Collier.

Piercy, M. (1982), *Circles on the Water*, New York: Alfred A. Knopf.

Piercy, M. (1998), *The Art of Blessing the Day: Poems on Jewish Themes*, Nottingham: Five Leaves Publications.

Powers, B. (1982), *Growing Faith*, Nashville: Broadman Press.

Pratt, M., Golding, G. and Hunter, W. (1984), 'Does morality have a gender?', *Merrill Palmer Quarterly* 30, pp. 321–40.

Proctor-Smith, M. (1990), *In Her Own Rite: Constructing Feminist Liturgical Tradition*, Nashville: Abingdon Press.

Quaker Women's Group (1986), *Bringing the Invisible into the Light: Some Quaker feminists speak of their experience*, London: Quaker Home Service.

Raymond, J. (1986), *A Passion for Friends: Towards a Philosophy of Female Affection*, London: Women's Press.

Reich, K.H. (1997), 'Do we need a theory for the religious development of women?', *International Journal for the Psychology of Religion*, pp. 67–86.

Reinharz, S. (1983), 'Experiential analysis: a contribution to feminist research', in Bowles, G. and Duelli Klein, R. (eds), *Theories of Women's Studies*, London; Routledge & Kegan Paul, pp. 162–91.

Reynolds, R.E. and Ortony, A. (1980), 'Some issues in the measurement of children's comprehension of metaphorical language', *Child Development* 51, pp. 1110–19.

Ribbens, J. (1989), 'Interviewing: an "unnatural situation"?' *Women's Studies International Forum* 12, pp. 579–92.

Rich, A. (1978), *The Dream of a Common Language*, New York: Norton.

Riegel, K. (1975), 'Toward a dialectical theory of development', *Human Development* 1, 2, pp. 50–64.

Riessman, C.K. (1987), 'When gender is not enough: women interviewing women', *Gender and Society* 1, pp. 172–207.

Rizzuto, A.M. (1979), *The Birth of the Living God: A Psychoanalytic Study*, London: University of Chicago.

Roberts, H. (ed.) (1981), *Doing Feminist Research*, London: Routledge & Kegan Paul.

Rubin, L.B. (1979), *Women of a Certain Age*, New York: Harper & Row.

Ruether, R.R. (1979), *New Woman, New Earth: Sexist Ideologies and Human Liberation*, Minneapolis: Winston Press.

Ruether, R.R. (1983), *Sexism and God-Talk: Towards a Feminist Theology*, London: SCM.

Ruether, R.R. (1985), *Women-Church: Theology and Practice*, San Francisco: Harper & Row.

Ruether, R.R. (1992), *Gaia and God: An Ecofeminist Theology of Earth Healing*, London: SCM.

Russell, L.M. (1974), *Human Liberation in a Feminist Perspective: A Theology*, Philadelphia; Westminster Press.

Russell, L.M. (1993), *Church in the Round: Feminist Interpretation of the Church*, Louisville, KY: Westminster/John Knox.

St Hilda Community (ed.) (1991), *Women Included: A Book of Services and Prayers*, London: SPCK.

Scanlon, J. (1993), 'Challenging the imbalances of power in feminist oral history', *Women's Studies International Forum* 16, pp. 639–45.

Schaef, A.W. (1982), *Women's Reality*, San Francisco: Harper & Row.

Scott Peck, M. (1993), *Further Along the Road Less Travelled*, New York: Simon & Schuster.

Schreiter, R. (1985), *Constructing Local Theologies*, London: SCM.

Segundo, J.L. (1977), *The Liberation of Theology*, London: Gill & Macmillan.

Segura, D. (1989), 'Chicana and Mexican women at work: the impact of class, race and gender on occupational mobility', *Gender and Society* 3, pp. 37–52.

Selman, R.L. (1980), *The Growth of Interpersonal Understanding: Developmental and Clinical Analyses*, New York: Academic Press.

Shields, V.R. and Dervin, B. (1993), 'Sense-making in feminist social science research: a call to enlarge the methodological options of feminist studies', *Women's Studies International Forum* 16, pp. 65–81.

Sheldrake, P. (2nd edn) (1995), *Spirituality and History*, London: SPCK.

Sher, G. (1987), 'Other voices, other rooms? Women's psychology and moral theory', in Kittay, E.F. and Meyers, D.T. (eds), *Women and Moral Theory*, Totowa, NJ: Rowman & Littlefield, pp. 178–89.

Sherif, C.W. (1979), 'Bias in psychology', in Sherman, J.A. and Beck, E.T. (eds), *The Prism of Sex: Essays in the Sociology of Knowledge*, Madison: University of Wisconsin Press.

Slee, N. (1989), 'Women's silence in religious education', *British Journal of Religious Education* 12, pp. 29–37.

Slee, N. (1992), '"Heaven in ordinarie": the imagination, spirituality and the arts in religious education', in Watson, B. (ed.), *Priorities in Religious Education: A Model for the 1990s and Beyond*, London: Falmer, pp. 38–57.

Slee, N. (1996), 'The power to re-member', in Hampson, D. (ed.) *Swallowing a Fishbone: Feminist Theologians Debate Christianity*, London: SPCK, pp. 33–49.

Slee, N. (2000), 'A Subject in Her Own Right: The Religious Education of Women and Girls', The Hockerill Lecture 2000, Hertford: Hockerill Educational Foundation.

Slee, N. (2001), 'Apophatic faithing in women's spirituality', *British Journal of Theological Education* 11, 2, pp. 23–7.

Smith, B.J. (1991), 'Raising a resister', in Gilligan, C., Rogers, A. and Tolman, D. (eds), *Women, Girls, and Psychotherapy: Reframing Resistance*, New York: Harrington Park.

Smith, D. (1974), 'Women's perspective as a radical critique of sociology', *Sociological Inquiry* 44, pp. 713–30.

Smith, D. (1977), 'Some implications of a sociology for women', in Glazer, N. and Waehrer, H. (eds), *Women in a ManMade world: A Socioeconomic Handbook,* Chicago: Rand McNally.

Smith, D. (1979), 'A sociology for women', in Sherman, J.A. and Beck, E.T. (eds), *The Prism of Sex: Essays in the Sociology of Knowledge*, Madison: University of Wisconsin Press.

Smith, D. (1988), *The Everyday World as Problematic: A Feminist Sociology*, Milton Keynes: Open University Press.

Smith, R.L. (1997), 'Professional and Faith Development in Women Religious Leaders', unpublished Ph.D. thesis, Claremont Graduate University.

Smith, W.C. (1963), *The Meaning and End of Religion*, New York: Macmillan.

Smith, W.C. (1979), *Faith and Belief*, Princeton, NJ: Princeton University Press.

Sölle, D. (1977), *Revolutionary Patience*, Maryknoll: Orbis.

Soskice, J.M. (1985), *Metaphor and Religious Language*, Oxford: Clarendon.

Spencer, A. (1982), *Seasons: Women's Search for Self through Life's Stages*, New York: Paulist Press.

Spender, D. (1980), *Man Made Language*, London: Routledge & Kegan Paul.

Spender, D. (1988), 'Talking in class', in Spender, D. and Sarah, E. (eds), *Learning to Lose: Sexism and Education*, London: Women's Press, pp. 149–54.

Spretnak, C. (ed.) (1982), *The Politics of Women's Spirituality: Essays on the Rise of Spiritual Power within the Feminist Movement*, New York: Anchor/Doubleday.

Stanley, L. (ed.) (1990), *Feminist Praxis: Research, Theory and Epistemology in Feminist Sociology*, London: Routledge.

Stanley, L. and Wise, S. (eds) (1983), *Breaking Out: Feminist Consciousness and Feminist Research*, London: Routledge & Kegan Paul.

Stephens, L. (1996), *Building a Foundation for Your Child's Faith,* New York: Zondervan.

Stern, D.N. (1985), *Interpersonal World of the Infant: A View from Psychoanalysis and Developmental Psychology*, New York: Basic Books.

Stevenson-Moessner, J. (ed.) (1996), *Through the Eyes of Women: Insights for Pastoral Care*, Minneapolis: Fortress Press.

Stevenson-Moessner, J. (ed.) (2000), *In Her Own Time: Women and Developmental Issues in Pastoral Care*, Minneapolis: Fortress.

Stewart, L.P., Cooper, P.J. and Friedley, S.A. (1986), *Communication Between the Sexes: Sex Differences and Sex-Role Stereotypes*, Scottsdale, AZ: Gorsuch Scarisbrick.

Stokes, K. (1989), *Faith is a Verb: Dynamics of Adult Faith Development*, Mystic, CN: Twenty-Third Publications.

Strauss, A.L. and Corbin, J. (1990), *Basics of Qualitative Research: Grounded Theory Procedures and Techniques*, London: Sage.

Streib, H. (2003), 'Faith development research at twenty years', in Osmer, R. and Schweitzer, F. (eds), *Faith Development and Public Life*, St. Louis, MO: Chalice Press.

Stroup, G.W. (1981), *The Promise of Narrative Theology*, London: SCM.

Stuart, E. (1995), *Just Good Friends: Towards a Lesbian and Gay Theology of Relationships*, London: Mowbray/Cassell.

Surrey, J.L. (1991), 'Self-in-relation: a theory of women's development', in Jordan, J.V. et al. (eds), *Women's Growth in Connection: Writings from the Stone Center*, New York: Guilford Press, pp. 51–66.

Tatum, B.D. (1997), 'Racial identity development and relational theory: the case of black women in white communities', in Jordan, J. (ed.), *Women's Growth in Diversity: Writings from the Stone* Center, New York: Guilford Press.

Tesch, R. (1990), *Qualitative Research: Analysis Types and Software Tools*, New York: Falmer.

Thistlethwaite, S. (1990), *Sex, Race, and God: Christian Feminism in Black and White*, London: Geoffrey Chapman.

Tillich, P. (1953, 1957, 1964), *Systematic Theology*, vols 1, 2 & 3, Hertfordshire: Nisbet & Co.

Treichler, P.A. and Kramarae, C. (1983), 'Women's talk in the ivory tower', *Communication Quarterly* 31, pp. 118–30.

Treasure, C. (1991), *Walking on Glass: Women Deacons Speak Out*, London: SPCK.

Trible, P. (1984), *Texts of Terror: Literary-Feminist Readings of Biblical Narratives*, Philadelphia: Fortress.

Turner, C.W. (1997), 'Clinical applications of the Stone Center theoretical approach to minority women', in Jordan, J. (ed.), *Women's Growth in Diversity: Writings from the Stone Center*, New York: Guilford Press.

Unger, R.K. (1983), 'Through the looking glass: no wonderland yet! The reciprocal relationship between methodology and models of reality', *Psychology of Women Quarterly* 8, pp. 9325–33.

Walker, A. (1984), *The Color Purple*, London: Women's Press.

Walker, L.J. (1984), 'Sex differences in the development of moral reasoning: a critical review', *Child Development* 55, pp. 677–91.

Walton, H. (2001), 'The wisdom of Sheba: constructing feminist practical theology', *Contact* 135, pp. 3–12.

Walton, H. and Durber, S. (eds) (1994), *Silence in Heaven: A Book of Women's Preaching*, London: SCM.

Ward, H. and Wild, J. (1995a), *Guard the Chaos: Finding Meaning in Change*, London: DLT.

Ward, H. and Wild, J. (eds) (1995b), *Human Rites: Worship Resources for an Age of Change*, London: Mowbray/Cassell.

Ward, H., Wild, J. and Morley, J. (eds) (1995), *Celebrating Women: The New Edition*, London: SPCK.

Watt, S.K. (1997), 'Identity and the Making of Meaning: Psychosocial Identity, Racial Identity, Womanist Identity, Self-Esteem, and the Faith Development of African-American College Women', unpublished Ph.D. thesis, North Carolina State University.

Webster, A. (1995), *Found Wanting: Women, Christianity and Sexuality*, London: Cassell.

Weems, R.J. (1988), *Just a Sister Away: A Womanist Vision of Women's Relationships in the Bible*, San Diego: LutaMedia.

Weiner, G. (1994), *Feminisms in Education: An Introduction*, Buckingham: Open University Press.

Westerhoff, J.H. III (1976), *Will Our Children Have Faith?*, New York: Seabury Press.

Westerhoff, J.H. III (1980), *Bringing Up Children in the Christian Faith*, Minneapolis: Winston.

White, V. (1985), 'Faith Stages, Affiliation, and Gender: A Study of the Faith Development of Catholic College Undergraduates', unpublished Ed.D. thesis, Boston University School of Education.

Whitehead, A.N. (1926), *Religion in the Making,* Cambridge: Cambridge University Press.

Whitehead, A.N. (1929), *Process and Reality*, Cambridge: Cambridge University Press.

Wilcox, M.M. (1979), *Developmental Journey*, Nashville: Abingdon.

Wiley, C.Y. (1991), 'A ministry of empowerment: a holistic model for pastoral counselling in the African American community', *Journal of Pastoral Care* 45, pp. 355–64.

Williams, D.S. (1993), *Sisters in the Wilderness: The Challenge of Womanist God-Talk*, Maryknoll: Orbis.

Wilmore, G.S. (1984, 2nd edn), *Black Religion and Black Radicalism*, Maryknoll: Orbis.

Winnicott, D.W. (1971), *Playing and Reality*, New York: Basic Books.

Winter, D. (1980), *Putting Theology to Work*, London: British Council of Churches.

Winter, M.T., Lummis, A. and Stokes, A. (1994), *Defecting in Place: Women Claiming Responsibility for Their Own Spiritual Lives*, New York: Crossroad.

Wood, J.T. (1994), *Who Cares? Women, Care, and Culture*, Carbondale, IL: Southern Illinois University Press.

Woodward, J. and Pattison, S. (eds) (2000), *The Blackwell Reader in Pastoral and Practical Theology*, Oxford: Blackwell Publishers.

Young, P.D. (1996), 'Experience', in Isherwood, L. and McEwan, D. (eds), *An A to Z of Feminist Theology*, Sheffield: Sheffield Academic Press.

Zappone, K. (1991), *The Hope for Wholeness: A Spirituality for Feminists*, Mystic, CN: Twenty-Third Publications.

Name Index

Acker, J. 49
Ackerman, D.M. 5, 12
Amirthan, S. 6
Anderson, K. 11, 56, 59
Anderson, S.R. 33, 34
Astley, Jeff 28, 29, 31
Atwood, Margaret 81, 178
Austin, J.L. 88

Ballard, Paul 5, 6
Barry, K. 49
Bassett, P.E. 32
Belenky, M.F. 25, 83, 86–7, 106, 133, 170, 171, 173
Bell, C. 44
Bennett Moore, Zöe 8
Blassingame, J.S. 76
Boff, Leonardo 6
Bonhoeffer, Dietrich 31
Bonino, J.M. 6
Bons-Storm, Riet 2, 5, 12, 43, 67, 68, 70, 83, 106, 125, 174, 180
Borker, R. 55
Bowlby, J. 22
Bowles, G. 44
Boyd, D. 24
Boyd, Marsha Foster 139, 146
Brabeck, M.M. 24
Bradley, R.B. 32
Brainerd, C. 21
Bridges, William 21, 39
Broughton, J.M. 24
Brown, G. 21
Brown, L.M. 84
Buber, Martin 62

Cameron, Deborah 55
Canham, Elizabeth 33
Cannon, L.W. 45
Chafe, W.L. 57
Chase, S.E. 57
Chodorow, Nancy 9, 22, 23

Chopp, Rebecca 3, 173, 176
Christ, Carol 9, 38–9, 67, 82, 109–10, 113, 115, 168, 179
Clark, Jean 109
Coates, Jennifer 55
Cone, James 6
Conn, Joann Wolski 4, 15
Cook, J.A. 44, 49, 51
Coon, L.L. 2
Cooney, J.A.M. 9, 34
Cooper-White, P. 22, 27
Corbin, J. 52
Cornwall Collective 3
Cotterill, Pamela 11, 45
Couture, P.D. 8
Cowden, M.A. 34
Cupitt, Don 68

Daly, Mary 67, 81
Davis, P.H. 27
De Beauvoir, Simone 110
Deforges, C. 21
DeMarinis, V.M. 5
Dervin, B. 45
Devor, N.G. 9, 34–5, 36, 160
Donaldson, Margaret 21
Donovan, Vincent 6
Duelli Klein, R. 44
Durber, Susan 172
Dykstra, Craig 28, 31

Eckhart, Meister 179
Edelsky, C. 55
Egan, H. 76
Erikson, Eric 9, 15, 17–18, 28, 29
Essevelt, J. 49
Estes, Clarissa Pinkes 83–4
Etter-Lewis, G. 45

Fageol, Suzanne 175
Finch, J. 11, 44
Fiorenza, Elisabeth Schüssler 2, 3, 6, 12

199

Subject Index

abdication and absorption of self 100–103
accompaniment of women 178–80
aims of study 4–5
alienation *see* faith development, women's
apophatic faithing *see* faithing strategies
arts
    in women's faith development *see* women's
        faith development
    use of in practical theology 8
    use of in religious education 175–80
awakenings *see* faith development, women's

'banking' model of teaching *see* teaching of
        women
belief 6
belonging, coming home 121–5

class in women's faith development *see* women's
        faith development
colour in women's faith development *see*
        women's faith development
conceptual faithing *see* faithing strategies
connectedness *see* relationality
context of study 2–4
conversational faithing *see* faithing strategies
conversational settings 173–5
creativity 129–31
criteria of analysis 58–9
cyclical method *see* pastoral cycle

data analysis 57–9
deadness, loss of feeling and reality 90–92
death 131–3
development *see* theories of development
developmental psychology 8–9, 15–28
dialectical theories of development *see* theories
        of development
difference and diversity in women's experience
        47–8, 84–5, 138–9, 172–3, 175
disconnection, fragmentation and division 92–6
discovery of creative voice or sphere 129–31

education of women and girls 168–81
empathy *see* faith development, women's
empowerment of women 49–50
experience, role of in theology 6–7
experience, women's 7, 37–8, 46–7, 133–4,
        170–73

faith
    women's images of 140–49
faith development
    definition of term, 1, 28–9
    theory 8–9, 16–17, 28–32, 163–8
    women's 2, 4, 32–7, 37–40, 163–8
        adolescent crisis in women's faith
            development 84–5
        alienation in women's faith development
            14, 81–107
        arts in women's faith development
            129–31
        awakenings in women's faith development
            14, 38, 39, 109–34
        class in women's faith development 25–7,
            52–4, 84–5, 101, 122, 133, 139, 154
        colour in women's faith development 85,
            94–5, 119–20, 139, 160
        empathy in women's faith development
            149–51
        friends and partners in women's faith
            development 72, 110–11
        integration in women's faith development
            154–9
        mentors in women's faith development 71
        naming in women's faith development 38,
            67, 70, 134
        nature mysticism in women's faith
            development 110
        nothingness in women's faith
            development 38, 82–3
        patterns of women's faith development
            14, 81–162
        processes of women's faith development
            13, 61–80